GOVERNMENTS OF WESTERN EUROPE

General Editor: NEVIL JOHNSON

Government in Spain

The Executive at Work

Government in Spain

The Executive at Work

BY

KENNETH N. MEDHURST

Lecturer in Government
University of Manchester

PERGAMON PRESS

Oxford · New York · Toronto
Sydney · Braunschweig

Pergamon Press Ltd., Headington Hill Hall, Oxford

Pergamon Press Inc., Maxwell House, Fairview Park, Elmsford,
New York 10523

Pergamon of Canada Ltd., 207 Queen's Quay West, Toronto 1

Pergamon Press (Aust.) Pty. Ltd., 19a Boundary Street,
Rushcutters Bay, N.S.W. 2011, Australia

Vieweg & Sohn GmbH, Burgplatz 1, Braunschweig

First edition 1973

Library of Congress Cataloging in Publication Data

Medhurst, Kenneth, 1938–
Government in Spain.

(The Commonwealth and international library.
Governments of Western Europe)
Bibliography: p. 237
1. Spain—Politics and government—1939–
I. Title.
JN8221.M4   320 9′46′082   72-13298
ISBN 0-08-016940-6

Printed in Great Britain by A. Wheaton & Co., Exeter

To my Mother and Father

Contents

EDITOR'S FOREWORD — xi

PREFACE — xiii

1. Before the Civil War — 1

The Historical Background — 1
The Causes of Instability — 6
    The political culture — 6
    The social and economic structure — 7
    The problem of class conflict — 11
    The regional problem — 11
    The problem of the Church — 14
    The problem of the military — 17
The Second Republic and the Civil War — 18

2. The Civil War and the "Nationalist Régime" — 21

Alignments during the Civil War — 21
Why the Republic was Defeated — 21
Post-Civil-war Political Problems — 23
    The nature of the "Nationalist régime" — 27
    The Nationalist régime and political parties — 29
    The problem of class conflict under Franco's régime — 33

Contents

The problem of the universities and "Intellectual Dissent"   38

The regional problem   41

The problem of the Church   42

The role of the military in post–Civil-war Spain   48

Conclusion   52

3. Franco's Political System   55

The Legal Basis of "the System"   55

The Genesis of "the System"   60

Franco   61

Franco and the Problems of Coalition Management   63

4. The Workings of the Government   76

The Problem of Internal Conflict   76

The Government and its Relationship with Major Interest Groups   77

The Major Centres of Influence within the Government   84

The Council of Ministers   89

Administrative Reforms   95

5. The Civil Service   102

Introduction   102

The Emergence of the Corps   104

The Triumph of the Corps   106

Recruitment   107

Promotion   109

Pay   110

The Fragmentation of the Administration   113

The Deployment of Personnel   113

Attempts to Reform the System   115

The Achievements of the Corps   117

6. The Ministerial Departments   119

Introduction   119

The French Legacy   122

The Active Administration   123

   The "Subsecretaría"   123

   The "Dirección General"   126

   The "Administración Periférica"   128

The Consultative Administration   132

   Ministerial "Gabinetes" and the "Secretaría General Técnica"   132

   Inspectorates   133

   Advisory councils   134

Conclusion   137

7. The State as the Promoter of Economic and Social Change   139

Introduction   139

The pre-Civil-war Situation   139

The post-Civil-war Situation   144

Agricultural Policy   145

Communications   150

Industrial Policy   151

Social Policy   155

   Housing   156

   Social security   157

   The control of prices and incomes   158

x   *Contents*

The organization of the public sector   159

Indicative Planning   164

The plans and social change   167

Education   168

Prices and incomes   171

Regional planning   173

Conclusion   180

8. Local Administration   181

Basic Principles   181

The Administrative Control of Local Authorities   197

Personnel   198

Tutelage   200

Local Finances   204

Conclusion   205

9. Control of the Administration   207

Political Controls—The Cortes   207

Legal Controls   217

The "Consejo de Estado"   219

Judicial controls   221

Financial controls   228

Conclusion   230

EPILOGUE   231

BIBLIOGRAPHY   237

INDEX   249

Editor's Foreword

WE KNOW very little about how contemporary Spain is governed. Though several scholars have written on the history of modern Spain and in particular on the emergence of the present régime, very few have studied how this régime has evolved and the kind of government it now provides. Dr. Medhurst's study is a significant contribution to filling this gap. In line with the two earlier volumes in this series, the main emphasis has been placed on the structure and tasks of government rather than on the interplay of political forces. Nevertheless considerable attention is paid to the way in which the present system of government emerged, to its subsequent development and to the principal political factors which shape its present structure and style. This attention to the historical and political context is all the more necessary in describing a system of government which for most readers must be relatively unfamiliar ground.

Dr. Medhurst's work is, I believe, the first account of Spanish government to be published in this country. By breaking new ground in this way he has demonstrated that contemporary Spain is by no means inaccessible to political and administrative research. It is to be hoped that his example will encourage others to pay more attention to this neglected part of Western Europe.

NEVIL JOHNSON
Nuffield College, Oxford

Preface

OF THE many people who have contributed to the production of this book I would particularly like to acknowledge my gratitude towards Mrs. Bernice Hamilton, of the University of York, who first encouraged me to take up the study of Spanish affairs; Professor W. J. M. MacKenzie of the University of Glasgow who first gave me the opportunity to pursue the interest, and Professor Brian Chapman, of the University of Manchester, whose friendship, encouragement and guidance have been a constant source of help. I would also like to express my appreciation for the advice of Mr. Nevil Johnson, of Nuffield College, Oxford, and the very thorough examination given to my manuscript by Mr. Derek Gagen of the University of Manchester. The people in Spain who have given me help are legion and all of them could not possibly be mentioned here (in any case some would undoubtedly prefer not to be mentioned). I would, however, like to say a special word of thanks to Professors E. García de Enterría and Amando de Miguel who have freely made available to me their invaluable experience and important background material. My first-hand knowledge of Spain was first made possible through a scholarship awarded by the Consejo Superior de Investigaciones Científicas to which body I would like to say a belated thank you.

Most of the research for this book has been done during the course of several visits made to Spain since 1962. Additional research was done in the library of Canning House whose staff have provided me with help that I have valued. During the necessary visits to London I have always been able to count on the hospitality of my good friends Mr. and Mrs. A. B. E. Clark to whom I am very grateful. Finally, I cannot lose the opportunity of thanking my wife for her patience and encouragement during long hours spent in writing.

The final version of the study was completed late in 1971 and it has been impossible to take any account of events after January 1972. I hope subsequent events will not affect the relevance of the bulk of the text. Whether it is relevant or not I, of course, remain solely responsible for all statements of fact and opinion included in this book.

CHAPTER 1

Before the Civil War

THE HISTORICAL BACKGROUND[1]

Modern Spain has a history of intense and frequently violent political conflict. Since Napoleon's invasion and the resulting "National War of Independence" (1808–14) the national polity has frequently been disrupted. French revolutionary ideas provoked a ferment bringing into conflict rival concepts of the State and radically opposed views about society's organization. From then onwards a politically active minority sought to create "Liberal Constitutional" forms of government within a society which, in the main, did not share or understand bourgeois liberal values. However, the roots of the later conflicts can perhaps be seen in the period before 1808.

Until 1808 Spain was an absolute monarchy. This was created by the "Catholic Kings" and their Hapsburg successors but after 1713 control passed to a branch of the French Bourbon dynasty. Thus Spain was drawn into France's orbit and educated minorities were exposed to French intellectual influences. Such influences were apparent (particularly during Charles III's "enlightened despotism", 1759–88) in plans for Spain's modernization. Efforts were made to rationalize the royal administration and to assert greater control over the patchwork of seigneurial fiefs, and autonomous regions and municipalities that had characterized the country's local government. Likewise, there were attempts to curb the influence of the great nobles and to subject the Church to greater government supervision. Thus it was hoped to remove obstacles to land reform and other schemes.

[1]For a good survey of modern Spanish history cf. Raymond Carr, *Spain 1808–1939*, Oxford, 1966. Cf. also Gerald Brennan, *The Spanish Labyrinth, An Account of the Social and Political Background of the Civil War*, Cambridge, 1950.

This eighteenth-century reform programme did not yield the anticipated fruits. Entrenched interests offered resistance and the monarch's own reforming drive was not sustained. Finally, there was the disruption caused by Napoleon's invasion. Nevertheless, it exercised a continuing influence upon portions of Spain's political leadership and was a factor in later political controversies.

Napoleon's invasion had dramatic consequences. The breakdown of monarchical authority precipitated the loss of nearly all Spain's American empire.[2] Within Spain itself there was an unprecedented outburst of nationalist sentiment and widespread popular resistance. Only small minorities, however, saw the upheaval as an opportunity for recasting political institutions. One group co-operated with the occupying power in the hope of imposing administrative reforms of the sort Napoleon introduced into France. More significant elements, drawn principally from Spain's small professional classes, were inspired by the example of the French Revolution whilst repudiating Napoleon's authoritarianism and collaboration with his agents. They summoned "the Cortes of Cadiz", in 1810, to draft a national constitution. This assembly's debates mark the genesis of nineteenth-century Spain's prevailing "liberal" political tradition. It entailed the search for a constitutional form of government resting on popular consent. The notion of the sovereignty of the nation was opposed to the idea of sovereignty vested in a monarch. On the other hand, plans for a centralized secular state owed something, not only to contemporary France, but also to Spain's reformers.

Divisions in the Cortes of Cadiz heralded enduring conflicts within the liberal camp. Those in the liberal tradition shared certain basic assumptions but were frequently divided by personal and factional struggles for the spoils of office. There were also two major ideological tendencies. Firstly, there were "Moderates" whose priority was the creation of a strong executive and who set strict limits to the practical consequences of the notion of popular sovereignty. They also tended to be socially conservative and to have pragmatic attitudes toward the question of Church–State relations. Secondly, there were "Progressives" who were more prepared to stress and to explore the democratic implications of the liberal tradition and to be militantly anti-clerical. They tended to encourage popular political participation, and to press for greater social equality. It was

[2]Cuba remained a Spanish colony until 1898.

out of such currents of thought that a republican movement later developed.

These divisions help to explain Spain's chronic instability after 1814. Instability was also due to the absence of popular support for political reform. The Cortes of Cadiz expressed the aspirations of the bulk of the politically aware, but most Spaniards were indifferent to or ignorant of national political issues. There were also significant minorities who strongly resisted change. Thus the returning monarch's efforts to restore absolute rule had some success. He inaugurated a period of conservative reaction which was punctuated chiefly by military coups. His succession was disputed by supporters of his daughter, Isabella, and his brother, Carlos, which precipitated the first "Carlist War" (1833–40). This terminated in a Carlist defeat chiefly, perhaps, because the Carlists lacked support in the army. Isabella's reign ended in 1868, with a military coup following a dangerous narrowing of the régime's base and a large withdrawal of confidence. Disparate elements, mainly united by the desire for office, replaced Isabella with another candidate. But each group wished the new monarchy to be its exclusive preserve and their divisions caused its collapse. This paved the way for the first (federal) republic (1873–4).[3] The republic, however, was short-lived. Its emergence represented not the strength of republican forces but the temporary disarray of their opponents. It failed, moreover, to maintain order. The final Carlist War (1870–5) was waged during this period and the State proved unable to check centrifugal regional forces. Another military coup (1874) restored the Bourbon monarchy and re-established order.

Despite such instability mid-nineteenth-century liberals left a significant legacy. A start was made on creating the machinery of a modern state even if, as will be seen, the desired results were not always forthcoming. Criminal and commercial law was codified. The famous para-military security force, the Civil Guard, was established. The foundations of a modern fiscal system were laid. A centralized state-controlled education system, on the French pattern, was established. Finally, the State promoted important road building schemes and presided over the construction of a railway network.

[3]There is a good study of this episode in English. C. A. Hennessy, *The Federal Republic in Spain. Pi y Margall and the Federal Republican Movement, 1868–1876,* Oxford, 1962.

The Restoration's architects established a form of parliamentary government operated by a Conservative and a Liberal party. These parties, however, lacked genuine popular bases and were manipulated by political bosses, or *caciques*. There were no stable party organizations and policies represented understandings between party "notables". As in eighteenth-century England, governmental changes preceded elections. Their outcome largely depended upon negotiations between national party leaders and local *caciques* who offered support to the Government in exchange for local political office or other rewards. A frequently illiterate and a largely apathetic rural electorate could generally be mobilized by the *caciques*. They could count on personal loyalties and apply informal pressures.

Under this system's auspices most progressive liberal demands were met. Universal suffrage, freedom of association and worship and the right to strike were, in principle, all eventually guaranteed. A period of stability was also provided. But the system's essential fragility ultimately became apparent. Though the two principal parties competed for the spoils of office their leaders had an underlying community of interests which blurred the distinction between them and left them insensitive to pressures for change. They failed to channel the demands of growing regional movements and of emergent working class groups. Thus extra-parliamentary and, sometimes, violent opposition gathered momentum.

A major crisis of confidence came in 1898 when Spain lost the remnants of her American Empire.[4] The political settlement of the restoration period never really recovered from this blow. A generation of intellectuals took the chance to scrutinize Spain's institutions and pressed for their modernization but they got no response from the intellectually bankrupt Conservative and Liberal parties.[5] They made more of an impression upon their opponents. Above all, the events of 1898 gave Catalan nationalism a mass following. Many Catalans were then becoming permanently alienated from the apparently ineffectual central government. Thus the established parties lost their foothold in Catalonia. Elsewhere, however,

[4] Spain simultaneously lost possession of the Philippines. These losses stemmed from defeat in the Spanish–American War. This conflict clearly exposed Spain's military and naval weakness. It also increased doubts about the efficacy of its political and administrative institutions.

[5] They constituted the so-called "Generation of '98". Their attitudes varied greatly but they were as one in seeking national regeneration through political and social changes. They influenced many of the Second Republic's leaders.

alienation from the political system was manifested more through increasing electoral abstentions than through a growth of opposition movements. The latter were too weak and divided to fill the political vacuum successfully.

Under these pressures the established parties themselves tended increasingly to fragment. This necessarily increased the importance of the monarch's role as arbiter in party disputes. It also pushed the monarchy toward greater dependence upon the army. Overt military intervention in politics ceased after the Restoration but the two-party system merely masked the continuing slackness of civilian controls. The retention of an unduly large officer corps, inflated by civil and colonial wars; large military appropriations often made at the cost of expenditure on public services; the appointment of War Ministers from amongst serving officers; and the right of military courts to try civilians for some offences, were indicators of the real situation. The weakening of political institutions made the situation still plainer. In 1917 opposition groups looked to groups of junior officers to force reform programmes upon the Government and so break the political deadlock. By 1918 this threat was neutralized but it was a warning signal.

In 1923 a portion of the army finally established a dictatorship under Lieutenant-General Primo de Rivera. Military disaster in Spanish Morocco precipitated the crisis.[6] Left-wing groups seized on the opportunity to discredit the monarchy and assert greater civilian control over the military. The army intervened to fend off these challenges. The dictatorship started with the goodwill of many who had lost confidence in parliamentary government and it enjoyed initial successes. It intervened to promote economic growth and (with French help) retrieved the Moroccan situation. But eventually it lost the loyalty of the army and all other major groups. Thus efforts to create a viable authoritarian state failed. The régime's collapse finally discredited the monarchy and the monarch withdrew.[7]

[6]Spain had long had an interest in North Africa although the creation of a Moroccan Protectorate was only formalized in 1912. Underlying her interest in the area was a desire to retain the trappings of a great power and to have control over the coastline opposite Spain. The Protectorate in practice became a military fief with little civilian control exercised from Madrid. The Spanish Foreign Legion, active in Morocco, became an élite combat unit and a training ground for leading soldiers—above all General Franco.

[7]Municipal elections, in April 1931, constituted the immediate occasion of King

The resulting vacuum was filled by republican parties (allied to Socialists) who in 1931 established the Second Republic. The enfeebled restoration parties did not survive Primo de Rivera's suspension of party politics.

As before, a republic's creation signified not the emergence of effective republican parties but the temporary disarray of their opponents.[8] The republican parties were not truly national. Their support was concentrated in particular regions and social strata. They were also parties of notables lacking well-structured organizations. Their programmes, moreover, frequently seemed negative in tone. They often appeared to be chiefly motivated by anti-clericalism, anti-militarism and anti-aristocratic sentiments and to lack the will to push through bold socio-economic reforms. They had some notable achievements to their name—notably efforts to increase educational opportunities. Their frontal attacks on traditional institutions, however, proved sufficient to alienate conservative elements who might have eventually accepted republican institutions whilst being insufficient to keep or win the support of those whose first priority was a drastic restructuring of society. The former moved toward an alliance with right-wing minorities who had never accepted the Republic's legitimacy whilst the latter espoused revolutionary solutions. Thus opinion became polarized between two coalitions of interests hostile to each other and both aiming to destroy "liberal–democratic" institutions. This polarization process culminated in the Civil War from which Spain's present political system emerged. Those close to the centre of the political spectrum proved quite unable to control the situation.

THE CAUSES OF INSTABILITY

The political culture

At the root of this instability lies a poorly integrated society torn by deep cleavages and containing little room for agreement upon fundamental

---

Alfonso's withdrawal. In urban areas, uncontrolled by traditional *caciques*, the elections indicated disaffection from the monarchy. For a study of the episode cf. M. Maura, *Así Cayó Alfonso XIII*, Mexico, 1962.

[8]Amongst the many books on the Republic attention can be drawn to Gabriel Jackson, *The Spanish Republic and the Civil War*, Princeton, 1965, and Richard A. H. Robinson, *The Origins of Franco's Spain*, David and Charles, Newton Abbot, 1970.

objectives. This is partly explicable in terms of a pronounced "particularism" seemingly characteristic of modern Hispanic culture.[9] It manifests
itself in a complex of attitudes inimical to the development of durable
political institutions. On the one hand, there is a belief that the State's
power may be legitimately used for private ends and, on the other, a
widespread suspicion of all authority and the practice of using personal
influence to protect oneself against the State's (possibly arbitrary) demands.
Sectional loyalties have tended to take precedence over loyalty to an
impersonal state and many have felt wholly alienated from official institutions. Thus a weak sense of legal obligation (typified by a tradition of
tax evasion) has been accompanied by mutual incomprehension in dealings between diverging interests. Equally, there have been tendencies
towards intransigence in pressing sectional demands or else towards
complete indifference to public issues. Consequently periods of considerable political apathy have alternated with bursts of sharp if not violent
struggle. The ready resort to extra-legal and violent action has characterized Spanish politics ever since the War of Independence. Popular
resistance then gave such activity a measure of legitimacy and surrounded
it with a certain mystique. It thus became an integral part of the nation's
political traditions.

Finally, particularism is apparent in the low propensity (outside Catalonia and the Basque Country) for joining or forming voluntary interest
groups.[10] This helps to explain Spain's lack of sustained political mobilization. It has also militated against the politics of bargaining and
compromise. The dearth of well-articulated interests has left politicians
free to indulge in radical rhetoric whilst ignoring fundamental problems.

The social and economic structure

Limited interest group activity can also be related to economic backwardness and low educational levels. Economic underdevelopment, rigid

---

[9]This theme is developed, particularly with regard to regional loyalties, in
J. Ortega y Gasset, *España Invertebrada*, Madrid, 1959. First published 1921.

[10]As will be noted below, the political culture and traditions of Catalonia and the
Basque Country are in a special category. These two areas have been more economically developed and have been characterized by higher levels of civic consciousness
than other regions of Spain.

social structures and unevenly distributed wealth have also contributed to
the problem of instability.

In 1936 most Spaniards were still engaged in agriculture.[11] Patterns of
landownership varied considerably, however, and created different problems in different regions. Catalonia and the Basque Provinces had fairly
prosperous and politically conscious peasantries who, as will be seen,
supported regional parties. In areas like Old Castile there was a poor
peasantry possessing highly fragmented and uneconomic landholdings (or
minifundia). These were, however, relatively homogeneous and stagnant
societies which had preserved traditional values and lacked major causes
of internal conflict. They tended to resist social changes and to remain
indifferent to national politics unless their interests appeared directly
threatened from outside.

Parts of Castile, and above all, the regions of Andalusia and Extremadura were characterized by large estates (or *Latifundia*) whose owners
were separated by a large economic and social gap from a mass of poor,
frequently illiterate, landless labourers and tenant farmers. The landowners came from the traditional nobility and Spain's commercial,
political and military élites. These originally distinct groups had tended to
coalesce and to develop common interests—sometimes cemented by
family ties. A portion of the nobility, because of its education, accepted
some of the thinking of "the Enlightenment" and so could coexist with the
chief beneficiaries of the "Liberal State". The latter included lawyers, and
financiers who speculated in the land thrown on the market following
nineteenth-century state attacks upon traditional corporations—notably
the Church. They also included leading *caciques* and generals. Some of
these elements were themselves ennobled and many merged into one
relatively homogeneous "upper class" sharing similar conservative values.
Only the traditional nobility firmly identified its interests with the
monarchy but all resisted demands for social change.

Landowners of this sort were frequently absentee landlords uninter-
ested in agricultural productivity. They preferred investing their profits in
urban real estate to reinvesting them locally. The neglect of areas suitable

[11]In 1930, according to an official census, 54 per cent of the working population
was engaged in agriculture, 24·3 per cent in the "secondary" sector and 21·7 per cent
in the "tertiary" sector. In 1940 the figures were 51·9 per cent, 24·0 per cent and 24·1
per cent, respectively.

for irrigation and large areas of monocultures were a measure of the situation. Such areas stagnated. Their labourers and tenant farmers constituted a "rural proletariat" living in primitive conditions. It was amongst them that, from the 1870s, anarchism attracted a mass following. The anarchist movement's growth highlighted the rural proletariat's alienation from the established order. It also indicated the shrewdness of anarchist leaders in associating themselves with traditional demands for land redistribution. The movement oscillated between quiescence and outbursts of violence, but the efforts of landowners (and the Civil Guard) to destroy it never wholly succeeded.

The upper strata of most townships, in this predominantly rural society, were composed of artisans, shopkeepers, self-employed professional men, civil servants and army (or naval) officers. They, with the conservative peasantry, have been labelled the *clases medias* to distinguish them from the *bourgeoisie* of more developed European countries. In the main they were little affected by the nineteenth century's great intellectual and political movements. They lacked a well-developed class consciousness or the sense of a distinctive (anti-aristocratic) historical mission. They depended economically upon the upper classes or upon the State. They tended to respect upper-class values and the most successful aspired to join that class. Given Spain's backward condition, serving the wealthy and public employment provided the chief outlets for the educated amongst them. Lawyers and engineers were in this category. Consultancy work on behalf of major economic interests was one of the few alternatives they had to the very real threat of "intellectual unemployment". The State, still more, was seen as a provider of security. Thus lawyers constituted the majority of Spain's better qualified administrators and a significant proportion of its politicians. Their influence was apparent in a legalistic administrative tradition. Engineers also filled senior administrative posts. They helped to forge a parallel technocratic tradition which viewed policy making as essentially a matter for technical experts and which placed a premium upon strong, stable government. These groups were obviously not radical innovators. Their first priority tended to be a secure career. Their principal political preoccupation was maintaining social stability and public order. Primo de Rivera's dictatorship recruited much of its political élite from such elements and Franco's régime has also been able to count upon their support.

One portion of the *clases medias* did tend to side with the forces of "movement" rather than the forces of "order". Republican parties attracted support from some artisans, school teachers and similar lower-middle-class groups. Likewise, republican and socialist movements drew many of their leaders from amongst professional men. These included some lawyers and significant proportions of the academic, medical and journalistic communities. Finally, there was a well-established tradition of radical student protest (going back at least until 1868). Vocal minorities within the student body were responsible, for example, for demonstrations which helped to destroy confidence in Primo de Rivera. These groups were concentrated, however, in a few major urban centres. In most places they were heavily outnumbered by more traditional middle-class elements who were disturbed by challenges to established institutions.

This social structure helped, in several ways, to retard and to influence the course of Spain's industrialization process. Firstly, the values of the socially dominant groups precluded capital accumulation and investment on the scale needed for rapid industrial growth. The loss of Spain's American Empire eliminated one major source of capital and remaining resources were insufficiently mobilized. Secondly, generally low living standards implied a small domestic market. Thirdly, the labour force was poorly qualified. Finally, reserves of technical and managerial expertise were limited. Higher education was an upper- and middle-class preserve and it was primarily geared to the training of traditional professional groups.

Major industries (with limited exceptions) emerged only toward the end of the last century and were heavily concentrated in these areas, notably Catalonia and the Basque Country, which had been thoroughly exposed to West European influences and had long-established commercial traditions. It was only in Catalonia, followed later by the Basque Country, that significant entrepreneurial groups developed. Earlier developments, particularly in the field of railway construction and mining, had depended on foreign capital.

Domestic capital eventually assumed the largest part in national development but this was supplied by a handful of large banks—most commonly with headquarters in the Basque Country. These dominated the nation's financial markets. Through their restrictive credit policies they acquired extensive industrial interests and promoted high concentrations of ownership in basic sectors like iron and steel. Domestic competition came only from small family businesses and tariff protection, reintroduced after 1891, provided a defence against more efficient foreign competitors. Thus home markets were controlled by relatively few enterprises all free to pursue restrictive practices. In particular they strongly resisted labour's demands for improved wages and conditions. Their resistance had the effect of fostering working-class militancy.

The problem of class conflict

Until the 1890s employers and the State regarded challenges from the working classes simply as problems for the police. Even in 1923 the working-class movement remained small. It was further hampered by divisions. Some workers supported republican movements; larger numbers supported the Socialist Party and its allied union confederation, the Unión General de Trabajadores (U.G.T.). They predominated in Madrid, the mining areas of Asturias and the manufacturing centres of the Basque Country. Their chief rival was the anarcho-syndicalist Confederación Nacional de Trabajo (C.N.T.) which held the initiative in Catalonia and Aragon and was well represented in and around Valencia and in Andalusia.[12] The former sought the creation of a centralized unitary state. The latter wished to replace the State by loosely federated workers' councils. Both movements were themselves divided. The Socialists were torn between advocates of an evolutionary approach, who prevailed until about 1933, and those attracted by revolutionary solutions. The C.N.T. was agreed about the wholesale destruction of the established order but its members disagreed over tactics. Proponents of terrorism were ranged against those preferring industrial action. Both approaches resulted in the intensification of class conflicts.

The regional problem

Tensions also arose from regional conflicts. Poor communications helped to preserve distinctive local or regional traditions. There were also marked regional variations in social structures and rates of economic development. Thus strong local loyalties survived. The near collapse of

[12]The emergence of anarcho-syndicalism in Catalonia owed a lot to large-scale migrations from Andalusia to the Catalan region.

state authority at periods of acute crisis indicates the strength of the resulting centrifugal forces. These forces help to explain, in their turn, why the State has lacked the strength to remove obstacles to national integration.

Such problems have been most intractable in Catalonia and the Basque Country. The end of the nineteenth century saw the growth of a strong Catalan movement which was followed by the emergence of a partially imitative Basque nationalism. To generalize about these movements is difficult. Those concerned had goals varying from the establishment of a limited autonomy to complete cession. Catalan political aspirations, for example, were first voiced by spokesmen for local industrialists prepared to work for concessions from within established institutions. They only succeeded, however, in arousing popular expectations that they could not satisfy and they were consequently outflanked by more radical elements able to mobilize mass support.[13]

There were also differences in the essential natures of the two nationalist movements. These, in part, reflected differences in the social structures of the two regions. Catalan nationalism was expressed through competing parties, divided along class lines, and it had a strong socially radical wing. It tended to be the forward-looking nationalism of a modern industrializing community with a large non-traditional middle class. Basque aspirations were voiced by one major regional party whose mass support was largely confined to the region's conservative peasantry.[14] It was not supported by the "upper-class" Basque financiers, who had close links with commercial and bureaucratic élites in Madrid, nor to any great extent by the region's industrial workers, who gravitated toward the Spanish Socialist Party. Equally, there was no counterpart to Catalonia's non-traditional middle class—such elements were thinner on the ground in the Basque Country. Thus Basque nationalism was of a more romantic backward-looking kind than its Catalan equivalent. It drew on memories of local privileges (or *fueros*), vestiges of which survived in the form of special financial arrangements negotiated between the Basque provincial councils and the Spanish Government.

[13]On local nationalist movements cf. M. García Venero, *Historia del Nacionalismo Catalan (1793–1936)*, Madrid, 1944, and *Historia del Nacionalismo Vasco (1793–1936)*, Madrid, 1945. Cf. also J. Solé-Tura, *Catalanismo Revolución Burguesa*, Madrid, 1970.
[14]There was a left-wing nationalist group but it had a small following.

Nevertheless, certain generalizations about these two movements are possible. Firstly, the survival of distinctive languages and cultures was vitally important to their development. These fostered the growth of a national consciousness and perpetuated the sense of a distinct identity.[15] Secondly, both movements were, in part, reactions against centralization and involved a sense of neglect at the hands of unsympathetic and incompetent national governments. The roots of this tension can be traced back to the circumstances of Spain's unification, which was largely the product of military conquest and which entailed the triumph of the centre (Castile) over the periphery. The tension was symbolized by the rivalry of the commercial centre of Barcelona and the bureaucratic centre of Madrid. Early nineteenth-century liberals aggravated the problem by replacing traditional administrative units with a system of legally uniform provinces which, particularly in the Basque and Catalan cases, were viewed as the instruments of a stifling central control rather than the embodiment of local interests. The fact that Catalan and Basque local authorities continued to show more vitality than those of other regions merely increased the frustration felt at being treated in the same way as areas with lower levels of civic consciousness.

Such reactions were intensified by the under-representation of Catalans and Basques in Spain's military élite, and, in the case of Catalans, by the small number of local people in prominent administrative posts.[16] This was often due to self-exclusion, for industrialization provided the educated middle classes of Catalonia and the Basque Country with career opportunities unavailable to their counterparts elsewhere in Spain. Resentment was nevertheless directed against those regions, notably Castile, whose *clases medias* were correspondingly over-represented.

Finally, there were clashes of economic interests. The concentration of industry in Catalonia and the Basque Country inevitably meant that these regions contributed much of the nation's revenues. Thus it was felt that backward regions were being subsidized at their expense and that these regions were acting as a brake on their own further growth. On the other

---

[15]Catalan nationalism first found expression in and through a literary revival.

[16] For statistical data on this point cf. "Within-nation differences and comparisons: the eight Spains", an article by Juan J. Linz and Amando de Miguel published in R. L. Merritt and S. Rokkan, *Comparing Nations, The Use of Quantitative Data in Cross-National Research*, Yale, 1966.

hand, Spain's national military, bureaucratic and political élites had a traditional ideological commitment to the notion of a unitary state and resented the idea of special treatment for Basques and Catalans.

The problem of the Church[17]

The Church was another source of conflict. Such conflict is partly explicable in terms of some of the distinctive features of Spanish Catholicism. Firstly, it has been characterized by an aggressive crusading spirit and by an intolerance of the unorthodox. Secondly, many have seen Catholicism as essential to the definition and maintenance of Spain's nationhood— a view which gained substance from the identification of priests and people during the War of Independence. Thus traditionalists have assumed that Catholicism was Spain's principal unifying force and threats to clerical interests have been represented as threats to national solidarity. Finally, and as a corollary of the above assertions, it has commonly been held that the State has responsibilities for protecting the Church and eliminating "error".

Such assumptions provoked strong reactions and counter reactions. The early liberals were militantly anti-clerical and used the State to confiscate Church property. This drove the Church to rely greatly upon the material assistance of socially privileged groups. Most priests, moreover, were recruited from the conservative peasantry of regions like Castile. It consequently became an increasingly conservative institution attracting its support chiefly from the upper classes and the traditional *clases medias*. It lost effective contact with the rural proletariat and with most urban workers. Thus aggressive anti-clericalism spread not only to the republican heirs of the early liberals but also to the organized working class. They repudiated the Church as an integral part of a social order whose destruction they sought. Religious and class divisions therefore increasingly overlapped.

Catholic spokesmen (lay and clerical) responded to this situation in different ways. The Carlists reacted most extremely. Their movement had

[17]For discussions of the clerical issue in Spanish politics cf. José Mariano Sánchez. *Reform and Reaction. The Politico-religious Background of the Spanish Civil War* (Chapel Hill: University of North Carolina Press, 1964). Cf. also J. Selwyn Schapiro, *Anti-clericalism*, Princeton, 1967.

aristocratic leadership and support from portions of the Basque peasantry and clergy. Above all it had a stronghold in the Province of Navarra (and the neighbouring Alava). The cause was dynastic but it attracted defenders of traditional regional and clerical privileges. Indeed, the Carlist Wars can be seen as the struggle of a proudly independent and intensely Catholic peasant society to resist the centralizing, secularizing and *laissez-faire* economic tendencies associated with the "Liberal State". Despite military defeat the Carlist movement survived, thanks to strong hereditary loyalties and the retention of a Navarrese base. Its leadership, however, fell increasingly into the hands of *Integristas*, or advocates of a theocratic state, for whom the dynastic and regional issues were secondary. Their first priority was the creation of an authoritarian state dedicated to the protection of traditional Catholic values and clerical interests.

Many Catholics, including most bishops, accept Carlist assumptions about Spain's essentially Catholic nature without adopting their extreme political postures. They were content with a Concordat of 1851 which arranged a *modus vivendi* between Church and State.

Whilst moderate liberals abandoned doctrinaire anti-clericalism, official Church leaders moved toward some acceptance of political change. Thus Spain became a confessional State, extending protection to the Church which, in return, accepted the maintenance of the traditional *Real Patronato*, permitting royal participation in episcopal appointments.

It was in this setting that, at the turn of this century, Spain witnessed a Catholic revival. This remained, however, an essentially upper- and middle-class phenomenon. Efforts to capture working-class loyalties through paternalistic confessional unions largely failed.[18] Catholic advances, moreover, reinforced middle-class anti-clericalism. Education, in particular, provided a battleground. Religious orders made big efforts in this area and in secondary education the Church assumed greater responsibilities than the State. This the State accepted as it lacked the resources to provide comparable facilities. Anti-clericals, however, reacted against the Church's efforts to keep the loyalties of Spain's potential leaders.

These efforts were sometimes frankly élitist. Priority was given to educating the social strata that supplied the nation's political and intellectual

[18]Catholic Unions are discussed by Juan N. García Nieto in *El Sindicalismo Cristiano En España*, Bilbao, 1960.

leadership. This was regarded as the surest guarantee of ecclesiastical interests. In the political arena a similar approach was apparent in the work of Acción Católica Nacional de Propagandistas (A.N.C.P.). This body, which was established in 1909 with Jesuit assistance, recruited potential political leaders from members of the more broadly based "Acción Católica" (Catholic Action). It was not a political party but a training ground for university-trained professional men entering public life, who were expected to defend Catholic interests within the framework of existing institutions. Officially it was indifferent to the nature of these institutions provided the Church was free to discharge its pastoral oblig- ations. It was prepared to accept the Second Republic, for example, provided the Church was exempt from punitive measures.

The A.N.C.P., in part, provided a model for Opus Dei (God's Work). [19] This body (founded in 1928) was also intended to combat anti-clericalism and was élitist in conception. It recruited from amongst able graduates in a position to capture politically and socially influential positions. Unlike the A.N.C.P.'s recruits, however, members of Opus Dei took religious vows. Affiliates, not admitted to full membership, were not subject to such strict discipline but they too were expected to pursue the movement's basic goal of re-Christianizing the world. Opus Dei also seems to have owed something to the Institución Libre de Enseñanza, an anti-clerical educational institute whose teachers and ex-pupils infiltrated quietly into influential positions on a considerable scale. Opus Dei was to prove more deliberately secretive, however, than the prototype whose influence it wished to combat.

The élitist orientation of Catholic groups underlined the extent of the Church's commitment to the established order. It also highlighted the absence of a basis for a Christian Democratic Party capable of mobilizing mass Catholic support for "liberal-democratic" institutions. Laymen were mobilized by Acción Católica and allied bodies but these were clerically controlled groups primarily involved in pastoral work. Their effective- ness, moreover, was limited by shortages of priests and low educational levels. Their greatest successes were in the most economically and socially developed regions where Catholic activists were drawn to local nationalist

[19] Its full name is the Sociedad Sacerdotal de la Santa Cruz y Opus Dei. On Opus Dei cf. Daniel Artigues, *El Opus Dei en España* and Jesus Ynfante, *La Prodigiosa Aventura del Opus Dei*. Both published by Ruedo Ibérico, Paris.

parties. The hierarchy's fear of providing a vehicle for *Integristas* and, from 1851, the absence of stridently anti-clerical governments, also delayed the mass mobilization of Catholics. The Church relied more on the State than upon its own laymen for defending its interests.

The problem of the military[20]

The problem of the military finally requires attention. The army emerged from the National War of Independence with greater prestige and more cohesion than any other purely national institution. That conflict also encouraged the army to view itself as the embodiment and final arbiter of "the general will". Civilian politicians soliciting military help in the seizure of power further encouraged such thinking. Thus military coups or *pronunciamientos* became frequent and the "man on horseback" or "Caudillo" a common phenomenon. Conventions arose, in fact, regulating the conduct of *pronunciamientos*. Commanders, often from outside Madrid, "pronounced" against the Government and hoped to rally sufficient support from colleagues to guarantee its overthrow.[21]

Nevertheless, most officers initially regarded themselves as "liberals". Military intervention was usually presented as the means of preserving or restoring constitutional government. This was partly because the early liberals regarded a professional army as a precondition of national unity and so defended its interests. Later the anti-militarism of republican and working-class movements combined with class and regional conflicts to foster more obviously authoritarian attitudes. Disturbances of public order offended against military concepts of discipline, and regional movements challenged the army's commitment to a unitary state. Simultaneously, antipathy grew toward civilian politicians. As the army became steadily more self-recruiting and socially isolated, so party politics were increasingly seen as unnecessarily divisive. Military disasters exacerbated such tensions. Soldiers tended to be made the scapegoats for the events of 1898,

[20]For a general discussion cf. Stanley G. Payne, *Politics and the Military in Modern Spain*, London, 1967.

[21]It is worth underlining that the chief threat to Spanish governments has not come from revolutionary upheavals in Madrid but from military leaders outside the capital. This contrasts with France's revolutionary tradition which has entailed disturbances of public order in the national capital. Partly for this reason Madrid has not, until very recently, had a special system of local government.

and later Moroccan reverses, whilst they blamed defeats on the incompetence of politicians. The army felt blows to national prestige with particular keenness and despaired of national regeneration through parliamentary government. Territorial losses also deprived it of a useful professional role. An officer corps, already demoralized by promotion blockages, was further frustrated by dwindling opportunities for rewarding service. The establishment of a Moroccan protectorate offered scope to some (and troops serving there came to be regarded as part of Spain's military élite), but most soldiers were left with no obvious role apart from acting as domestic policemen. Encouragement to play this part came from those traditional political, bureaucratic, economic and even ecclesiastical élites who constituted the principal outside contacts of military leaders. As tensions heightened they increasingly looked to the army for assistance and encouraged it to view itself as the ultimate guarantor of public order and national unity. The propensity to intervene overtly in politics and to espouse authoritarian political attitudes consequently increased.

THE SECOND REPUBLIC AND THE
CIVIL WAR

All these conflicts intensified during the Second Republic. Its first government tried to ensure army loyalty by reducing its numbers, curbing its privileges and promoting republicans. A republican para-military force, the "Asaltos" (Assault Guards), was established as a counterweight to the Civil Guard. The Church was dis-established, anti-clerical legislation was passed and popular manifestations of anti-clericalism went largely unchecked. In the socio-economic sphere a start was made on land redistribution and protective labour legislation sought greater bargaining power for trade unions. Finally, Catalonia secured some autonomy. All this induced clerical, business and agrarian interests to form a new party, la Confederación Española de Derechas Autónomas (la C.E.D.A.), which seemed, to opponents, to threaten the republic's existence. Its leader was initially prepared to work through parliamentary channels but many grass-roots supporters and some financial backers were less committed to the Republic. [22] These groups, drawn from the traditional *clases medias* and

[22] C.E.D.A.'s leader, J. M. Gil Robles, has published an informative volume of memoirs, *No fue posible la paz*, Barcelona, 1968.

from the upper classes, blamed the Republic for breakdowns in order and feared for established institutions. The party particularly aroused suspicions, on the left, by parading some of the trappings of contemporary fascist movements.

On the left the Republic's creation met with great enthusiasm and Socialists participated in its first government. Disillusionment, however, quickly followed. Agrarian reforms came slowly and, confronted by depression and unemployment, the Government resorted to orthodox monetary policies and retrenchment. Such factors, plus an unprecedented expansion of the U.G.T. into disturbed rural areas, pushed the socialist movement towards a more revolutionary posture. Competition from the C.N.T. reinforced this tendency. Elections held in 1933 therefore saw some left-wing disarray and large working-class abstentions. Conservative groups, by contrast, tended to rally round C.E.D.A. Thus a government emerged requiring the latter's support. It antagonized the left by reversing earlier reforms and it also got involved in disputes over the extent of Catalan autonomy. C.E.D.A.'s eventual entry into the Government provoked an outright Catalan challenge to the State's authority, which quickly collapsed, and a more serious workers' rising. This occurred in the mining area of Asturias in October 1934, with support from the U.G.T., the C.N.T., and the small, relatively new, Communist Party. The rising was quashed, thanks to troops commanded by General Franco, but its consequences were far reaching. Firstly, it firmly established Franco's reputation on the Spanish right. His position as a national figure, gained in the course of a spectacular military career, was confirmed. More importantly, the rising precipitated a polarization of opinion. On the right support grew for groups proposing authoritarian solutions to national problems. The most influential was Renovación Española whose supporters, in business, the army and the Church, advocated a corporate state. [23] Secondly, there was the Carlist Comunión Tradicionalista which trained a militia for use against the Republic. Finally, there was the Falangist Party which had little importance before 1936, apart from participating in street violence that did much to discredit the Republic. On the left the groups which co-operated in Asturias formed a "Popular

[23]Its leader was Calvo Sotelo, a former high-ranking civil servant and later Primo de Rivera's finance minister. His assassination in July 1936 was perhaps the immediate occasion of the military uprising.

Front" which, in February 1936, contested elections. They defeated a similar right-wing coalition and a government emerged needing their support. Moderate republican parties, torn by factionalism or with their reputations tarnished by scandal, were weakened or virtually eliminated.

Electoral victory encouraged left-wing forces to overestimate their strength. A substantial parliamentary majority stemmed from a narrow popular majority. Nevertheless, such fears of social revolution were aroused that even the most traditionally apathetic of the *clases medias* began to mobilize in their own defence. The Government's inability to maintain order lent credence to their fears. Urban terrorism increased and unofficial land seizures commenced. Ultimately a group of military leaders planned a *pronunciamiento* aimed at restoring stability. Their rising was not, however, wholly successful. Significant groups of officers and considerable portions of the rank and file stayed loyal to the Government. There was also stiff opposition from armed working-class organizations. Thus much of Spain, including major cities, stayed out of insurgent hands. Their rising, moreover, finally provoked a social revolution in areas remaining beyond their control.[24] A civil war became inevitable.

[24]For working-class politics of the period. cf Stanley G. Payne, *The Spanish Revolution*, London, 1970.

CHAPTER 2

The Civil War and the "Nationalist Régime"[1]

ALIGNMENTS DURING THE CIVIL WAR

Divisions within the army highlight the difficulty of generalizing about war-time alignments. Apart from the Carlists and orthodox Monarchist leaders no major group in Spanish society was exclusively allied with one side. Many simply made common cause with those who gained control of the locality in which they found themselves when war broke out. Nevertheless, alignments pointed to the basic cleavages in Spanish society. The Republic was supported by the organized working classes and most Catalans and Basques (outside of Navarra and Alava). The insurgents could count on a majority of the *clases medias*, the bulk of the upper class, most army officers, and a majority of active Catholics. Only in the Basque Country did large numbers of practising Catholics oppose the insurgents. They supported the local nationalists who, in exchange for the recognition of an autonomous Basque Government, adhered to the republican cause.

WHY THE REPUBLIC WAS DEFEATED

Several factors help to explain why, in April 1939, the insurgent "Nationalists" were ultimately victorious. They were of essentially three kinds—diplomatic, military and political. On the diplomatic front the Republic was hampered by the attitudes of the great European powers. Republican leaders regarded the war as the first round in a more general conflict between "fascism" and the "liberal-democracies" but Britain and France, fearful of provoking an international war, tried to persuade all the great powers to remain neutral. In practice this meant that the Republic

[1]The classic English work on the Civil War is Hugh Thomas, *The Spanish Civil War*, 2nd ed., Penguin Books, 1965.

21

received no assistance from the British and French Governments whilst Nazi Germany and Mussolini's Italy, anxious for a foothold in Spain, were virtually free to help the Nationalists as they saw fit. The Republic was therefore driven to depend largely upon the Soviet Union which was probably more interested in keeping the war going than in securing an outright republican victory. On the military front two factors favoured the Nationalists. Firstly, they proved more efficient than their opponents in the task of rapidly recruiting and training a well-disciplined army. Secondly, Soviet assistance proved less reliable than the aid supplied by Germany and Italy. There was some irony in this for most Nationalists, unlike their enemies, regarded the conflict as an essentially Spanish affair and discounted its international significance. They simply took what help they could find in the pursuit of domestic objectives. Finally, internal political divisions proved more damaging to the Republic than to the insurgents. Both sides encompassed competing groups but the popular enthusiasm which the outbreak of war provoked obscured their long-term conflicts of interest. These became more apparent as the enthusiasm waned. On the republican side there was tension between those pre-occupied with the defence of recent political gains and others who wished to subordinate everything to the task of securing victory. Thus there were conflicts between the central republican government, with overall responsibility for the war effort, and the Basque and Catalan authorities who were anxious to protect their hard-won prerogatives. There were further debilitating conflicts over the whole question of the nature of the State's authority.

Behind republican lines the social revolution of 1936 entailed a wholesale collapse of central authority. Economic control passed to local workers' councils under whose auspices the economy quickly ran down. Likewise, military power passed to decentralized militias whose revolutionary enthusiasm could not compensate for the absence of an effective command structure.

It was the Spanish Communist Party, allied with moderate Socialists, who took the lead in reconstructing state machinery better adapted to the exigencies of war. In July 1936 the party was relatively small. Most potential members had been pre-empted by the Socialists and the C.N.T. Four factors explain why it subsequently asserted itself. Firstly, Soviet aid added to its bargaining power. Secondly, its immediate objectives coincided with those of significant elements in the Socialist Party. Thirdly, its pragmatic espousal of moderate social policies enabled it to mobilize mass support amongst the *clases medias* caught in republican territory, whose interests had been threatened by earlier revolutionary developments. They reversed previous trends and successfully presented themselves as a party of stability and order. Finally, its discipline and ruthlessness served to override opposition and to capture key political posts.

The party, however, never wholly dominated republican Spain. Many allies resented its methods and suspected its intentions. The resulting feuds had an ennervating effect upon the prosecution of the war and left an enduring legacy of mistrust on the Spanish left. Ultimately republican morale completely collapsed and an end to resistance was heralded, characteristically, by a *pronunciamiento* directed against those wishing to continue the struggle.

The Nationalists were also divided. Their principal unifying force was a revulsion against disorder. The chief binding principle was a belief in the nebulous ". . . notion of an objectified historical Spain—disfigured and betrayed by Masons of the Republic".[2] The nature of the ". . . true Spain to be restored by violence"[3] was a contentious matter. They were, however, saved from the damaging feuds of their enemies. The insurgent generals, having seized the political initiative, were free to impose an artificial unity upon their followers. Moreover, their leader, General Franco, succeeded in welding the disparate elements under his command into a durable coalition.

POST-CIVIL-WAR POLITICAL PROBLEMS

Before examining Franco's régime more closely, an attempt will be made to isolate the turning-points in its history and the major problems it has confronted. This will signpost the way through subsequent discussions.[4]

During the 1940s the central issue in Spanish politics was the régime's survival. Its defeated enemies were in no position to fight back but they

[2]Cf. Raymond Carr, *Spain, 1808–1939, op. cit.* p. 644.
[3]*Ibid.*
[4]For a general survey of recent Spanish history cf. George Hills, *Spain*, London, 1970.

hoped that a combination of international pressures and internal divisions would provoke a collapse. Abroad the régime's reputation was mortgaged because of its links with the Axis powers. Hitler's efforts to draw Spain in the Second World War were successfully resisted but postures adopted in the process harmed her post-war international standing. The move from "neutrality" to "non-belligerency" when Germany invaded France; the sending of the "Blue Division" to fight alongside Germans on the Russian Front; and the assertion of claims to Gibraltar and to a larger North African empire all alienated the Allies. After 1945, therefore, Spain was subjected to diplomatic isolation and economic blockade. Spain was excluded, for example, from the Marshall Plan and from the United Nations.

International pressures were intended to foster political changes but they proved counter-productive. By presenting himself as a spokesman for national interests in the face of foreign threats Franco was able to consolidate his régime just as the fissures in it were becoming more apparent. The divisions arose, partly, from disputes over the "New State's" definitive form. The Nationalist camp contained republicans, orthodox monarchists, Carlists and the advocates of a fascist totalitarian state—all hoping to gain acceptance for their solution to Spain's political problems. Initially Franco prevaricated but inactivity became increasingly difficult. Monarchists, encouraged by the World War's outcome, became particularly impatient.[5] Ultimately the international boycott helped Franco to rally such support to his régime and so strengthened his hand that he felt free to impose his own solution. He declared Spain a monarchy but left himself free to nominate a monarch at an unspecified future date and under conditions of his own choosing. He became, in effect, Head of State for life.

This coup was followed by an intensification of the "cold war" and significant shifts in international attitudes. The United States government made conciliatory gestures, culminating in 1953 in the establishment in Spain of American air and naval bases and in grants of military and

---

[5]It is worth mentioning here that many monarchists were anglophiles. They felt their bargaining position had been strengthened by the victory of the Allies. Starting in 1943, pressure built up, but in 1945 with Falangist help Franco rounded up potentially dangerous monarchist leaders and disrupted the organization that they had created.

economic aid.[6] Later that year "provisional" agreements between the Vatican and Spain's Government, to which the Church had reluctantly agreed in 1941 in the interests of its pastoral work, were embodied in a Concordat. Eventually, in 1955, Spain was also admitted to the United Nations.[7] Such developments signalled an end to Spain's isolation. At home, they killed many doubts about the régime's durability and respectability. In the 1950s few continued to expect a quick collapse. The régime's own confidence was revealed, for example, in renewed claims to Gibraltar.

In the 1950s economic problems acquired a special importance in Spanish political debate. Initially international circumstances and the régime's national revivalist temper impelled it to adopt a policy of "autarchy" (or the search for national economic self-sufficiency), requiring massive state intervention. The economy's basic structure, however, was not greatly changed, and when, in the early 1950s, there was a measure of economic recovery, its basic weaknesses became very apparent. In 1957 Franco responded to this situation by changing the Government's economic managers and by permitting a shift of emphasis in official policies. Autarchy had already been criticized in business and academic circles as an unrealistic policy. After 1957 economic management was increasingly entrusted to skilled "technocrats" committed to revising the policy. They advocated a relaxation of state controls and a freer flow of overseas trade as the best path towards economic efficiency.

Their initial stop-gap measures proved insufficient to check mounting inflation, the depletion of exchange reserves and an increasing balance of payments deficit. Thus, in 1958, they launched a full-scale deflationary or "Stabilization" programme. This marked the start of Spain's full acceptance into the international financial and trading communities. In return for credit restrictions, public expenditure cuts, tax increases, an easing of restrictions on foreign investment, and some liberalization of trade, international support grants were made available to assist in a devaluation of the peseta. Spain also joined such bodies as the O.E.E.C. and G.A.T.T.

[6]Spain, for ideological reasons, remained excluded from N.A.T.O.

[7]During the years of isolation and after, Spain cultivated special relationships with some Latin American and Arab powers. Their support was important in gaining acceptance for Spanish membership of the United Nations. Portugal was also one of the few allies Spain could count upon during the years of isolation.

Later the World Bank's advice was sought on the economy's future development. Acting partly on its advice a development plan (for 1963–7) was launched. Immediately before and during this plan's course Spain experienced unprecedented economic expansion. Continuing difficulties with agriculture were partly compensated for by impressive industrial growth. In the process, however, Spain ran into the familiar problems of economic management in a mixed industrial economy. Delays in implementing a second plan highlighted the problems. Before initiating it the Government felt obliged to take more deflationary measures, to further devalue the peseta and to revise growth targets in a downward direction.

Economic liberalization was accompanied by tentative essays in political liberalization. They were in response to two kinds of pressure. Firstly, Spain's new economic managers felt that long-term economic security depended upon some association with the E.E.C. and they recognized that this must entail some relaxation of authoritarian controls. Secondly, the Government has had to face mounting internal pressures for political change from new generations less preoccupied with order and stability than those who experienced the events of the 1930s.

The debate on political liberalization has now merged into a wider discussion about the nature of the régime which will succeed Franco. Between 1947 and 1966 no formal measures were taken to deal with this question. In 1966, however, an "Organic Law" was enacted which provided some framework of constitutional law for the post-Franco era, including some clarification of a future monarch's prerogatives. Finally, in 1969, Franco nominated Alfonso XIII's grandson, Prince Juan Carlos, as the prospective King. There are two things about these arrangements which show that Franco's answer to the succession problem is essentially that of *continuismo*—or the continuance of authoritarian rule. Firstly, Franco bypassed Alfonso XIII's son, who is in the liberal-monarchist tradition, in favour of a candidate trained under his own auspices. Secondly, Franco states his intention to "install" and not "restore" the monarchy.

This solution is seen as a special triumph for the technocratic elements, whose influence, within Franco's régime, has steadily grown since 1957. They pressed Juan Carlos' candidature in order to provide a legal framework within which they could continue to pursue their élite-directed modernization programmes. Opposition to the arrangement has therefore not only come from the régime's outright opponents, but also from rigidly authoritarian and intensely nationalistic elements within the régime. The resulting conflicts underlie much of Spain's current political debate.

The nature of the "Nationalist régime"

It is against the background of these general trends that one must examine post-Civil-war efforts to resolve Spain's perennial conflicts. As will be seen, the régime to emerge from the war differed from contemporary totalitarian régimes in never trying to deny completely the society's pluralistic nature. Franco's Spain came to be equated, by domestic and foreign enemies, with Nazi Germany or Fascist Italy, but this was never an accurate picture. Fascist elements within the Nationalist camp advocated the proclamation of one official ideology and the mobilization of mass support for a state that would regulate all significant aspects of national life. In practice, however, the régime continued to draw support from and to acknowledge the existence of distinct and often conflicting groups. Moreover, the initiative always lay with entrenched and usually conservative interests whose first priority was preserving stability and who preferred passive acceptance of the established order to mass political participation or enthusiasm. They wanted a traditional authoritarian state capable of resisting pressures for radical social change. Particularly during the formative years Nationalist leaders accepted some of the appurtenances of a national-revivalist régime and sometimes indulged in radical nationalist rhetoric, but the régime represented an essentially conservative reaction against challenges to Spanish society's traditional patterns. This was apparent in studied efforts to represent its institutions as revivals of traditional bodies. The régime's legislature, for example, is described by the old term "Cortes" and not as a "Parliament". Likewise, the traditional name "Consejo del Reino" (Council of the Realm) was given to an institution, representative of Franco's main bodies of support, which he created to advise him on the succession problem.[8] The choice of such names signifies a conscious attempt to portray the régime as the guardian of traditional Spanish values that the "Liberal State" was commonly believed to have imperilled.

[8]Such institutions were frequently "dignified" rather than "efficient" parts of the political system but this does not alter the main point.

In practice the Nationalist régime could not ignore the Liberal State's legacy nor the politically significant forces to have emerged in Spain since the early nineteenth century. Thus, in its efforts to create an enduring form of authoritarian rule, it was impelled to see that no major social group remained wholly free from state control. In principle this was an attempt to harmonize conflicting interests.

In practice it has entailed the outlawing of overt opposition. Thus there has been no right to associate outside officially approved organizations. A law, enacted as late as 1964, forbade associations advocating independent trade unions or a competitive party system. Similarly, all channels of political communication are liable to state control. The press, for example, was subject to prior censorship until 1966 and editors could be compelled to publish official statements. A law of 1966 relaxed such controls but freedom of expression remains subject to several and often ill-defined limitations.[9] Journals held to have infringed official regulations are liable to the seizure of the offending issue, fines or suspension of publication. There is a right of appeal to the courts but this does not necessarily compensate for the economic damage that can be inflicted. Moreover, editors officially "warned" three times can be dismissed without appeal. Finally, it should be borne in mind that all journalists have to be trained in an officially controlled School of Journalism. The State generally permits more criticism of official policies than it did before 1966 and, especially in academic publications, it tolerates *sub rosa* discussions of controversial issues but publishers can still be harried, forced out of business and prevented from communicating with mass audiences. The press is permitted to reflect and to express a variety of viewpoints but the closure of the independent-minded newspaper *Madrid*, towards the end of 1971, confirmed that sustained and outright opposition will not be tolerated.[10]

---

[9]*De facto* censorship was relaxed with a change of Information Minister, in 1962, but the law was not changed until 1966. Cf. Ley de Prensa e Imprenta, 18 March 1966.

[10]The limited evidence available indicates that high percentages of Spaniards do not regularly receive political information and comment via the press. Their sources of information and comment are more likely to be the more rigidly controlled radio and television networks. In part the relatively low levels of newspaper readership may be due to the absence of controversy, and possibly both a cause and an effect of the "depoliticization" of significant segments of society in post–Civil-war Spain.

The Nationalist régime and political parties

The régime's approach is best seen in its attitude to political parties. In July 1936 army leaders proscribed most political activity. On the whole this ban was easily enforced. Left-wing parties were dissolved, right-wing parliamentary parties were discredited and groups like Renovación Española lacked large popular bases. The Carlists and Falangists, however, fell into a different category.[11] Their militias provided rearguard assistance and their propaganda helped to mobilize support for the war. Its content seemed relevant to a conflict that was being presented in highly charged ideological terms. Both attracted considerable support. Carlism, however, remained an essentially Navarrese movement. The Falangists therefore claim most attention.

The Falange Española y de las Juntas Ofensivas Nacional Sindicalista was created from mergers between three small groups. The chief one, the Falange Española, was founded in 1933 by José Antonio Primo de Rivera, a son of the dictator. It was a complex phenomenon but it may be regarded as a Spanish variant of Fascism, owing something to contemporary Italian and German models. It offered a radical nationalist alternative to the left-wing revolutionary movements. Thus a small élite would seize power, by force if necessary, and establish a totalitarian state able to play an imperial role. Support would be mobilized by official *sindicatos*—or unions—geared to promote radical socio-economic reforms.

The party attracted little support before 1936. A nucleus of idealists coexisted with students attracted by a cult of violence. Several factors explain this. Firstly, Spain's neutrality in the First World War left her without Germany's and Italy's problem of absorbing a generation of disillusioned nationalists. Secondly, the C.N.T. pre-empted potential working-class support. Thirdly, the *clases medias* experienced no economic crisis sufficient to foster radical attitudes. Finally, Spain's upper classes, forewarned by similar movements elsewhere, suspected the party's radicalism.

After February 1936 it expanded rapidly. Many then viewed it as a last defence against social revolution. Later, in Nationalist territory, it

[11]On the subject of the Falange cf. Stanley G. Payne, *Falange. A History of Spanish Fascism*, London, 1961. Cf. also the same author's article in H. Rogger and E. Weber (editors), *The European Right*, London, 1965, pp. 168–207.

frequently seemed the only credible political force. But several factors prevented it from capitalizing upon its accesses of strength. Its leaders were nearly all caught in republican territory and were imprisoned or executed. Most new recruits came from the *clases medias*. They had mobilized in defence of the established order and remained fundamentally conservative. Of the rest, many were opportunists or left wingers seeking refuge. Finally, Nationalist Spain's ultimate political arbiter, the army, remained suspicious of the party.

Nevertheless, in the then heated atmosphere, an organization was required to harness popular energies, to provide an official ideology, and to absorb and discipline hostile populations. Military leaders also wished to reassure their German and Italian allies. The Falangists and (to a lesser extent) the Carlists were obvious instruments for these purposes. Thus in 1937 the army's supreme commander, Franco, forcibly merged these ill-matched movements to form Nationalist Spain's one legal party, the Falange Española Tradicionalista y de las J.O.N.S. Both groups lost their freedom of action. Franco was designated party chief, or "Caudillo". He effectively appointed the party's chief policy-making body, the National Council, and its principal executive organ, the *Junta Política*. He also nominated a Secretary General to control the party's bureaucracy. These powers were used, moreover, to isolate committed Falangists and Carlists. They became outnumbered on the party's official bodies by representatives of other groups. Finally, all army officers automatically became party members.

The feeble resistance to these developments underlined and subsequent events confirmed the essential weakness of the Carlists and the Falangists. Carlists were appeased by concessions to the Church but Falangists secured few of their objectives. The National Council, for example, prepared a "Labour Charter" in 1938 which paid little more than lip-service to Falangist ideals.[12]

After the Civil War most Carlists withdrew to their regional stronghold. Only a minority actively co-operated with the régime. A nucleus of committed Falangists continued to urge the creation of a dynamic totalitarian party, but without success. The conditions for mobilizing mass support no longer existed. In the aftermath of war most Spaniards

[12]This is the "Fuero del Trabajo" of 9 Mar. 1938. It was modified and republished in the *Boletin Oficial del Estado* (henceforth described as B.O.E.) of 21 Apr. 1967.

eschewed political activity and took refuge in private life. Falangists, far
from extending their base, saw many existing supporters return to their
traditional apathy. Even militants usually preferred conformity to anything likely to disrupt the régime. Thus efforts made (in 1940) to launch
an active youth movement and attempts (in 1940–1) to get official *sindicatos* to mobilize working-class support were both easily checked by
conservative political, military and business leaders. Likewise, Falangists
failed to maintain a network of party agencies, created during the war
with a view to supervising parallel state institutions, and they did not
succeed in making party membership a prerequisite for access to senior
administrative and political posts. Finally, their militia was effectively
neutralized.

Several factors explain these circumstances. First, there was, everywhere,
a reaction against ideological conflict and a weariness of violence. Many
were further demoralized by post-war economic privations. Repression
also played its part. A law of 1939 on "Political Responsibilities" armed
military courts with wide and retrospective powers designed to root out
potential opposition leaders.[13] They sentenced large numbers to death or
to lengthy prison sentences and were frequently used to settle old political
scores. A minority of Falangist intellectuals urging "national recon-
ciliation" was ignored. The régime's working- and radical middle-class
opponents were therefore forced into sullen acquiescence. Within the
Falangist Party itself Franco's nominees, in positions of leadership, used
their patronage to erode the remaining independence of party militants.
They deliberately created a network of vested interests in the *status quo*.
Falangists were appointed to governmental agencies and local government
bodies. Many were compromised by the corrupt handling of official
contracts and licences. The net effect of such developments was an
enervating and oppressive atmosphere quite inimical to the success of a
radical national revivalist movement.

After 1945 the party lost still more ground. This was related, in part at
least, to the outcome of the World War. The Axis powers' defeat subsequently made it a liability rather than an asset in Spain's dealings with
foreign powers. The decline in influence was apparent at all levels.
Locally it was reflected in continuing drops in membership. At the

[13]Such courts continue to be convened. Cf. The section below on the military for
further references to them.

national level loss of party control over the politically important activity of censorship was an indicator of the situation. The party even began to lose its identity. Franco increasingly replaced references to it with references to the vaguer concept of a "Movement" embracing all government supporters. Falangists staffed the Movement's bureaucracy but its policy-making organs largely remained appointed bodies lacking real independence. Likewise, Falangists continued to receive government appointments but as members of coalitions in which they were clearly outnumbered by the representatives of rival groups.[14] Only once, in 1956, were there determined efforts to revive the party and to reassert its independence, but they failed. Indeed, in 1958 Franco unilaterally decreed "the Fundamental Principles of the Movement" that contained little specifically Falangist content and gave vague assurances to all the régime's constituent groups.

All this indicates that the original Falangist party had become an amorphous, if highly bureaucratized institution, providing few opportunities for genuine popular political participation. In practice it retains only two important functions. It serves as an official propaganda instrument which, particularly in times of political crisis, provides the régime with ideological "window dressing". It also acts as a patronage network providing jobs for some of those who rallied to the Nationalists in 1936 and subsequently followed political careers under the Movement's auspices. Its central and provincial bureaucracies and its plethora of affiliated organizations offer additional sources of employment to portions of those *clases medias* who have traditionally looked to the State for their material security. Such essentially conformist elements have made no sustained attempts to encourage popular political participation or to generate positive popular support for the régime.

Nevertheless, the Movement remains Spain's only forum for legitimate political activity. Since 1966 Franco has spoken of permitting "clashes of opinion" and diverse discussion groups have formed. They include small groups of independent Falangists who favour the creation of an authoritarian republic pursuing radical social policies and a neutralist foreign

[14]In 1955 provision was made for the indirect election of fifty National Council members—on the basis of one from each Province. The elections are, however, carefully supervised by the Movement's central Secretariat. Also, the Council's expansion makes it still less effective as a policy-making organ.

policy. There is also a liberal monarchist group. Such groups point to the existence of perhaps three main tendencies within the Movement's higher echelons; those favouring the *status quo*; those advocating some institutionalization of dissent under the general auspices of the Movement; and those who urge a more thoroughgoing liberalization process. The Organic Law of 1966 and a law of 1968, redefining the Movement's organizational principles, make it clear, however, that independent parties, free to bid for popular support, will not be legalized. It is equally plain that the Movement is unlikely to become a dynamic institution, capable of providing a framework within which Spain's fundamental conflicts may be resolved.

The problem of class conflict under Franco's régime

This is particularly true of class conflicts. In principle the Nationalists rejected the notion of class conflict. The State was to harmonize the interests of capital and labour. Thus a law of 1940 obliged all employees (except public officials, professional groups and domestic servants) and employers to join official *sindicatos* created on the basis of one for each sector of the economy.[15] A hierarchy stretched from the local to the provincial and national levels. At each level employers were to be represented on consultative bodies (known as "economic sections") and employees were to be represented on similar bodies (known as "social sections").[16] Spokesmen for both sides could meet together, on theoretically equal terms. Executive powers, however, were vested in a chain of centrally appointed officials headed by a *Delegado Nacional* responsible to the Movement's Secretary-General.[17] Likewise, elections to the con-

[15]Cf. "Ley de Unidad Sindical", 26 Jan. 1940. The Syndical structure is described in F. Witney, *Labour Policies and Practices in Spain*, New York, 1965. An official explanation comes in C. Iglesias Selgas, *Los Sindicatos en España*, Madrid, 1965, and an opposition critique cf. Cuadernos para el Diàlogo, *Numero Extraordinario*, XII, Madrid, 1968.

[16]There are also special "sections" representing managerial grades.

[17]From 1957 to 1969 these two offices were combined in the person of Sr. Solís who had a seat in the Council of Ministers. He was succeeded, in the major reshuffle of 1969 by two ministers—one at the head of the Movement and one responsible for the *Sindicatos*. The latter is a business man with no previously known political connections. This is further evidence of the decline of the Falangists and of their replacement by non-political technocrats.

sultative bodies were indirect—thus permitting the official screening of candidates.

In addition strikes were banned and, as a *quid pro quo*, the employers' power to dismiss was restricted. Collective disputes were thus officially precluded. Conflicts between individual employers and employees were referred to special labour courts dependent upon the Labour Ministry.

The principles underlying this system were borrowed from the original Falangist plan for a "National Syndicalist State". The plan, however, has not been realized. Falangists have continued to staff the syndical bureaucracy but they have been unable to implement their party's pre-Civil-war conception. In practice the *Sindicatos* have served as instruments for controlling rather than mobilizing workers. Most workers have therefore never regarded them as genuinely representative institutions. They have perhaps obtained some acceptance in newly industrialized areas lacking trade-union traditions but elsewhere their legitimacy is questioned. Their effectiveness in defending workers' interests also appears to vary from region to region. They are perhaps least effective in southern rural areas where landowners still hamper the enforcement of land reforms and welfare programmes. They are most effective in industrial areas where employers and employees have been long accustomed to union activity. But everywhere employers generally have greater bargaining power.

This is principally because workers have no effective strike weapon. Restricted powers of dismissal have, in reality, done more to encourage economic inefficiency than to compensate for bans on withdrawals of labour. Over-manning has been encouraged and mobility of labour discouraged, but the bargaining hand of employees has not been strengthened.[18] In practice they have less freedom than employers to organize in defence of their interests. Although small and some medium-sized enterprises tend to work through the official syndical channels, the biggest companies have been able to maintain private and less formalized arrangements for concerting resistance to working-class pressures. Representatives of the largest employers have also been able to short-circuit the *Sindicatos* in their dealings with government departments. Labour's case, however, (at anything above plant level), is almost always put by centrally appointed

[18]It should also be noted that enterprises in economic difficulties can get government permission to lay off workers. In practice this is done fairly frequently and sometimes on thin pretexts.

officials. There have been occasions, during widespread unofficial strikes, when the Government has treated with unofficial workers' leaders but these have represented *ad hoc* responses to emergencies and not a lasting change of policy.

Labour's position was weakest from 1940 to 1958. During those years the Labour Ministry determined wages and conditions and the *Sindicatos* were mainly responsible for enforcing official decisions. Falangist Labour Minister saw that workers' interests were not wholly ignored but the general tendency was to keep their living standards at low levels.

Most workers were therefore not reconciled to the régime. This helps to explain a limited resumption of opposition activities after 1950. By then the régime felt more secure and relied less on coercion.[19] Also, Spain was again open to foreign influences. Finally, capital accumulated during the years of isolation, later supplemented by American aid, encouraged economic expansion. Thus expectations were aroused which the régime could not satisfy. In these circumstances left-wing groups, which had never been wholly dormant, began to revive. The Socialist Party regained adherents in traditional strongholds and the Communist Party made headway. For example, it partially filled the gap left in southern Spain by anarchists.

The impact of these groups was, however, limited. Intermittent police activity removed leaders and disrupted their organizations. The leaders, moreover, were divided. There were divisions between indigenous and exiled leaders and between those within Spain itself. The Communist Party, in particular, remained suspect to its left-wing competitors. Finally, many workers had become more interested in economic than ideological issues.[20]

Opposition groups consequently had more success on the industrial than the political front. Illegal strikes exposed the weakness of official

[19]Less active and widespread repression does not necessarily mean a reduction of the State's capacity for capricious and arbitrary behaviour toward its opponents. Legal charges can be kept pending against individuals for lengthy periods or they may be arrested long after committing the offences with which they may be charged. Equally, "emergency powers" can be invoked to have large-scale round-ups of opposition leaders. Thus the Government retains the means for harassing opponents and disrupting their organizations.

[20]Opposition groups are the subject of comment in Sergio Vilar, *Les Oppositions a Franco*, Paris, 1968.

unions, the survival of an independent working-class consciousness and the success of unofficial leaders in mobilizing support. Official leaders responded by pressing for reforms designed to revitalize the syndical apparatus. Concessions were eventually made. They came in an attempt to compensate Falangists for the Government's espousal of more liberal economic policies and for the loss of Falangist influence implied in this shift of emphasis. Thus, in 1957, more open elections for shop stewards were permitted and, in 1958, a form of collective bargaining was instituted. Minimum wages were still decreed but, subject to compulsory arbitration in the event of deadlock, employers and employees could negotiate detailed local agreements. Later, "non-political strikes" were legalized.

These measures failed to achieve their objectives. On the contrary they have aroused new expectations without satisfying basic demands. Collective bargaining, for example, has stimulated militancy without drastically strengthening the bargaining power of workers' representatives. Many have lacked the expertise needed to exploit the system or have been frustrated by the syndical bureaucracy's slowness in handling claims. Also, the system of compulsory arbitration has encouraged employers to look for state assistance in resisting wage demands. The Government, for its part, has tended to concentrate more upon stabilizing wages than prices. Increased production has yielded wage increases but demands for income redistribution are unsatisfied and there are indications of a growing gap between better and poorly paid workers.

Similarly, the more open system for electing shop stewards has done more to reveal the extent of dissent than to transform official institutions. The elections permitted Socialists, Communists and members of Catholic workers' associations to capture positions within the official structure. Moreover, these groups joined to form unofficial Workers' Commissions which, particularly after 1964, spread throughout Spain. But hopes of transforming the *Sindicatos* from within, which were particularly high amongst Catholic unionists, proved illusory. This was especially true of attempts to explore the possibilities of strike action. The Government viewed most strikes as essentially "political" and the courts upheld the right of employers to dismiss strikers. Thus the *Sindicatos* have conducted purges of local activists and employers have been able to sack unofficial workers' leaders.

Frustrated expectations have been reflected, in the 1960s, in fairly steady increases in the scope and intensity of industrial conflict. During the years of the most rapid economic growth (1963–6) there were regions like Asturias and industries like iron and steel in which the incidence of industrial conflict was particularly high. Moreover, since 1970, there has been an increase in industrial disputes with an essentially political motivation; disputes registering disapproval of official policies and aimed at undermining confidence in the Government. Indications exist, however, that economic growth may prevent a revival of class conflict on the pre-Civil-war scale. A much larger salaried and non-traditional middle class is now emerging. There are also indications that skilled industrial workers now have some (albeit limited) prospects of social mobility. Equally, many workers, now apparently preoccupied with material security rather than revolutionary social changes, have, with other groups, some stake in an emergent "mass consumer society". Finally, agrarian conflicts may, to some extent, diminish for industrialization has attracted much of the rural proletariat to urban areas. By 1960 below 40 per cent of Spain's working population was engaged in agriculture.[21] Rural living standards still lag well behind those generally found in urban areas but fewer people (in both relative and absolute terms) are affected by this situation than was the case in 1936.[22]

Nevertheless, serious inequalities of income and significant groups of workers who do feel alienated from the present society make it certain that class conflicts will remain an important feature of Spanish politics. It is equally clear that the existing *Sindicatos* cannot resolve these conflicts. Indeed, the failure of moderate opposition groups to transform them from within has probably strengthened the hand of more militant elements. A new Syndical Law was enacted in 1971 in another attempt to breathe life into official unions but subsequent events indicate that the reform was

[21]By 1969, according to official figures, only 30 per cent of the working population was engaged in agriculture. This remains a large figure when compared with most other West European countries but it is a drastic reduction on pre-Civil-war figures. In 1969 industry employed 37 per cent of the working population and services 33 per cent.

[22]It also seems probable that anarchism, given the relatively complex state of contemporary Spanish society, now appears to be a less viable solution than it did before the Civil War.

quite inadequate for the purpose.[23] Though its preparation was accompanied by consultations that would have been inconceivable in 1940, the net result was an extremely limited change. In some cases the changes are little more than changes in terminology. The basic principles of the system remain unaltered. Massive strike waves, like those of October 1971, which have affected most of Spain's major industrial centres, indicate the extent of working-class frustration in this situation and the very limited support that exists for National Syndicalism. This does not necessarily present an immediate threat to the Nationalist Régime's safety. Indeed, it could be argued that in the short run unofficial union activity may be of some assistance to the régime for it provides a safety valve for dissent and a means of gauging the state of working-class opinion. In the long term, however, it presents policy-makers with a dilemma which they can resolve in only one of two ways—by a reversion to widespread repression or through more thoroughgoing reforms.

The problem of the universities and "Intellectual Dissent"

The Movement has also failed to eliminate dissent in the universities and amongst professional groups. The Nationalists regarded the universities with suspicion because of their part in producing the Republic's political leadership. They also probably recalled the part played by students in Primo de Rivera's downfall. Thus a law of 1942 empowered Falangists to supervise the content of university education and obliged all students to join their student union, "Sindicato Estudiantil Universitario" (S.E.U.). Control was always imperfect. Academic freedom was restricted but Falangist doctrine made little positive impact. Until the early 1950s, at least, Education ministers effectively made appointments to university chairs. Appointments were officially made through the traditional system of *oposiciones*, or academic disputation before a tribunal. In practice the tribunals could be packed. Likewise, ministers personally appointed university rectors. As the ministers came from Catholic groups their appointees were as likely to be members of Opus Dei, for example, as committed Falangists. Also, S.E.U., like other unions, was principally an

[23]This law and the general problem of industrial conflict is discussed in M. Martinez Cuadrado, *Anuario Político Español, 1970*, Madrid, 1971, pp. 695–750 and 359–438. The text of the law (approved by the Cortes on 16 Feb. 1971) appears on pp. 710–28.

instrument of control. Most members gave it only a nominal allegiance. Thus when opposition revived, in the 1950s, universities became centres of dissent and the tradition of student protest revived.

Initially there were few active dissenters and they concentrated upon freeing universities from Falangist control. They received some encouragement from an Education Minister, appointed in 1951, who tried to reduce the importance of political criteria in academic appointments. His mild reforms led, in 1956, to a direct clash, at Madrid University, between Falangists and their opponents. This precipitated a political crisis and the minister's dismissal.[24] The crisis had significant repercussions. It convinced many seeking for a more open political system that major changes could not be introduced from within the régime. Its impact was greatest in the universities where opposition could crystallize rapidly.

Three significant univeristy reform movements eventually formed— one led by distinguished academics and the others led, respectively, by Communist and Christian Democratic students. They all pressed for increased academic freedom and for more representative student organizations. S.E.U. ultimately became so patently unrepresentative that it was replaced by associations whose officials, at lower levels, were elected. The associations remained subject to official supervision, however, and electoral abstentions indicated an absence of student support. Official institutions, were *de facto*, supplanted by unofficial bodies. They are now, belatedly, receiving state recognition.

Criticism of university conditions has sometimes broadened out into a questioning of the political system. Thus opposition parties frequently recruit leaders from the universities. A small Social Democratic Party and Christian Democratic groups depend upon university-based leadership.[25] The traditional Socialist Party and the Communists (now divided into a pro-Moscow faction and a majority inclined to take a more independent line) also have considerable intellectual support.

Higher education remains a largely middle- and upper-class preserve.

[24]This minister, Sr. Ruiz Jiménez, has subsequently moved into opposition. He is a prominent leader of Christian Democratic opinion and has founded a periodical, *Cuadernos para el Diálogo*, which has become a prestigious vehicle for the expression of moderate opposition views.

[25]In some of these cases leadership is provided by former Falangists who have been moving into opposition since it has become clear that the original Falangist aims were not going to be realized.

Growing opposition, within universities, therefore indicates a spreading of dissent to portions of society which, in preceding generations, were largely conformist. Even the children of prominent Nationalist leaders are now sometimes involved. This may partly explain why, in 1969, student disturbances led to the declaration of a national emergency. Another factor may have been fears, inspired by events in France in 1968, of students spearheading a more widely based opposition. The opportunity was certainly taken to disrupt university-based and working-class opposition groups. Government members who regarded such drastic steps as counter-productive regained the initiative but the time for conciliatory gestures may now have passed. Groups who have been urging greater university autonomy are now being hard pressed by militant Marxists and radical Christian Democrats who repudiate all dealings with the Government. Universities are therefore likely to remain centres for dissent.[26]

During the 1960s overt opposition has spread beyond the Universities to other intellectual and professional groups. Thus prominent intellectuals have publicly protested against arbitrary uses of power. Protests have also come from organized professional bodies. After 1939 professional associations were subjected to state supervision and their office holders were often government appointees. Later, greater autonomy was permitted but they still usually limited themselves to defending narrow professional interests. Recently, however, some bodies have become involved in political controversies. A notable example was that of the College of Lawyers which, in 1969, requested the abolition of special procedures for the trial of political offenders and asked that political prisoners should not be treated as common criminals. It appears that, in the absence of an institutionalized opposition, established professional bodies are becoming channels for expressing dissent. It also appears that traditionally conservative professional groups, confronted by an authoritarian state, are being driven, by the values of their professions, into more radical positions.[27]

[26]Disturbances at the University of Madrid, in Jan. 1972, seem to confirm this view. On the University problem cf. P. Lain, *Entralgo El Problema de la Universidad*, Madrid, 1968, and J. L. Aranguren, *El Problema Universitario*, Barcelona, 1968.

[27]Defence lawyers in trials of a political nature inevitably become spokesmen for opposition groups.

The regional problem

The Nationalists also attempted to apply authoritarian solutions to regional conflicts. Catalonia and the Basque Country lost their autonomous status and the Basque Provinces of Guipúzcoa and Vizcaya lost their traditional financial privileges. Navarra and Alava, by contrast, retained their privileges as a reward for adhering to the Nationalist cause. Efforts were also made to weaken the Catalan and Basque cultures by forbidding the use of their languages on public occasions or for educational purposes. Nevertheless, the regional problem remains. Periodic conciliatory gestures highlight the survival of regional loyalties which the State cannot ignore. Thus systematic efforts to destroy cultural traditions now seem to have been abandoned. In 1966 Guipúzcoa and Vizcaya's provincial councils even felt free to petition (albeit unsuccessfully) for the restoration of their old rights.

For many Catalans and Basques, however, small conciliatory gestures remain insufficient. Particularly in the Basque Country demands for autonomy, and even secession, continue and have considerable local support. In Catalonia there has been constant friction between the local population and the State's representatives. Barcelona has witnessed examples of passive resistance which twice, at least, have induced the Government to remove agents who had offended local susceptibilities. Similarly, the Basque Nationalist Party survives and retains the loyalty of much of its traditional constituency. Moreover, the emergence of stronger left-wing Basque groups, notably E.T.A. (Freedom for the Basques), indicates growing intransigence and impatience amongst sectors of the post-Civil-war generation. They resort to terrorism and advocate revolutionary social changes.

Such groups are not in the mainstream of Basque nationalism. Most Basque nationalists probably oppose their methods and reject their Marxist orientation. Nevertheless, a stiffening of state resistance, particularly since 1967, to all expressions of nationalist sentiment, has exacerbated local hostility towards the central government and awakened some sympathy for the radical elements. This was apparent during the major political crisis of Christmas 1970, occasioned by the trial before a military court of E.T.A. members accused, in certain instances, of assassination. The trial seems to have been an essentially political device. It was intended to demonstrate the Nationalist Régime's determination to resist Basque Nationalist demands. In practice it helped to consolidate Basque opinion. [28]

The crisis shed interesting light on the regional issue's continuing sensitivity. Falangists and some groups within the army went to the length of encouraging popular demonstrations designed, in part, to urge the taking of a stern line with Basque nationalists. They revealed the Spanish Right's still strong emotional attachment to the concept of a unitary Spanish State. Indeed, the threat of secession is one issue which might still provoke overt military intervention.

Despite this evidence there are reasons for supposing that the regional issue, though still a potential source of instability, may ultimately prove less explosive than it was before the Civil War. Firstly, industrial growth outside of Catalonia and the Basque Country, notably around Madrid, means that the old gulf between Spain's centres of political and economic power has now to some extent been bridged. Conflicts of economic interest should, in the long term, be less intense than they were before 1936. Large-scale migrations to the Basque and Catalan Provinces, from other regions, might also, in the long run, lower tensions. On the other hand, the capacity of the local communities, particularly in Catalonia, to absorb migrants, suggests that the basis remains for strong regional parties. [29]

The problem of the Church

The religious problem also received attention from the Nationalists. Pre-Civil-war attacks upon the Church not only alienated Catholics who had originally been prepared to accept the Republic but they also reactivated pro-clerical sentiments amongst many previously indifferent members of the *clases medias*. Thus most Catholics were on the Nationalist

[28]For accounts of these events, written from an opposition viewpoint, cf. G. Halimi, *Le Procé de Burgos* and K. Salaberrio *El Proceso de Euskadi en Burgos*. Both published in Paris, 1971. My own study of the Basque problem, done for the Minority Rights Group, will appear in 1972.

[29]For this issue cf. Juan J. Linz's article, "The party system of Spain: past and future", in S. M. Lipset and S. Rokkan (editors), *Party Systems and Voter Alignments*, New York, 1967. At present, in Catalonia, class conflict bulks larger than the regional issue but reactions amongst workers and intellectuals, to the Burgos trial, show that the issue is not dead.

side in the Civil War and their military leaders encouraged them to view the conflict as a "crusade". Likewise, the hierarchy (with few exceptions) publicly supported the Nationalist cause. This greatly strengthened the "New State's" claims to legitimacy. In return the Church received privileges sufficient to satisfy all but the most militant *Integristas*.[30] They were so extensive that some Catholic leaders foresaw the possibility of uniting Spaniards within the framework of a "new Catholic culture". Anti-clerical legislation was repealed. The State subsidized clerical stipends and Church building. On matters such as divorce, Canon Law became Civil Law. Ecclesiastical censorship was imposed alongside state censorship. Catholic instruction became compulsory throughout the educational system and most secondary schools were left completely in Church hands. Finally, Protestants lost the right to hold public office, to worship publicly and to proselytize. They were also periodically harried by state officials. Catholic organizations, by contrast, were exempt from most of the restrictions usually placed upon freedom of association. They were free to organize in pursuit of social and pastoral objectives.

The State, however, demanded some control over the Church. Thus it successfully pressed for a revival of the "Real Patronato". A procedure was instituted (in 1941) for appointing bishops which, in effect, gave the State a veto. The Concordat of 1952 gave permanent form to this and other agreements between the Church and State.[31]

Active support from Catholics has further strengthened the régime. The Movement has its chaplains and some bishops have sat in the Cortes. More importantly, prominent Catholic laymen have participated in the Government. Catholic Action (through its adjunct A.N.C.P.) has supplied ministers. As some of these could have fitted equally well into the right wing of a Christian Democratic Party they have, through their participation, helped to still the doubts that many middle-class Catholics came to have about the régime. Above all, Opus Dei has furnished the Government with important reserves of political and administrative expertise.

[30]For a general review of the post-Civil-war Church cf. William G. Ebenstein, *Church and State in Franco's Spain*, Princeton, 1960. For a sociological survey cf. J. M. Vazquez, *Realidades Socio-religiosas de España*, Madrid, 1967.

[31]The procedure is as follows: the Government in consultation with the Papal Nuncio chooses six names from which the Vatican selects three. The final choice rests with the Government. Negotiations are customarily conducted by the Foreign Ministry.

Until 1936 Opus Dei had few members and was relatively insignificant. Its opportunity came with the Nationalist Régime's emergence. It created a climate particularly favourable to Opus Dei's élitist brand of Catholicism and propitious for its chosen tactic of quietly infiltrating positions of responsibility. Its first success was the appointment of a sympathizer as Education minister. His patronage enabled some young Opus Dei adherents to secure footholds in the universities. In particular, members of the organization gained control over the autonomous state institution created to co-ordinate and to promote Spain's scientific and academic research—the Consejo Superior de Investigaciones Científicas (C.S.I.C.). This provided an operational base, financial resources and the chance to cultivate useful overseas contacts. Later, adherents moved out from their academic bases into the civil service. Also, control was gained over the "Banco Popular" which paved the way for a major expansion of influence within the financial, business and publishing communities. Finally, official recognition from Pope Pius XII gave it special influence and prestige in ecclesiastical circles.[32]

The appointment of two adherents to the Government (in 1957), with responsibility for economic management, was recognition of the influence which Opus Dei already exercised within the Nationalist Régime. It was also a recognition of its reputation for recruiting competent, honest, cosmopolitan and well-qualified technical experts. Their overseas contacts promised to ease Spain's incorporation into the international financial community and they had the skills deemed necessary for directing an increasingly complex economy. The organization represented a blending of Spain's technocratic and authoritarian Catholic traditions that fitted in well with the temper of Franco's régime.

After 1957 Opus Dei's political influence steadily increased. Ultimately, in October 1969, a Government was formed which was largely composed of its members or sympathizers. Under the auspices of such men experiments in economic liberalization and "indicative planning" have been conducted. With the help of allies in both the public and private sectors they have attempted to modernize Spain's economy and administrative machinery.

Opus Dei's spokesmen insist that it is an apolitical organization and that

[32]It was made a "secular institute", directly dependent on the Vatican and, unlike Acción Católica, independent of local episcopal control.

members pursue their careers subject only to the Church's general moral guidance. They attribute the ubiquitous nature of its membership to the individual efforts and hard work of adherents. Opponents, however, are encouraged by its success and by the secrecy surrounding its activities to view it as ". . . a conspiracy or a mutual benefit society".[33] It is true that sympathizers within the Government are not there as Opus Dei's delegates and that their participation has not prevented fellow members from criticizing official policies. Thus newspapers run by leading Opus Dei sympathizers have run foul of the censor.[34] Equally, Opus Dei has no political programme. It does, however, produce men of a broadly similar outlook who share a general belief in "technical progress but political and religious conservatism".[35] Commitment to economic and administrative modernization has been accompanied by suspicion of recent changes within the Church and resistance to a thorough democratization of Spanish society. Likewise, it seems improbable that adherents captured so many influential positions without much co-option and mutual aid.

The organization's very success has now produced some loss of élan. Its own recruiting drives and the possibilities of advancement offered to members have probably attracted some opportunists and led to declines in morale. Thus some members have left in disillusionment and others have had their reputations tarnished. The "Matesa scandal" of 1969, involving the misappropriation of public funds, led to the bringing of charges of corruption against ex-ministers, civil servants and businessmen associated with Opus Dei. This had not done immediate damage to the organization. On the contrary the efforts of its enemies, within the Government, to use this incident to discredit Opus Dei backfired. They were replaced in the

[33]J. W. D. Trythall, *Franco*, London, 1970, p. 226.

[34]Recently there has been talk of two major political tendencies within Opus Dei. One is associated with Sr. López Rodó and the technocrats within the Government. The other, led by Sr. Calvo Serer, has come out in favour of evolution towards a liberal democratic system. It has links with a fairly wide range of political groupings some of whom can be clearly classified as part of the opposition to the régime. Calvo Serer has been associated with *Madrid*, a prominent Madrid evening paper, which has clashed with the régime over questions of civil rights and allied issues. As noted earlier, this paper was finally closed down late in 1971. Calvo Serer, however, originally occupied an authoritarian position and his faction seems as preoccupied with the problems of technical efficiency and modernization as those associated with López Rodó.

[35]Cf. J. W. D. Trythall, *op. cit.* p. 227.

reshuffle of 1969 by adherents of Opus Dei.[36] Ultimately, however, its reputation for probity and efficiency seems likely to suffer and the bargaining power of opponents, in ecclesiastical and governmental circles, could be strengthened.[37] Nevertheless, it has sufficient internal discipline and cohesion to survive, for the foreseeable future, as a significant political force. The creation of an Opus Dei university in the Carlist stronghold of Navarra certainly indicates an attempt to create an independent and enduring operational base.

Despite links with the Church, Franco's régime has never eliminated friction between Church and State. Whilst some clergy and prominent laymen unreservedly welcomed the régime's advent, others were more reserved. A minority of the latter, chiefly consisting of *Integristas*, were hostile. Others reluctantly accepted it as a bulwark against disorder. They were divided between those hoping, through co-operation, to transform the régime from within and those who feared that co-operation would eventually hamper its pastoral work—particularly amongst workers. Initially the former group accounted for most clergy and nearly all bishops.[38]

Such qualified support explains the initial difficulty, of Church and State, in agreeing upon episcopal appointments. It also explains why bishops, despite their mode of appointment, have frequently opposed the Government on specific issues. Links with Nazi Germany, press censorship and social and economic policies have all been publicly criticized at different times. Episcopal pressure has, for example, been instrumental in the raising of minimum wages and some bishops have encouraged workers' associations, established by Acción Católica, to compete with official unions.

During the past decade such conflicts have intensified. There has been mounting criticism of specific government policies and a growing tendency to question the régime's entire structure. Groups of priests, sometimes with episcopal blessing, have openly identified themselves with strikers. In 1969 the Spanish episcopal conference, as opposed to

[36]Prominent adherents implicated in the Matesa scandal have now benefited from an amnesty.

[37]Within the Church there is considerable friction between the Jesuits and Opus Dei.

[38]The chief exception was the Basque clergy which, in the main, identified itself with local nationalist opinion. Priests are still playing a prominent part in moderate and militant Basque movements.

isolated bishops, advocated the right to strike and to form independent unions. There have also been clashes over the limits of the Church's pastoral responsibilities. The State maintains that some of the Church's social activities are essentially political in nature and so are violations of the Concordat. Many Catholic spokesmen regard such activities as part of their pastoral responsibilities.

Several factors explain these developments. Firstly, pressures from Rome and contacts made at the Vatican Council have fostered significant shifts in episcopal attitudes. Church leaders have experienced increasing doubts about the régime's compatibility with the Church's most recent social and political teaching. Secondly, the episcopate has had to face growing pressure from its own followers. Since 1939 the priesthood's general educational and social level has risen so that many younger clergy are now more aware than their seniors of contemporary ecclesiastical debates. Likewise, limited but growing sections of the laity are beginning to question some traditional tenets of Spanish Catholicism. In the social and political spheres this has entailed growing opposition to the Church's identification with the *status quo*. It is now being argued that the Church should not seek state protection or a socially privileged position but should accept Spanish society's pluralistic nature and co-operate with other groups in efforts to promote social change. Such thinking has even influenced portions of the Government. Thus a law, enacted in 1967, relieved Protestants of many disabilities. Other Churchmen, however, have drawn more radical conclusions. They range from extreme radicals, partly inspired by Cuban models, to more numerous elements seeking to make Acción Católica an instrument for mass political action. Most bishops still resist efforts to mobilize Catholics in these ways. Their own values and pressures from traditionalists incline them to take that course. The strength of these pressures can be gauged by the bitterness of opposition to the 1967 law on religious liberty. Nevertheless, pressures for change cannot be ignored and most of the episcopate itself now supports some change of social and political structures.

At the heart of conflicts with the State lies the question of the "Real Patronato". Recently the Spanish Church and the Vatican have left several bishoprics vacant rather than co-operate with the State in filling vacancies. Church leaders no longer accept this limitation upon their freedom of action.

In 1971 the Spanish episcopal conference in fact rejected Vatican proposals for modifying traditional arrangements as insufficiently radical. The State, for its part, probably wishes to retain some control over clerical appointments whilst reducing its financial obligations to the Church. The immediate outcome is therefore likely to be a revised rather than an abolished Concordat. An eventual separation of Church and State cannot, however, be precluded.

Efforts to use Catholicism as a politically unifying force have clearly failed. Indeed, the activities of groups like Opus Dei and the continued opposition of many Catholics to social change means that anti-clericalism will probably remain a live issue.[39] On the other hand, new alignments within the Church could eventually lead to the formation of a Christian Democratic party and so make the issue less divisive than it was before 1936.

The role of the military in post-Civil-war Spain

It now remains to examine the problem of the military in post-Civil-war Spanish society.

Army support is obviously vital to a régime whose origins can be traced to a military rebellion. Since 1939 the army has performed an internal policing role that has been indispensable to the Nationalist régime's security. Thus the country is divided into twelve military regions (of eighteenth-century origin) each under a Captain-General appointed by Franco and garrisoned by troops that could speedily isolate revolutionary outbreaks. The Captains-General are figures of major political importance. They, for example, review the sentences of military courts empowered to try civilians for acts of terrorism and similar offences of a political nature.[40]

---

[39]Changes within the Church and the fear of changes within Spanish society have provoked strong reactions from a minority of ultra-conservative Catholics. One group, "Guerillas of Christ the King", has indulged in acts of violence aimed at intimidating left-wing Catholics. They sometimes act with police complicity.

[40]The trial of political offences by military courts goes back to the Civil War and was regularized by post-war legislation. Difficulties have always arisen from the imprecise nature of the jurisdiction of the courts. Moreover, they necessarily involve a very summary form of justice. In the early 1960s tentative efforts were made to liberalize the system. Civilian defence lawyers were permitted and, in 1964, a

It is therefore important to explain why the army, sometimes in the face of policy decisions adversely affecting its interests, has not withdrawn its support.[41] The answer lies partly in the army's relationship with the Government and with other groups supporting the régime, which will be discussed later. Here the army's own composition and attitudes require examination.

Personal loyalty to the Commander-in-Chief has undoubtedly played a part. Within the Spanish army Franco has great prestige and an outstanding professional reputation. Moreover, he has maintained good relationships with army leaders through frequent personal contacts.[42] These ties have been cemented by shared values and experiences. Commanders of the Civil War generation were sometimes divided by personal, professional and military rivalries but their thinking had been moulded by the same military academies, campaign experiences and political upheavals. This generation has now been largely replaced by those occupying middle ranking or junior posts during the war but their experience of that conflict fostered authoritarian political values and a strong attachment to Franco's régime. Indeed, loyalty to the régime and devotion to Franco may be greater amongst this group than amongst Franco's peers. Their support much reduced the possibilities of a coup.

Franco's powers as Commander-in-Chief have been used to check generals showing signs of independence. Regional commanders are periodically reshuffled to prevent close ties developing between senior officers and their subordinates. Also, examples are sometimes made of generals engaging in political controversy. Thus the Captain-General of the Granada region was dismissed following criticisms of moderate

---

civilian "Tribunal of Public Order" was created to try all but the most serious political offences. This Tribunal provides defendants with better facilities than military courts. In 1968, principally in response to the activities of E.T.A., the military was again given responsibility for the trial of all political offences, ranging from illegal association and propaganda to acts of violence or assassination. The military now must explicitly waive its rights to try a case before it can be heard by the "Public Order Tribunal". In practice the army generally does this but sometimes, as at Burgos, military authorities, acting on their own initiative or on orders from the Government, proceed with their own more summary form of justice.

[41]Chapter 3 for examples of decisions adversely effecting the military.

[42]For example, Franco has regular audiences with military leaders, separate from those with civilians and representatives of foreign governments.

elements within the Government made during the crisis of Christmas 1970. By the same token the key Madrid command was awarded to a general who had remained unconditionally loyal to the Government. Lower down the scale promotion by seniority promotes conformity. The poor pay of junior officers contrasts with the rewards available to their superiors, and it causes dissatisfaction, but automatic promotion up to the rank of colonel encourages them to remain loyal.

Even so the 1970 crisis exposed cleavages within the army. At the highest level there are two main schools of thought. Firstly, there are senior officers who now regard themselves as non-political. They are unconditionally loyal to Franco's régime and concentrate upon the performance of professional duties. During the 1970 crisis they proved reluctant to involve the army in political disputes. They have also made clear their willingness to accept the official solution to the succession problem. Their general outlook remains conservative and authoritarian but they have no independent political aims. Their support has made possible some modernization of the military establishment and cuts in the proportion of the national budget devoted to defence.[43] Secondly, there are more rigidly conservative generals who not only resist any relaxation of authoritarian political controls but also continue to see the army as Spain's ultimate political arbiter. Their demand for punitive measures against Basque Nationalists precipitated the 1970 crisis and during its course they reaffirmed the army's responsibility for defining and defending national interests. Officers of this kind are suspicious of the liberalizing measures of the currently dominant technocrats. They favour a continuation of the Nationalist Régime under more clearly authoritarian auspices.

Both groups, and especially the former, have followers amongst lower-ranking officers.[44] There are indications, however, that some of those,

[43]In the 1969 budget for the first time since the Civil War, at least, more was set aside for housing and public works than for defence purposes.

[44]It should be stressed that these remarks refer to regular army officers. There is conscription in Spain and beneficiaries of higher education, in particular, may receive commissions and then pass into the military's reserves. Conscripts, however, have limited opportunities for influencing military thinking and as members of the reserves have little direct contact with regular troops. Moreover, as members of the reserve they are liable to military discipline in the event, for example, of engaging in public controversy deemed harmful to the army's reputation. Conscription thus becomes a form of political control. Equally students whose "call up" has been

below the rank of colonel, recruited since the war, have more radical attitudes. This may be partly explicable in terms of changing recruitment patterns. The army remains a largely self-recruiting body drawing heavily on its traditional catchment areas, but recently larger numbers of officers have come from the sons of N.C.O.s. Officers' sons have often been attracted by the better pay of other services or have followed their contemporaries into the universities. The new officers have some of their predecessors' social prestige but have less economic security. There are also conflicts between the traditional values of the officer corps and the values of the social strata from which they come. Thus there is some tendency to adopt more radical postures. Some are left-wing Christian Democrats and others, described as "Nasseristas", are willing to establish a military régime pursuing radical domestic policies and a neutralist foreign policy. These are minority groups but they reveal a changing climate of opinion within the military. Such changes are best seen in the attitudes of recent recruits to their profession. Many junior officers wish to abandon the role of internal policeman and to convert the army into a more thoroughly modernized force capable, perhaps, of contributing to N.A.T.O.[45]

These changing attitudes indicate that the army might ultimately accept democratically elected governments and civilian controls. Nevertheless, the training and social isolation of most officers have preserved many traditional attitudes. Thus attacks upon military privileges or serious political instability could entice the military back into the political arena. Generals favouring intervention might then find enough support to make a coup viable. Recent appointments, however, indicate efforts to isolate belligerent commanders and to ensure army support for Franco's solution to the succession problem. Moreover, Spanish society is now so complex that no régime could survive long without help from civilian technocrats. The army's attitudes remain vitally important but an overtly military dictatorship is not the most probable successor to Franco's régime.

---

deferred, or workers in reserved occupations can be drafted into the army in retaliation for engaging in opposition political activities.

[45]For this and other evidence about the army's changing composition cf. J. Busquets Bragulat, *El Militar de Carrera en España*, Madrid, 1967.

CONCLUSION

It is clear from the foregoing discussion that, since 1950 at least, the pluralistic nature of Spanish society has reasserted itself. The ennervating fear and apathy of the immediate post-Civil-war era has, in some quarters, gradually given way to a renewal of political awareness and activity. The result has frequently been a reaction against the policies, if not the very existence of the Nationalist Régime, and a growth of overt and tacit dissent. The régime has itself done something to aid this process. Recent very tentative experiments in political "liberalization" were designed (in part) as an answer to demands for change but they have generally succeeded only in whetting an appetite for further changes. "Modernizing" or "liberalizing" elements within the régime are in fact unwilling or unable to face up to the logic of the situation they have helped to create. They generally regard active repression as distasteful or counter-productive but cannot consistently pursue the alternative of a thoroughgoing liberalization, which is now probably the only way of satisfying opposition demands. They are inhibited by their own élitist approach to politics and by the ambivalence of their attitudes toward authoritarian rule. Of perhaps greater importance, they are inhibited by the rigidly authoritarian elements with whom they must coexist. Pressure from such authoritarian groups makes it virtually impossible to direct a planned return to a more open political system. Events in the past decade have indicated that the more conservative elements now in power (and some Falangists) will react very strongly against the manifestations of dissent which such a liberalization programme is bound to encourage. The latter groups, moreover, can count on the continuing political apathy of large sections of Spanish society and (at times of crisis, at least) the active support of portions of those groups who have traditionally looked to the State for their security. For example, there are still extensive bureaucratic interests with a stake in the present political system. Thus those prepared to rely upon repression are free to initiate periodic police measures that have the effect of disrupting the organization of the opposition. In the short run such measures serve to maintain a certain stability but they do nothing to solve the long-term problem of opposition to the régime. Dissent has difficulty in securing adequate channels of expression but it clearly cannot be eliminated. Indeed, repression has sometimes had the effect of radicalizing opposition groups and of driving into temporary alliances groups who had previously been deeply divided. It is possible, for example, that the prestige of the Spanish Communist Party has increased as a result of the practice, common amongst the most conservative governing elements, of describing all serious opposition as Communist inspired.

Some commentators have argued that Franco could have provided a way out of the impasse by launching a political party of the Gaullist variety with himself at the head. This, however, would be quite alien to his approach to politics and unacceptable to many of his closest allies. There is evidence that open political conflict might now be less intense than it was before the Civil War but the country's present leaders find the risks entailed in such conflict quite unacceptable. The willingness of some opposition groups to use violence and the State's present capacity to contain opposition tend to strengthen the resistance to change. The result, in practice, is an uneasy state of equilibrium. On the one hand there are many Spaniards (probably the great majority) who are content to remain on the political sidelines and who do not come into open collision with the State. Some of these may feel personally constricted by the political conformism that the present régime seeks to promote but are not actively oppressed by it. At most they may resent some of the more arbitrary aspects of the present system of rule and the contrast between Spain's apparently anachronistic political institutions and the institutions of countries to the north. On the other hand, the existence of still sharp conflicts within Spanish society, including a generational conflict between those who knew the upheavals of the 1930s and a younger generation generally less concerned with security and stability, has led during the 1960s to some intensification of opposition activity. Numerically limited but vocal elements within the working classes, the universities, the Church, national minorities and even the army are tending to oppose official policies with increasing vigour, despite all the obstacles placed in their way. After Franco's departure, a central issue in Spanish politics will be whether these groups can gain the initiative from the moderate reforming elements within the régime or whether they will invite a reversion to more widespread and systematic repression.

In the meantime Spain continues to be governed with the minimum of active popular political participation. Determined official efforts to mobilize public opinion are only made during a crisis like that of Christmas 1970, when domestic and foreign pressures appear to present the régime with a particularly serious threat. National policy-making therefore goes on with very little direct reference to the wishes of the bulk of Spaniards. The general state of public opinion obviously cannot be wholly ignored by the country's rulers; the régime's survival and stability ultimately depend on its capacity to contain potentially destructive forces. Nevertheless, only very limited élite groups can legally campaign on behalf of their own interests and can directly influence those placed in positions of formal political or administrative responsibility. The latter, moreover, can operate under such a cloak of secrecy and are so protected against the sustained pressure of an informed public that they must inevitably enjoy immense discretion in the taking of decisions. It is this which justifies the study of the machinery of Spanish government which forms the major part of this book. Thus, in subsequent chapters stress will not only be laid on the coalition of essentially conservative political forces that have formed the basis of Franco's personal dictatorship but attention will also be paid to the operations of the Council of Ministers, the structure and influence of the civil service, and the organization of ministerial departments. There will also be an investigation of the State's growing responsibility for economic and social matters and an examination of local government. Finally, there will be some scrutiny of those few formal checks to which, in principle at least, the Spanish Government is subject.

Throughout the course of this argument particular attention will be paid to recent attempts to modernize Spain's economic and administrative institutions. Particularly since 1957 there has been a growth in the power and influence of technocrats committed to economic and administrative modernization whilst leaving political and social structures essentially unaltered. By placing the stress on economic prosperity and administrative efficiency, they hope to stabilize the present political system and to offer solutions to Spain's perennial political problems. An attempt to examine the viability of this approach will constitute one of the underlying themes of the following chapters.

CHAPTER 3

Franco's Political System

THE LEGAL BASIS OF "THE SYSTEM"

"Franco's political system" can trace its origins back to the rising of July 1936. This was conceived as a traditional *pronunciamiento*, aimed against the Republic's left-wing government. Ten generals, including Franco, formed a "National Defence Council" which assumed the State's powers in the areas falling under their control. It was not seen as the nucleus of a rival state.

The Civil War's outbreak compelled military leaders to reconsider the situation and they improvised instruments of rule to direct the conflict, administer conquered territory, and provide their authority with an apparently legitimate basis.

The first and decisive step was a decree of 29th September 1936 dissolving the Council and making Franco both Commander-in-Chief of the Armed Forces and "Head of the Government of the Spanish State" vested with all its powers.[1] Franco's colleagues chose him for three reasons: his prestige, particularly in military circles; his command of Moroccan-based troops who, at the war's outset, were of crucial military importance; and the fact that he was not closely associated with any one political faction and could therefore unite the Nationalists' disparate following.

Franco's undefined political position left the "New State's" final form an open question. His colleagues expected to resolve that question at a later date. In reality the September 1936 decree provided the legal basis for a lasting personal dictatorship. Franco (and his advisers) slipped in the

---

[1]An English version of this decree and most of the other items of legislation mentioned in this chapter are to be found in the International Commission of Jurists' report—*Spain and the Rule of Law*, Geneva, 1962.

ambiguous formula, glossing over distinctions between the Head of Government and the Head of State, and to that extent prejudged the issue. He could subsequently claim to be the new régime's founder and embodiment. He was also fortified by the concentration in his hands of legislative and executive powers. Colleagues regarded this as a temporary necessity providing for effective war-time leadership. The situation, however, has remained essentially unaltered.

As a step toward the creation of "normal" institutions, a law of 30 January 1938 created a Council of Ministers, under Franco's chairmanship, which was recognized as the national government. However, the Head of State still enacted all laws and countersigned decrees issued by ministers when performing their executive functions. A further law of 8 August 1938 made this legal supremacy more explicit. It stated that, in emergencies, the Head of State could legislate without consulting ministers. This gave him theoretically unlimited powers, for he decided what constituted emergencies and when they existed.

The creation of the Cortes, by a law of 17 July 1942, did not fundamentally alter this position. It was not conceived as an independent legislature but as a body assisting Franco to exercise his legislative powers. It involved purely voluntary restrictions upon his authority.

There was a list of important matters normally requiring the Cortes' approval if they were to be given the full weight of law. They included the annual budget, all grants of taxation and other matters of major social and economic importance. But its authority was limited in several important ways. Firstly, Franco retained the right to legislate without reference to the Cortes—a right which he has exercised on few but always important occasions. A law of 1946, modifying the legislation that created the Cortes; the "Fundamental Principles of the Movement"; and the original draft of the Organic Law of 1966 all resulted from Franco's personal initiatives.[2] The power has been used, in other words, for matters of a "constitutional" nature. Secondly, Franco retained a right of veto. This is rarely used for the Cortes has never seriously challenged the Government and because it can be circumvented in other ways.[3]

[2]The Organic Law was in fact formally enacted by Franco on 10 Jan. 1967, but it was put to and approved by the Cortes on 22 Nov. 1966 and further approved by a referendum held on 14 Dec. 1966.

[3]Cf. Chapter 9 for a more detailed analysis of the Cortes' role.

One problem has been the imprecision of the line dividing matters that lie within the Cortes' jurisdiction from matters which are the executive's exclusive responsibility. The idea of an executive rule-making authority, independent of the legislature, is not new but is one of the features of the "Napoleonic State" introduced into Spain by nineteenth-century reformers. They took certain powers and responsibilities to be inherent in the executive function. Thus the executive was free in emergencies to take exceptional measures in defence of the State's security.[4] Equally, the executive could invoke "Police Powers" to enforce laws, ensure the smooth running of public services and maintain public safety.[5] Finally, the administration's internal organization was regarded as the executive's exclusive responsibility.[6]

In principle administrative regulations issued under these headings, by ministerial order or government decree, cannot modify laws approved by the legislature. In practice it has always been hard to stop the executive using its rule-making authority to alter the spirit of laws. It has been particularly hard in the absence of an institutionalized opposition. Legislation, enacted in 1957, expressly forbade the abrogation of laws by administrative regulations and administrative courts have recently been acting upon this principle with greater vigour. The executive has subsequently been more cautious, but until it can be subjected to searching public criticism old practices are unlikely to be eliminated.

The Cortes may also be circumvented by "decree laws". The decree law had traditionally been used when Parliament, in a crisis, gave the Government emergency grants of legislative power. The law of 1942, however, empowered the Government to legislate by decree whenever there was a war or "an emergency". In reality this power has been used extensively, for the Government alone defines an emergency. Its use can be justified, for example, when confronting natural disasters but it has also been used to vote supplementary grants and even to fight prostitution. The Cortes was originally required to ratify decree laws but after 1946 it merely had to be "informed". As a concession to criticisms of this, within

---

[4]For this theme cf. A. Guaita, *Derecho Administrativo Especial*, Tomo 2, Zaragoza, 1962, pp. 51 and 52.

[5]Cf. F. Garrido Falla, *Las Transformaciones del Concepto Jurídico de Policía Administrativa*, Madrid, 1962.

[6]Cf. Ley de Régimen, *Jurídico de la Administración del Estado(B.O.E.,*31 July 1957).

the Cortes, a special commission of that body was established, in 1957, to deal with decree laws. It is only empowered, however, to state whether or not an "emergency" really exists. Its views, moreover, are not binding. Thus there has been no substantial change.[7]

Finally, the Cortes may itself be encouraged to make specific grants of legislative power to the administration. In such cases the Cortes establishes general principles and government departments elaborate them. This now increasingly happens with complex technical measures. Thus a law of 1957 empowered the Government to create special administrative systems for Madrid and Barcelona. The Government later determined the nature of the systems.

In 1945 a "Bill of Rights"—or "Charter of the Spanish People"—was issued, guaranteeing rights customarily incorporated into such documents. It apparently limited the Government's freedom of action. The Charter, however, contains two "escape clauses". One states that the exercise of rights "may not affect the spiritual, national and social unity of the community" which can of course justify the repression of opposition. The other indicates that the effectiveness and the enforcement of "constitutional" rights depends upon the enactment of subsequent and more detailed legislation. This has frequently been slow to materialize and has limited the exercise of rights in significant ways. The law of 1964, regulating the right to associate, comes into this category. The Government is further empowered to suspend the Charter's chief provisions if it decides that a threat to the State's security exists. This power was most recently invoked following the crisis of Christmas 1970.

Also in 1945 Franco invoked his own legislative power in order to provide for the holding of referenda. This, too, appeared to impose limits upon the Government's freedom of action. It was made plain, however, that a referendum should only be held when Franco himself decided that ". . . the exceptional importance of any law makes it advisable or the public interest so demands . . .".

This provision was in fact a prelude to the Law of Succession (submitted

---

[7]For a discussion of the Decree Law cf. R. Gómez-Acerbo Santos, "El ejercicio de la Función Legislativa por el Gobierno", *Revista de Administración Pública*, No. 6 (1951), pp. 99–124. Cf. also M. Fraga Iribarne, *El Reglamento de las Cortes Españolas*, Madrid, 1959, pp. 167–78. A list of recent decree laws appears in M. Martínez Cuadrado, *op. cit.*, pp. 577–8.

to a referendum in 1947) which made Spain officially a monarchy whilst effectively confirming Franco's rule for life. It also created a new category of "Fundamental Laws" only to be repealed or modified by further referenda. These were the "Constituent Laws of the Cortes", the "National Referendum Law", the "Charter of the Spanish People", the "Labour Charter", and the "Law of Succession" itself.

A referendum was next used, in November 1966, to ratify Franco's proposed "Organic Law". This was a complex measure. It was partly designed to amend existing Fundamental Laws in the light of recent political changes. It was also intended to provide for the future. In particular provision was made for appointing a Prime Minister. This might have significant long-term implications but has not transformed the existing situation. Franco (when and if he chooses to make use of the provision) will effectively appoint and dismiss the premier. Likewise, he retains the right to legislate on constitutional matters, to issue decree laws, and to invoke the executive's traditional rule-making power.

The referenda of 1947 and 1966 were partly designed to give the régime the appearance of popular support. In this it scored significant tactical successes. In 1947 approximately 82 per cent of the electorate was reported to have approved official proposals and in 1966 the figure was still higher.[8] This can be partly explained by such factors as official control over the electoral apparatus, deliberately exaggerated government claims, and the one-sided nature of preceding public debates. It is certain, how-ever, that at those particular times large numbers of Spaniards did rally to the régime. Naturally, it does not follow that the results would have been so decisive at other times.

The Law of Succession and the Organic Law were also part of a series of steps, taken since 1936, in an effort to create some semblance of con-stitutional law, to legitimize the Nationalist Régime's authority and to institutionalize Franco's essentially personal and dictatorial prerogatives. But at the bottom each step has been an improvised response to changing political circumstances and not part of a planned return to constitutional government. The Council of Ministers was re-created (1938) for adminis-trative convenience; the Cortes was established (1942) to make the régime more representative at a time when its association with the Axis powers

[8]The preamble to the law claims that it was approved by 85 per cent of all eligible voters.

was becoming a serious embarrassment; the "Bill of Rights" and provision for referenda (1945) were intended to make the régime more
acceptable in post-war Europe; the Law of Succession (1947) was a
device for silencing monarchists and catching a favourable tide of public
opinion; finally the Organic Law (1966) is to provide for the future and
for the successor to Franco. Nothing, however, has fundamentally altered
the legal situation created in 1936.

THE GENESIS OF "THE SYSTEM"

To understand this situation one must move from discussions of
Franco's legal powers, which merely provide the technical instruments of
his rule, to an examination of the underlying political realities. Reflections
upon legal technicalities reveal little about the régime's real nature and
cannot explain its survival.

Franco's original appointment was viewed as a temporary expedient,
but through a blend of political skill and good fortune he created a lasting
personal dictatorship and indefinitely postponed the establishment of more
clearly institutionalized forms of authority. Indeed, the failure to create
viable impersonal sources of authority is partly due to the extent to which
all necessarily hinges on his personal skills and reputation. The referendum
of 1966 provided some confirmation of this. The proposed Organic Law
was so complex that relatively few are likely to have digested all its
contents. Sophisticated voters, moreover, had to give one Yes or No
answer to a measure that they may have partly accepted and partly
rejected. Thus the referendum tended to resolve itself into a vote of
confidence in Franco himself rather than in his proposals.

The strength of Franco's position originally arose from the heterogeneous nature of the forces whose leadership he assumed. He came to
power through the army which in a civil war was inevitably the ultimate
source of authority. Apart from wishing to resist civilian controls and to
establish some authoritarian form of government, its leaders were united
by no clearly defined ideology or plan of action. This left open the question of a political formula acceptable to the Nationalists. Amongst them
the army was the chief but not sole element. The pre-war polarization of
opinion left it at the head of all Spain's right-wing forces. They, too, shared
a desire for victory but lacked any other clear unity of interest or purpose.

As the war progressed a system of rule had to be fashioned from these elements. Civilian help was required to provide administrative expertise and, ultimately, to relieve the Government from a total dependence upon force.

One solution might have been for Franco to found his own political movement. Initially this possibility was explored but the basis of such a movement did not then exist. Later, Franco's chief political adviser advocated a régime based on the Falangist Party's support.[9] This advice was partly followed when Franco forcibly merged the Falangists and Carlists into one monopolistic and personally controlled movement.[10] The Original Falangists had totalitarian aspirations which, for tactical reasons, Franco did not publicly dispel. He made statements designed to rally Falangist support and to impress foreign allies, but there was no genuine desire to create a totalitarian system. The Government's dictatorial apparatus had some attributes of a totalitarian régime but those pressing for a régime comparable to Nazi Germany or Fascist Italy were unsuccessful. The Falangists were too weak to press their demands and army leaders were too conservative to accede to them. The party instead became an instrument, lacking independence, for Franco to manipulate.

The alternative he selected was a government of "national concentration". This was a coalition which co-opted representatives of all the major groups in Nationalist Spain, stiffened by "non-political" experts from the civil service and business life. The system was devised to direct the war but, thanks partly to Franco's adroit manoeuvering, coalition government became an enduring instrument of rule.

FRANCO

Franco's success is partly explicable in terms of a special combination of personal qualities and attitudes. In some ways he is the representative product of a traditional Spanish middle class and military background. His basic political convictions are few and fairly simple but firmly rooted. Above all he is a traditional nationalist anxious to assert Spanish influence

[9]This was his own brother-in-law, Ramón Serrano Suñer. He had been a prominent member of "la C.E.D.A." and was to become Minister of the Interior and Foreign Minister.

[10]Cf. Chapter 2 for the background to this development.

and interests. This goes with a conception of national unity in which class and party conflicts have no place. He believes national unity and public order can only be preserved by an authoritarian state linked to those institutions, notably the army and the Church, which are deemed to embody Spain's characteristic values and traditions. Like many colleagues Franco had no sentimental attachment to the monarchy; he wanted a government that would defend military interests and uphold a particular conception of public order.

In other respects he stood apart from fellow officers. This was partly a question of his professional standing but also of his political attitudes and shrewdness. He approached the projected rising of 1936 cautiously but once committed he quickly seized and exploited his opportunities. He seemed to develop some sense of an historic mission and, perhaps fortified by an attachment to conventional Catholic values, trusted in his ability to fulfil it. His military career showed him capable of ruthlessness, but experience of Moroccan tribal politics and of political life under the Republic apparently developed qualities of realism and flexibility unusual in somebody of his background.[11]

Franco's skills are mainly tactical. He has, however, shown a clearer understanding of contemporary social and political forces than most of his colleagues. After the war he did not rely wholly upon force for disciplining the working classes but took a personal interest in the development of social-security provisions. Similarly, he is not blind to the Spanish economy's structural problems. His diplomatic successes have frequently arisen from factors beyond his control which he has nevertheless turned to good effect. Thus, during the Second World War, he secured economic assistance from both sides without direct involvement. Later he exploited the "Cold War" to obtain an American alliance that gave his régime accesses of moral and material strength. More recently his realism has been apparent in his treatment of Spain's remaining colonies and by his attitudes towards the E.E.C. Confronted by nationalist demands he granted Spanish Morocco its independence and has personally

---

[11]His handling of the rising in Asturias indicated his capacity for ruthlessness but the rising also appears to have fostered an interest in social problems. For explorations of Franco's character and his unique position in Spanish political life cf. the following biographies: George Hills, *Franco. The Man and His Nation*, London, 1967; Brian Crozier, *Franco*, London, 1967; J. W. D. Trythall, *op. cit.*

promoted policies designed gradually to develop other African territories
and to prepare them for eventual independence.[12] Also, though un-
enthusiastic about the E.E.C. he appreciates the possible dangers of
Spain's complete exclusion and has permitted "European-minded"
ministers to make preliminary approaches.[13]

None of this reflects a coherent set of beliefs or ideology. His over-
riding aim is to preserve his régime, which he equates with the national
interest. This prescribes limits to his freedom of action but within them he
is a pragmatist dealing with problems on their merits as they arise and
willing to work with anybody who will serve his ends. This pragmatism
partly explains his survival.

FRANCO AND THE PROBLEMS OF COALITION MANAGEMENT

The political forces within "Nationalist Spain" embraced widely
ranging interests. They included Falangists, "liberal monarchists", proponents of a corporate State from Renovación Española, Carlists,
associates of Primo de Rivera, conservative Catholics from Opus Dei,
moderate Catholics from Acción Católica, and supporters of the disbanded
C.E.D.A.[14]

Franco deliberately continued to leave his own position unclear. His
public pronouncements contain vaguely worded appeals to varying traditions and interests and give some reassurance to nearly all his supporters.

[12]In July 1968 Spain's West African colonies of Fernando Poo and Spanish Guinea
were given independence as part of one new state—Equatorial Guinea. The timing was
probably part of an effort to win support in the United Nations for Spanish claims to
Gibraltar. Later, in January 1969, Ifni (a remnant of the Moroccan Protectorate) was
handed over to Morocco. Spain now retains Spanish Sahara and Ceuta and Mellila
(two cities on the North African coast).

[13]In Feb. 1962 Spain formally applied for associate membership of the E.E.C
French opposition to an enlargement of the community ended this attempt though
it was apparent that there was very strong opposition from other quarters, notably
the Benelux Countries. In July 1970 a preferential trading treaty was signed but
membership remains impossible for the foreseeable future.

[14]The diversified nature of Franco's support is discussed in Juan J. Linz, "An
authoritarian régime: the case of Spain", published in E. Allardt and Y. Littunen
(editors), *Cleavages, Ideologies and Party Systems* (Helsinki: Transactions of the
Westermarck Society, 1964).

They also stress the things binding them together and blur over their conflicts of view and interest. In particular memories of the Civil War are kept alive and fears of fresh conflicts played upon.

During the war itself all but a minority of Carlists and Falangists accepted Franco's leadership. Afterwards, however, latent conflicts over the régime's final form came to the surface. In these circumstances Franco's position depended upon retaining freedom to act as a political arbiter and to manoeuvre between competing groups. He achieved this by refusing to identify himself with any one section of opinion and by playing off one group against another, granting partial satisfaction to all of them but giving way completely to none. The Government changes of 1969, which will be examined later, perhaps marked a departure from these tactics, but by then Franco was virtually irreplaceable. Thus the régime, generally speaking, has not been the property of a single faction and no opposition has emerged sufficiently strong to upset the delicate balance of forces underlying Franco's authoritative bargaining position.

The chief danger could come from the army, upon which the régime ultimately depends. Franco's use of balancing tactics to restrain military opposition is therefore particularly interesting. Many conservative army officers hoped to destroy the Falange after 1939. Franco shared some of their antipathy yet he kept the party alive. One reason was to have an alternative pillar of support that could free him from complete dependence upon the military. Falangists have lost ground but as long as they exist Franco can threaten the conservative majority amongst his followers, particularly in the army, with a revival of their influence.

In both 1941 and 1942 Franco confronted political crises arising from rivalry between the army and the Party. In the first case the appointment of an anti-Falangist officer as Minister of the Interior provoked a reaction within the party. The Minister was publicly insulted and under pressure Franco dismissed those held responsible. However, to prevent the army getting the upper hand, he chose this moment to reconstruct his government with larger numbers of Falangists. In 1942 the Interior Minister and the Carlist Army Minister, General Varela, seized an opportunity to discredit Franco's pro-Axis Foreign Minister, Serrano Suñer, whom they identified with the Party and whose great influence they resented. Franco had acquired reservations about such a powerful minister and took the chance to dismiss him. But Varela had openly canvassed other generals to put pressure upon Franco. He could not accept independence of this sort so, as a reminder of where control ultimately lay, Varela and his colleagues were replaced by ministers more acceptable to the Falange.[15]

Such tactics particularly helped Franco to increase his freedom of manoeuvre over the monarchial issue. The monarchists were poorly organized but when, toward the end of the World War, some army leaders supported growing demands for a restoration, it became a sensitive issue. Franco neutralized the danger by encouraging Falangist opposition. When the issue was settled it was on his and not monarchist or Falangist terms.

A crisis in 1956 demonstrated the existence of limits to these tactics. By then the Falangists were weaker and their opponents in the army, the Church and the business community had become firmer in resistance to their demands. Therefore when demonstrations at Madrid University provoked Falangists to employ violence the army reacted strongly. It feared a breakdown in order and the implied challenge to its authority. Franco consequently forced the Falangists to withdraw. The alternative might have been direct military intervention and a settling of accounts likely to upset the basis of his system. But to reassure Falangists, and as a warning to army leaders, Franco began to listen to the former's plans for remodelling political institutions. This time there were strong protests not only from the army but also Church and business leaders, so Franco beat a partial retreat.[16] Franco's freedom of manoeuvre is reduced, in other words, if the army threatens to clash openly with other groups or if fairly unified opposition develops amongst the military and other influential elements. The power left to Franco, in such circumstances, can be no more than the power to obstruct or veto proposals emanating from his followers. This has always been sufficient, however, to enable him to regain and retain the initiative.

Several special factors have helped him to do this for so long. The first is his prestige and the reserves of credit upon which he can therefore draw in periods of crisis. His reputation, established on the Spanish right before 1936, was given a wholly new dimension by war-time successes and by the way these were exploited in official propaganda. Subsequent triumphs added to this and put his authority beyond doubt. Though he may arouse

[15]These crises are discussed in Stanley G. Payne, *Falange, op. cit.*, pp. 225–38.
[16]*Ibid.*, pp. 250–67.

less positive enthusiasm amongst younger generations of Nationalist supporters this is compensated for by less intense hostility in the country as a whole. Franco led one part of Spain to victory over another but now he can claim to be established as more of a national leader. In some cases he enjoys a personal standing amongst those opposed to his régime and, in many other cases, his authority has been accepted out of indifference or habit. This fortifies his position *vis-à-vis* his political allies for there is nobody else so clearly capable of upholding their special interests.

Franco's personal system is also maintained by the fluidity and overlap existing amongst different groups of supporters. A complicated pattern of informal relationships provides channels for interaction and reciprocal influence. For example, there have been personal links between leading army officers and Churchmen, resulting in some cases from contacts made in Renovación Española—whose members gave the régime valuable support and influenced its thinking. Also, large banks and companies have tended to appoint generals to their boards because of the prestige conferred and the access to official circles which this opens up. Within the business community itself there is a system of interlocking directorates and family alliances that is associated, at some points, with agrarian interests. [17]

The careers of some members of the régime's political élite illustrate this point. A former Army Minister, Lieutenant-General Barroso, was a landowner with monarchist connections. Lieutenant-General Alonso Vega, who was Interior Minister from 1957 until 1969, had business interests and links with Opus Dei. [18] Finally, an ex-Finance Minister (who became Governor of the Bank of Spain) has been associated with Opus Dei and occupied posts in the army, the *sindicatos*, the civil service and on the board of a bank.

These multiple points of contact between distinct groups help to perpetuate that minimal basis of shared values and material interests which first brought the Nationalists together. In particular the political élite acquires some coherence for leaders emerge whose authority is regarded as more or less legitimate by diverse and even conflicting interests.

This engenders a general climate of acceptance for the régime without

[17]Cf. Juan J. Linz, "An authoritarian régime: the case of Spain", *op. cit.*
[18]He was also head of the Civil Guard prior to his ministerial appointment. He died in July 1971.

removing those conflicts which Franco has turned to his personal advantage. On the contrary, there are continued differences of emphasis—like
those dividing most army and Church leaders on social questions. In
addition, the overlapping of groups creates communities of interest and
lines of cleavage cutting across other loyalties. This makes coalition
management easier because allegiances fluctuate according to the issues or
personalities involved and so impede the emergence of independent
political forces with lasting strength. This is particularly true in the army's
case. It could overthrow the régime if it developed sufficient unity of
purpose but in practice it tends only to unite in defence of professional
interests. Its leaders are politically divided.[19] Those military figures
appointed to Franco's governments, for example, have separately been
identified with all the régime's major political tendencies.

Franco also has the benefit of an effective intelligence system. He
gathers into his own hands information flowing from the competing
services of the police, the armed forces, and the Party. Private meetings
of important politicians are reported to him and on his orders even
ministers' telephones have been tapped. Official channels of information
are supplemented by private contacts, particularly in the armed forces but
also in the Church, business circles and even the universities. This keeps
him informed of movements of opinion within the régime and amongst
opponents. The system's existence helps to deter independent political
action and enables Franco to anticipate trouble. In 1940, for example,
some Falangists and a prominent general were implicated in a plot to
remove him, but it was quickly uncovered.[20] Effective opposition cannot
easily form in such circumstances.

The same system enables him to seek out suitable candidates for
appointments in his government and to check on the reliability of those
recommended to him. Franco's use of his great powers of patronage is in
fact another important stabilizing factor. Their use to guarantee the army
and the Party's loyalty has already been examined. Their use in forming
governments will be examined below.

The factors which have held the régime together have also conditioned
the quality of the day-to-day performance of successive governments. Its
survival has depended on holding together sharply conflicting interests

---

[19]Cf. Chapter 2 for an examination of internal army divisions.
[20]Cf. Stanley G. Payne, *Falange, op. cit.*, pp. 212–14.

and as a consequence governments have been coalitions with most of the problems associated with that type of rule.

The chief difficulty has been welding ministers of divergent interests into an effective team. This partly depends upon decisive leadership which Franco has generally been unable to supply. In the absence of an independent basis of support he has only been able to act through his régime's constituent groups and his authority has depended upon the avoidance of commitments that might reduce his ability to arbitrate between them. Therefore, though major decisions require his approval, he has not usually tried to impose his solutions to problems nor laid down clear guide lines for action. He might now have the prestige to impose his will more frequently and the crisis of Christmas 1970 indicates that in an emergency he is still capable of asserting himself, but old habits have persisted and with increased age he has generally proved less active. One solution is the appointment of a Prime Minister capable of taking difficult decisions without directly implicating Franco, and replaceable if policy changes become necessary. Such a figure might be able to provide more decisive leadership than has previously been possible. The "Organic Law" makes formal provision for this and the appointment, in 1969, of Admiral Carrero Blanco as the Council of Minister's Vice-Chairman may be a practical step in the same direction.* He now assumes considerable responsibility for the daily management of affairs. Until recently, however, Franco refused to contemplate the emergence of a leader who might become a serious rival and Carrero Blanco owes his appointment to his unquestioned devotion to the Head of State. Moreover, there must be doubts about the authority Carrero Blanco or any other comparable figure, will be able to wield, when they can no longer claim to act on Franco's behalf.

Until very recently, at least, Franco has interested himself in most important problems and has sometimes taken significant initiatives, but these have usually been sporadic and taken on an *ad hoc* basis rather than as part of a general programme. His role in stimulating the extension of social security provisions may be seen in this light.

Because of this Franco has not created a large group of personal advisers equipped to supply his lack of technical expertise, to provide regular and independent sources of administrative information or to aid

*Since this book went to press Franco announced his intention of making Carrero Blanco Prime Minister at a future date.

in formulating policy. The most he has are two small and separate groups of military and civilian aides, or "households", who manage his daily programme and prepare reports on current developments from the information made available by formal and informal "intelligence" sources. This private "intelligence" system furnishes technical advice and information but it is fragmentary and sometimes self-interested. At best it helps Franco to evaluate ministerial proposals and so to retain some influence over the final shape of important decisions. To a large extent he must (in most fields) rely upon his ministers' advice.

There are certain matters considered vital to his régime's interests in which he will take the lead. They constitute a special "domain" in which the major policy decisions must ultimately rest with Franco. The matters in question are the organization of the régime's basic institutions, control of the army, the maintenance of public order and foreign relations.

The first two have been considered already and require no further comment. The maintenance of public order involves a number of concerns. It implies an interest in all those social or political matters likely to effect the régime's security. Under this heading comes trade-union affairs, and the general supervision of press comment. Above all it entails the surveillance and handling of opposition activities.

Franco's precise role in formulating foreign policy has varied according to circumstances and his relationships with successive foreign ministers. At the Second World War's outbreak, for example, the Foreign Minister was confined to handling relations with the Allies. Franco did not trust him in dealings with the Axis powers which were entrusted to Serrano Suñer, acting under his own supervision. Later this unsatisfactory arrangement was ended by Serrano Suñer's move from the Interior to the Foreign Ministry. There he enjoyed some autonomy in the conduct of affairs because of the broadly similar nature of his and Franco's own views. By contrast the Foreign Minister from 1945 to 1957, Sr. Martín Artajo, was, on the main issue of coming to terms with the victorious Allies, the executant of policies whose main principles were established by Franco. On other issues he relied heavily on the Foreign Ministry's advice. More recently, Sr. Castiella (1957–69) and Sr. López Bravo (1969) have been allowed some freedom to pursue policies of which they are personal advocates—notably establishing closer links with the E.E.C.[21]

[21]Following Castiella's replacement by López Bravo some observers felt that they could detect some marginal shifts in Spanish foreign policy. Claims to Gibraltar

In all matters of major national concern, however, Franco has closely watched current development. This may partly explain, for example, the firmness and underlying consistency of Spanish policy towards Gibraltar. On this issue Franco's views have coincided with those of radical nationalists. He remains anxious to reunite Gibraltar with Spain.

On most matters of domestic policy Franco has generally been content to let the initiative lie with his ministers. Until 1969, at least, they formed coalition governments of the sort first created in 1938. The strength of various groups changed with circumstances and new elements were incorporated but all the original components kept some representation. Even the present government is not monolithic. In fact during the régime's evolution conventions developed regulating the distribution of offices. Service ministers have always been officers of the respective armed forces. Education Ministers have always come from one of the Catholic groups and the Justice Ministry, which handles Church and State relations, has usually been controlled by Carlists. Foreign Ministers have been appointed with an eye to external developments and since 1945 they have come from the right-wing Christian Democratic or Opus Dei elements. The Secretary-General of the Movement is invariably a Minister without Portfolio and Falangist sympathizers have also controlled the Labour and Housing Ministries.

This sort of formula has helped to solve many problems. It has given important groups some stake in the régime and by handing responsibility for policy-making in given areas to ministers associated with the affected interests these have had chances to defend themselves and to obtain partial satisfaction for their claims. It has also done something to maintain channels of communication with significant sections of opinion which, in the absence of open political discussion, might have completely broken down thus permitting a dangerous accumulation of tensions. Falangist Labour ministers, for example, have helped to keep working-class interests before the Government and through minimum wage and social security programmes have perhaps blunted the hostility of workers.

It has also meant that no major social force could remain wholly immune from state influence. The régime rests upon a society containing

---

seem to have been pressed less vigorously whilst defence and aid agreements with the U.S.A. were renewed in 1970 on terms that Castiella is believed to have resisted. Both men have been instrumental in establishing links with Eastern Europe.

a plurality of interests. But the pluralism is of a restricted kind, for none of the organized groups to be tolerated have enjoyed complete autonomy and all have been to varying degrees implicated with the Government and its policies. This gives the Government a measure of legitimacy in significant areas of the society. In addition it promotes a degree of ambiguity about the régime's position, which is one of its chief strengths, for lines of division between supporters and opponents become blurred. For example, the lay head of Catholic Action (Martín Artajo) was, in 1945, made Foreign Minister.[22] He had the Primate's blessing which caused the Church to be closely identified with the Government. This quietened the doubts of some Catholics and left others in an ambivalent position. One section of Catholic Action, fearful for the Church's reputation amongst the working classes, were hostile to the move, yet their links with people inside the régime inhibited effective opposition and made it difficult for them to co-operate with the Government's outright opponents. Equally, there were obvious advantages for Franco in promoting dissension within this particularly well-organized and respected body. As more elements have been incorporated into the régime it has become increasingly difficult to pin down the positions occupied by particular individuals or groups.

Such tactics have also enabled the régime to neutralize challenges to its authority. The Monarchists and Artajo himself, in the case just cited, hoped to reduce the harsher aspects of authoritarian rule and to promote the monarchical cause by working from within the Government. But once inside he was hemmed in by more authoritarian elements and too absorbed by routine tasks to exert effective pressure. The monarchy was officially restored but this merely divided the monarchists further whilst leaving Franco firmly in control.

Attempts to liberalize the educational system made by another moderate Catholic, Sr. Ruiz-Jiménez, had limited success and were supported by Franco himself in the face of opposition from soldiers opposed to all loosening of authority, from conservative Catholics (notably members of Opus Dei) fearful for the Church's hold on education and from Falangists who feared they would lose political control in the universities. Ruiz Jiménez was, however, dismissed in 1956 when the political implications

[22]For this incident and the background to it cf. the chapter on the Church, in J. Hughes, *Report From Spain*, New York, 1947, pp. 46 and ff.

became clearer and so another attempt at change from within eventually failed.[23]

Appointments to the Government have also been made in order to cut the ground from beneath powerful individuals who, if left outside, could become focal points for opposition. After the 1956 crisis Franco gave ministerial office to Barroso, the army's leading monarchist, and retained Arrese (the Movement's Secretary-General) whose plans for reviving Falangist influence had been dropped. For identical reasons prominent politicians are rarely driven completely into the wilderness. Dismissed ministers frequently receive some other post thus compromising their effectiveness as critics.[24] Ministers may even be denied the opportunity to embarrass the Government by resigning at a time not of Franco's choosing. During the 1956 crisis Arrese and a Falangist colleague tendered their resignations but Franco would not accept them. Arrese was (in 1961) permitted to resign from the Housing Ministry, following cuts in its budget, but by then the Falangists had been more or less neutralized and his departure was not a major embarrassment to the régime.

Franco's freedom to decide upon appointments has been limited by his over-riding desire to preserve his régime. Once, during the 1941 crisis, a whole list of appointments was submitted to him by Falangists and accepted in order to conciliate the Party.[25] In 1945 prominent monarchists even refused to accept office.[26] There is, however, a more fundamental problem. The Party has attracted few new recruits and there is no other clearly prescribed path to the top in Spanish politics. Personal contact and even accident therefore play an unusually large part in the selection process. The clearest indicator is the number of government posts which have been held by Franco's own personal associates. The same factors also partly account for the large proportion of ministers recruited from the bureaucracy.

Nevertheless, the limits within which Franco has operated, when replenishing his régime's political élite, have been fairly wide. His follow-

[23]On these efforts at "reform from within" cf. D. Ridruejo, *Escrito en España*, Buenos Aires, 1964, pp. 116–20.
[24]It is usual, for example, to appoint ex-ministers to the Cortes.
[25]Cf. Stanley G. Payne, *Falange, op. cit.*, p. 224.
[26]This reluctance to serve, on the part of some monarchists, tended to diminish after the "restoration" of 1947.

ing's heterogeneous nature has made possible a variety of permutations. This degree of flexibility has enabled him to maintain his basic pattern of rule whilst adjusting to changed domestic and foreign circumstances.

Franco has reconstructed his governments only nine times in thirty-three years. These changes have never been wholesale but have involved reshuffles in which some ministers have been moved around and others replaced. The changes have usually occurred in response to crises of confidence within the régime caused by external or domestic events and their interaction. A shift of emphasis occurred, for example, in 1945. By then the Falangists had proved to be a liability rather than an asset in the régime's conduct of foreign affairs. The balance was therefore tilted a little in favour of Catholic and monarchist elements and more reliance was placed on administrators with civil service or business backgrounds. This was done to attract additional domestic support and in the hope of co-operating with the United States and its European allies. The Catholic and monarchist groups were further strengthened in 1951 when hopes of an American alliance had become real.

In 1957 and 1961 significant changes were made in response to domestic events. The crisis of 1956 and chronic economic difficulties induced Franco to incorporate two adherents of Opus Dei into the Government. They gave the régime new political strength and brought greater technical expertise to the handling of economic problems.

In 1961 the Government's handling of labour disputes strained its relations with the Church and damaged its reputation abroad at a time when it was seeking association with the E.E.C. The control of Opus Dei's adherents over economic policy was therefore strengthened and younger men (like the new Minister of Information and Tourism) believed to favour some relaxation of authoritarian controls were brought into the Government. Further changes in 1965 confirmed this picture.

The most recent reshuffle occurred in October 1969. It appeared to represent something of a new departure. Two factors suggest this conclusion. Firstly, it entailed more comprehensive changes than previous reshuffles. Thirteen ministers, out of a total of eighteen, then received their first ministerial appointments. Secondly, the new government was more homogeneous than any of its predecessors. A majority of its members were members or sympathizers of Opus Dei and this group's most notable ministerial opponents (including the Foreign Minister, the Minister of

Information and Tourism and the Secretary-General of the Movement) were dismissed. Other groups, notably the Falangists, were correspondingly weakened.

Some observers concluded from this that the Government was effectively appointed by Franco's deputy, Carrero Blanco (a sympathizer of Opus Dei), rather than by himself. This seems a likely explanation for a government constructed on lines so different from others in the post-Civil-war era. Three additional points, however, require emphasis. Firstly, it is unlikely that the appointments were made without Franco's consent. They are to be seen in the context of his partial withdrawal from political activity and of his preparations for an orderly succession. The youth and professional backgrounds of most of the new ministers indicate efforts to create a cohesive and competent team which, perhaps under Carrero Blanco, could hold the régime together after Franco's departure. Franco's mediating role in the crisis of Christmas 1970 shows that he has not yet wholly abandoned his prerogatives. Secondly, the new government's homogeneity can be exaggerated. Ministers have been selected as much for their technical competence as for their links with Opus Dei. Also, traditional patterns of coalition rule have not been wholly abandoned. The Government still includes at least one Carlist and one Falangist. The Opus Dei sympathizers, moreover, do not have identical outlooks and sometimes maintain links with other groups. The new Housing Minister, for example, is an Opus Dei sympathizer but he also has Falangist associations. Finally, it must be observed that other groups are in reserve should the present team encounter difficulties. Elements within the army and the Movement and representatives of Catholic groups like Acción Nacional Católica de Propogandistas remain in the wings.[27]

This reshuffling process has enabled the régime gradually to replenish its political élite with ministers capable of initiating new policies whilst preserving a basic continuity. Various groups have put men at the Government's disposal and have been made responsible for different policy-making areas. Franco's practice of remaining partially detached from all of them means that when mistakes have occurred or it has been necessary to repudiate a policy he has been able to pin most of the responsibility on

[27]Cf. Chapter 1 for a reference to this group. It is also worth noting that the military (which always constitutes a special case) is well represented in the present Government.

the ministers concerned and has been able to replace them without serious damage to his own authority. When the policy of autarchy, for example, was shown to be unworkable the ministers most closely associated with it were replaced by adherents of Opus Dei. They were left free to pursue more liberal economic policies.

It is significant that the net effect of changes since 1957 has been to strengthen the Government's technocratic or civil service element. Recruitment from this quarter has in fact solved Franco's problem of finding dependable replacements for ministers of his own generation. Above all it has enabled him to recruit ministers of a much younger generation not implicated in the Civil War. The absence of well-defined and graduated steps in the climb to the top has indeed made it possible to pick out some younger men from the ruck and give them their chance earlier than contemporaries in countries with more settled patterns of promotion.[28] With no party capable of mobilizing mass support or encouraging widespread political participation the bureaucracy becomes an obvious recruiting ground.

This mode of recruitment raises two problems. Firstly, it impedes the emergence of genuine political leaders who, because of their distinctive attitudes and their freedom from entanglements with bureaucratic interests, are able firmly to impose their will on the administration and to give a decisive lead in the formulation of new policies. Also, there must be doubts whether leaders recruited on this basis can command the support needed by those seeking to guide the régime smoothly through the transitional period following Franco's departure. But in the short run, at least, they have strengthened the régime by increasing its level of technical competence and giving it a measure of appeal to some sections of the younger generation preoccupied with the problems of modernization.[29] In particular they have given priority to fostering the economic growth on which they pin their hopes as an answer to the problem of maintaining political stability after Franco.

[28]The recruitment of ministers should not be regarded, however, as a wholly random process. An unpublished paper circulated by a well-known Spanish sociologist pointed to certain uniformities in the careers of ministers. The study confirmed the frequent importance of a successful career in the higher reaches of the civil service and of subsequent appointments to political offices below the rank of minister.

[19]They perhaps appeal more to those brought up in the post-war period of economic difficulty than to the next generation who have generally experienced less privation.

CHAPTER 4

The Workings of the Government

THE PROBLEM OF INTERNAL CONFLICT

Franco's system of coalition rule has left his governments without a well-developed sense of common purpose. Ministers have tended to be held individually rather than collectively responsible for their conduct of affairs. Sometimes there have been public disputes between ministers.[1] Ministers identify with varying traditions and the interests and assumptions they do share have generally provided an inadequate basis for generating coherent programmes in terms of which competing claims could be evaluated, priorities ordered or clear objectives defined.

Special factors have intensified this lack of unity. In the absence of independent political parties ministers have no effective structure upon which to rely for support apart from their own departments. This is particularly true of civil servants promoted to the Government, who sometimes are almost unknown outside the administration prior to their appointments. Given the Movement's run-down state it even applies to Falangists. Thus ministers identify closely with established departmental traditions and interests, defending their prerogatives against encroachments from other departments and, where possible, extending departmental influence by annexing new functions. The factors influencing a department's conception of its interests will emerge later. The main point here is the unusual extent to which administrative interests and political concerns become entangled. The first thing to preoccupy ministers examining the proposals of colleagues has tended to be whether they involve intrusions upon or curtailments of their department's jurisdiction. There has been intense interministerial competition, particularly for

[1] Usually such public disputes have entailed the use of "coded" messages whose meaning is clear to the initiated. Falangists and adherents of Opus Dei, for example, have conducted disputes of this type over social and economic policies.

control over areas of parallel or overlapping responsibility. This partly explains why even ministers of similar outlooks fail to co-operate in the tackling of common problems as occurred, for example, when the Presidencia del Gobierno (or Prime Minister's office) and the Finance Ministry, both led by adherents of Opus Dei, clashed over the question of administrative reform.

The opportunities for such conflicts have grown with increases in the Government's size. This is largely a response to the universal tendency for the governments of industrializing societies to assume new responsibilities and to extend the scope of existing ones. Thus established departments have been divided and new ministries created. In 1951, for example, the Ministry of Industry and Commerce became two separate departments and the Ministry of Information and Tourism was established to administer services formerly managed by the Education and Interior Ministries. The appointment, in 1965, of a minister responsible for economic planning was part of the same tendency.

Political factors also explain this growth. Thus, during the Civil War there was a single Defence Ministry which was afterwards trisected to satisfy the special claims of each force and to break up a potentially dangerous concentration of power. Similarly, a Housing Ministry was created not only to co-ordinate the work of hitherto scattered agencies but also to create a job for the Falangist leader Arrese which would channel his energies in ways acceptable to the Falange and yet away from unsettling political controversies.

THE GOVERNMENT AND ITS RELATIONSHIP WITH MAJOR INTEREST GROUPS

Departmental conflict has been further intensified by the practice of appointing ministers associated with a particular group to departments directly affecting that group's interests. The motive for such appointments has been to incorporate each group into the régime, but the groups have simultaneously been given opportunities for defending their sectional interests and maintaining entrenched positions. [2] Thus underlying conflicts

[2]The importance attached by interest groups to having a ministry with which a special relationship may be maintained can be illustrated by recent campaigns conducted by the medical profession to secure the creation of a Ministry of Health.

have been perpetuated rather than resolved. Ministers recruited on this basis have tended to share the general attitudes and interests of the political and social groups from which they come rather than those of their ministerial colleagues from different backgrounds. This is apparent, for example, in conflicts over the appropriate handling of strikes. Falangists, anxious to maintain "National Syndicalism", and military men, keen to preserve public order, are more likely to favour stern disciplinary measures than the technocrats of Opus Dei whose priorities are promoting economic growth and improving Spain's relations with her European neighbours.

For identical reasons each major interest group has tended to establish close relationships with, at most, a limited number of departments. They deal with the ministries to which they have ready access and where they are assured of a sympathetic hearing. In these cases formal channels of communication are supplemented by informal contacts, usual amongst people with similar backgrounds; they provide the possibility of a dialogue sustained against a background of common interests and assumptions. Consequently groups press their claims through particular sectors of the administration and ministers are responsive to limited sets of interests. Official union leaders, for example, can exercise some influence within the Labour Ministry whilst business and agrarian interests bring pressure to bear upon the economic departments. Ecclesiastical influence has been more pervasive but has been principally exercised through the Foreign, Education and Justice departments which most affect clerical interests and have been under specifically Catholic leadership. The Armed Services constitute the most clear-cut case. Their well-developed sense of corporate identity impels the service ministers to align themselves in defence of their respective professional interests. Therefore the demands of particular groups have tended to be formulated in isolation, which inevitably leads to conflict at higher levels. For example, there is strong inter-service rivalry over the allocation of resources. Similarly Falangists and members of Opus Dei have clashed over priorities in the economic and social fields.

Nevertheless, ministers have never been mere mouthpieces of sectional interests. There are several obvious reasons for this. Firstly, ministerial careers ultimately depend upon Franco and their first loyalty must be to him. Secondly, ministers develop their own views and interests which can bring them into conflict with the groups they are presumed to represent.

Ministerial responsibilities may create an awareness of problems which can only be tackled at the expense of special interests—the desirability of army and educational reform being two cases which will be examined later. Likewise, a minister's view of his department's interests can conflict with the interests of those with whom he deals. The Labour Ministry, for example, sees its task as essentially regulative in nature and this has brought it into competition with the *Sindicatos* for control over the management of labour relations, even though both have usually been under Falangist leadership, for union leaders believe their future depends on some acknowledgement of popular pressure for greater union autonomy.

Also, there is no group sufficiently independent or homogeneous to develop a clear-cut point of view that can be pressed upon ministers. This is apparent from earlier statements but it can be underlined with particular reference to the business community. The many small business interests are inadequately organized and lack ready access to ministerial departments. This leaves the field open for major economic and financial institutions. Their importance to the economy gives them potentially great bargaining power which could be used to help shape the general lines of national economic policy. A relatively recent study suggests, however, that they do not fully exploit their position.[3] The representatives of big banks and companies have formal and informal contacts with ministerial departments which are denied to less significant groups. They can make representations through officially constituted chambers of commerce or, more importantly, they can get into direct contact with civil servants and ministers through unofficial trade associations. Such contacts tend to be made, however, on the basis of personal links and they entail approaches to positions scattered throughout the administration. They do not necessarily involve a concerted exercise of pressure. The need for technical advice in formulating policy and for co-operation in its implementation, coupled with the favourable predisposition within the economic departments to business interests, means that their influence is great and widespread on such matters as obtaining tariff protection or the awarding of credit facilities, but it tends to be exercised on an *ad hoc* and piecemeal basis. They therefore play a largely defensive role and, though major concessions are extracted from the administration, departments have

[3]Cf. Juan J. Linz and Amando de Miguel, *Los Empresarios ante el Poder Público*, Madrid, 1966.

considerable freedom to choose between competing claims and to determine the general lines of policy.

Ministers can reinforce this freedom of action by using their powers of
appointment. Those from a group like Opus Dei, possessing some
cohesion, can promote fellow members to positions of importance within
the administration. This facilitates the execution of their policies, provides
opportunities for furthering the interests of allies outside the administration and offers some protection against pressure from other quarters.

The freedom of manoeuvre enjoyed by ministers can be illustrated by
references to relationships with the Church and army. Sr. Ruiz Jíménez,
for example, was not prevented by his Catholic background from
initiating plans for the reform of secondary education, entailing greater
control over Church schools.[4] Similarly, in 1958, Barroso proposed to
modernize the army by placing greater reliance on sophisticated weapons
and making corresponding cuts in manpower. This was a particularly
delicate matter as it involved replacing many Civil War veterans by
younger technically qualified officers.[5]

On the other hand, these cases also illustrate the limits within which
policy-makers work and the nature of the influence which major interest
groups can exercise.

The drafting of Ruiz Jíménez's plans was both preceded and followed
by consultations with educational and Church authorities whose advice
and co-operation were necessary to the reform's success. At both stages
there was hard bargaining during which Church leaders brought their
moral authority to bear in order to win significant concessions, such as
the right to nominate their own school inspectors, which blunted the
reform's effectiveness. In the case of Barroso's reforms, the need to guarantee the army's loyalty meant that sweeping changes could only be
launched in agreement with the general staff and by regional commanders. Subsequent delays in their implementation and the final shape
of things suggests agreement was difficult to achieve and was bought at
the price of major concessions to important groups within the army. The
result was in fact a compromise between advocates of a modernized army
and defenders of traditional interests, particularly those stressing the

[4]Cf. *Hispanic American Review*, Stanford, Mar. 1953.
[5]Cf. Arthur P. Whitaker, *Spain and Defense of the West*, New York, 1962, pp. 75–
76, for reference to this.

importance of an army equipped to perform its internal policing function.

Deadlock in such bargaining may be broken by appealing over the minister's head to Franco. Thus negotiations about a law of 1945 on primary education ran into difficulties when the minister concerned was carried along by colleagues opposed to granting the Church big privileges. The Primate himself then approached Franco and by threatening to disassociate himself publicly from the régime extracted the concessions he was seeking.[6]

It is apparent therefore that the power of major interests is large. In particular the Church's moral authority and the army's political importance mean that they have been able to exert strong pressure when they have closed ranks in defence of special interests and that they have had strong bargaining positions from which to moderate attacks upon their strongholds. Their importance to the régime has meant that if opposition was sufficiently strong they could, in the last resort, exercise a veto power. Responsibility for initiating policy, however, has lain firmly with the Government.

The final reason for seeing ministers as something more than the mouthpieces of sectional interests is that, as members of the Government, they may be obliged to accept a certain responsibility for decisions vigorously opposed by themselves and the groups with which they are associated. Indeed, the participation in the Government of members of the groups may make it easier to impose unpopular decisions upon them for they then accept its authority as legitimate.

This is best illustrated by referring to the military which is, in principle, in the strongest position successfully to oppose the Government.

In 1956, for example, Franco agreed to give Spanish Morocco its independence. Initially he had followed a policy of aiding nationalists in the neighbouring French Morocco whilst ignoring similar demands from within Spain's protectorate. In this way he hoped to retain control of Spanish Morocco and yet promote Spanish influence in the Arab world. When France granted its protectorate independence the policy boomeranged. Franco then recognized that Spain's position in Morocco had become untenable and that the only way of retaining the friendship of Arab countries was to follow France's example. This decision would

[6] Cf. J. Hughes, *op. cit.*

probably have destroyed previous Spanish governments of this century. Given its great stake in the protectorate the army might have been tempted to intervene. Its loyalty was in fact strained but there were none of the difficulties experienced by the French in Algeria.[7]

Military pressure did, however, win the concession of retaining the enclave of Ifni. In 1957 this was subject to the threat of attack from Morocco. The Government's failure to take preventative measures provoked resentment amongst military leaders but they made no attempts to take the law into their own hands. An attack finally came and caught the Government unawares. Its authority was re-established, however, and on terms opposed by the Army Minister. He is believed to have advocated a strong counter-offensive. Franco accepted the Foreign Minister's advice to negotiate and the army acquiesced.[8] Thus even in a case where divisions tended to harden along civilian versus military lines the army was kept under control.

The most important decision affecting military interests taken since the Civil War was to seek an alliance with the U.S.A. The initiative on Spain's side came from Franco but ran counter to many Spanish military traditions.[9] In this case opposition was reinforced by Church leaders and Falangist spokesmen. Confronted by hostility from all these important groups it took two years before agreement was reached. The time was used to wear down opposition and to negotiate terms that would make the arrangement acceptable to the army. In the process the army successfully pressed for large grants of military aid which strengthened its position. Its opposition, however, was eventually removed.

Military leaders played a prominent part in negotiating with the U.S.A., defence planning being considered their preserve. But when in 1963 negotiations for the renewal of defence agreements ran into difficulties Franco broke the deadlock by replacing military negotiators by a diplomat who was given considerable latitude to conclude an agreement. In

[7]For references to the Spanish army in North Africa cf. *Hispanic American Review, op. cit.*, 1956 and 1957.

[8]There was a joint French–Spanish operation in response to a further attack but this was executed with full government approval. As noted before, Ifni was finally handed over to Morocco in 1969. This provoked no obvious response from the army.

[9]Hostility to the U.S.A. in military circles can be explained, in part at least, by the events of 1898. A detailed discussion of Franco's dealings with the U.S.A. is to be found in Arthur P. Whitaker, *Spain and Defense of the West, op. cit.*

the most recent Spanish–American negotiations civilians have played a similarly prominent part.[10]

This evidence suggests that the inclusion in the Government of military spokesmen does not mean that major decisions are always taken in accordance with their views or the military's short-term interests. On the other hand, they and other ministers remain sensitive to the demands of powerful interests and they can, from within the Government, defend interests and extract concessions which leave these groups entrenched in their own separate and established positions. Thus the centrifugal forces within the Government are perpetuated.

The lines of division within the Government have, however, rarely been clear or consistent. Members of identifiable groups like the Falange or Opus Dei have shown some general tendency to co-operate with each other but alliances have otherwise fluctuated according to the issues or personalities involved. The only discernible pattern is a division between "conservatives" who are nervous about the relaxation of authoritarian controls and "moderates" who believe the régime's best hope of survival is to rely less upon coercion and more upon the modernization of economic and administrative structures. There is a tug-of-war between these two tendencies which may cut across other alignments. This was apparent during the political crisis of 1969. Pressure from conservative army officers, supported by military men within the Government, obtained the declaration of a national state of emergency. It was designed as an opportunity for disrupting the activities of opposition groups. Once its immediate purpose had been served the technocratic ministers primarily concerned with economic problems, who had always opposed such drastic measures, fought back. They believed repressive measures to be counter-productive and harmful to Spain's international standing. Their pressure led to the premature lifting of the emergency. In 1970 there were similar arguments within the Government over the fate of the Basque separatists sentenced to death by a military court. The commutation of the death sentences, after lengthy debate, indicated a hard-won victory for the "moderates". Nevertheless, the situation remains confused for

[10]It should be stressed, however, that the agreements renewed in 1970 continued to lay particular stress on military as opposed to other forms of aid and co-operation. For a discussion of the agreements and for details of their terms cf. M. Martinez, Cuadrado *op. cit.*, pp. 510–12 and 517–25. It is noteworthy that, throughout, Spain has retained sovereignty over U.S. bases

ministers of similar outlook constantly conflict when departmental interests are at stake. Likewise, members of the same faction may be divided over fundamental issues. Thus, during the above-mentioned crises, Opus Dei sympathizers were found amongst the "moderates" and the "conservatives".[11]

THE MAJOR CENTRES OF INFLUENCE WITHIN THE GOVERNMENT

Such fluidity rules out the possibility of consistently solid and irreconcilable blocs and so provides some basis for the coexistence of conflicting elements within the Government. It also makes it possible for particular ministers to play especially assertive roles. They partially fill the vacuum created by a lack of decisive leadership from the top and by the absence of very clearly defined ministerial alignments. The ministers concerned exercise a major influence on the formulation of policy because of a special relationship with Franco, their prestige within the régime or the department they head. It is hard to say who they are at any given moment because changing circumstances or political miscalculations can reduce an individual's standing and diminish his influence with Franco. Some observations, however, are possible.

The outstanding member of recent governments has been Admiral Carrero Blanco. He is Franco's official deputy and also has a singularly close personal relationship with him. He has come to public prominence relatively recently but almost from the régime's outset Franco entrusted him with politically important tasks. There has been an identity of views and mutual confidence between the two men. The Admiral's influence has been reinforced by the increasing importance of his department, the Presidencia del Gobierrno (Presidency or Prime Minister's office). It was traditionally the premier's private office and technically Franco remains its head with Carrero Blanco as his deputy, but the former's style of leadership meant that in practice it developed as an independent agency. Initially Carrero Blanco was excluded from the Government which in

[11]The events of 1969 are reviewed in M. Martinez Cuadro (editor), "Cambio Social y Modernización Política", *Anuario Político Español*, 1969, pp. 221–44. For a similar review of the 1970 crisis cf. M. Martinez Cuadrado, *ibid.*, 1970, especially pp. 232–65 and 283–306.

effect gave him the status of Spain's only "Minister without Cabinet rank". But his department gained increasing significance as a repository for important functions excluded, for political or administrative convenience, from the jurisdiction of traditional ministries. These included the civilian administration of overseas territories and the gathering of official statistics. This importance was formally recognized in 1951 when, though still officially without ministerial status, Carrero Blanco was appointed to the Government.[12]

As a sympathizer of Opus Dei he gave adherents of the movement a base in the Presidency from which to implement their administrative reform projects. This has enabled them to extend their influence throughout the administration and to promote corresponding increases in the Presidency's importance. It was through this channel that Franco's attention was drawn to the technocrats of Opus Dei who progressively assumed responsibility for economic policy.

The initial move was to establish an office within the Presidency under an important member of Opus Dei, Sr. López Rodó, to study the question of administrative reform. The first practical result was a law of 1957 codifying legislation on the Government's powers and composition and seeking to increase its efficiency. For the first time a theoretical distinction was explicitly made between the Heads of State and of Government (or Prime Minister).[13]

A list was drafted of the Head of Government's tasks with the proviso that those of an administrative nature could be delegated to the Presidency. But at this level, of course, the distinction between administrative and political questions is slight and often unreal so, in practice, Franco has permitted the Presidency to assume responsibility for matters with a political content which he might have reserved to himself. These include attempts to coordinate departmental activities and to supervise the execution of government policy. Being detached from the ultimate source of executive power the department lacks the authority needed to guarantee success in these endeavours and other special reasons, which will become apparent, limit its effectiveness. Yet as the repository of so many legal powers the Presidency is well placed to exert a widespread influence on the shaping of domestic policy.

[12]Cf. A. Guaita, *El Consejo de Ministros*, Madrid, 1959, pp. 34–36.
[13]This was the "Ley de Régimen Juridico de la Administración del Estado".

This potential has been partly realized through further attempts at administrative reform and, in particular, through the establishment of machinery for economic planning. This will be examined later. It is sufficient to say here that López Ródo was made the Government's planning officer and that in 1965 he was made "Minister without Portfolio" to strengthen his authority in dealing with departments responsible for the plan's execution. As leader of the administrative reform movement and as a prominent Opus Dei member he exercised considerable influence from outside the Government. The priority given to economic planning now makes him a prominent figure within the Council of Ministers itself. It is significant that two of his lieutenants, hitherto employed in the Presidency, were given ministerial appointments in the government reshuffle of 1969. Thus the Presidency is now represented in the Government by two powerful ministers, one of whom (Carrero Blanco) has done more than any other single individual to fill the gap created by the relaxation of Franco's grip on the daily conduct of affairs.

The Presidency has frequently had to vie for influence with the Finance Ministry. The latter's departmental traditions and interests have fostered conflict and competition even when the Finance Ministers themselves have been Opus Dei sympathizers (which has been the case since 1957). The holder of the purse strings is invariably powerful but this has been particularly true in Spain. Franco's system of coalition rule has made it difficult to agree upon the criteria to be imposed on the Ministry when allocating resources. Thus the department's own view of its function has been especially important. Until 1957, at least, this was largely conceived of in terms of curbing expenditure and not of regulating economic development. After 1957 there was a shift in emphasis but its extent was limited by the persistence of traditional departmental attitudes and by the Government's generally conservative complexion.

When Ministries submit their estimates and bargain over budgetary allocations the Finance Ministry frequently exercises a veto power or substantially modifies the spending department's priorities. Similarly, current expenditure has to be cleared with the Ministry which has a representative in each (civilian) department to sanction the payment of credits. Such controls were devised to ensure that money was only released for approved purposes but they are now frequently used to withhold funds and so to influence the speed of a policy's execution, to modify it or even to prevent its effective implementation. Finally, management of taxation and monetary policies helps the department to determine the general availability of funds and the terms upon which they may be used.[14]

By law major questions of fiscal and monetary policy must be decided by the Council of Ministers. However, the technical arguments Finance Ministers can marshal make it difficult effectively to oppose them. The same is true of other financial decisions taken at this level. These include important new investment decisions, the settlement of disputes between the Finance Ministry and other departments over the approval of estimates or the award of credits and, finally, the financing of important administrative reforms. The nature of the Finance Minister's influence in these government discussions was highlighted in 1964 following the initiation of the Presidency's schemes for civil service reform. The Presidency's plan was substantially revised by the legislation making the necessary financial provisions. This involved quite distinct criteria. In such circumstances the department assumes the proportions of a "super ministry" capable of influencing nearly the whole field of government policy.[15]

This influence is more limited when large or important groups within the Government achieve a considerable degree of unanimity or Franco's support is won for a project. Perhaps the clearest illustration is the level of defence expenditure. Franco's attention to military interests, their importance to the régime and the pressures that can therefore be exerted mean that they appropriate large slices of Spain's budget. Recent reductions in the percentage of the budget devoted to defence have probably been due as much to the military's own modernizing elements as to the exertion of greater financial discipline.

This makes it clear that service ministers must be counted amongst the key figures in any Spanish government. They play an essential part in defence planning and army ministers, at least, can also influence decisions affecting internal security. The military's internal policing function places them in that position. Their overall impact on national policy must not, however, be overstated. It is often of a negative nature. They generally

[14]Cf. "Los 'Enclaves' Financieros en la Administración Pública", *Documentación Administrativia* No. 83, Nov. 1964, pp. 79–80, and M. Beltrán Villaba, 'Las disfunciones del presupuesto convencional', *ibid.* No. 93, Sept. 1965, pp. 23–37.

[15]Cf. The observations of A. Nieto, *Revista de Derecho Financiero y de Hacienda Pública*, Dec. 1964 (pp. 951–82).

lack the expertise needed to have a positive influence upon wider questions of economic and social policy.

The Interior Ministry is the department most intimately concerned with domestic security. Its responsibility for maintaining order, controlling the police, licensing public assemblies, registering voluntary associations, monitoring the state of public opinion and supervising local administration necessarily makes it a major centre of influence within any government.[16] Franco's practice of appointing its head from amongst personal and well-trusted associates is one measure of its importance.

Finally, brief mention must be made of the Foreign Ministry. As already observed, this department and its heads haver ecently enjoyed considerable freedom in the formulation of foreign policy. They have also exerted considerable influence on domestic affairs when these have had a bearing on international relations. Franco, for example, permitted Castiella to pursue his objective of a law on religious tolerance which was partly conceived as a gesture to European opinion.

Those ministers exercising widespread influence could be said to constitute an "inner cabinet". But their personal and political divisions have prevented them from forming a coherent group able to supply the sense of direction Franco has often failed to provide. The implications this has for the Government's effectiveness will be made clearer by examining the formal decision-making machinery.

---

[16]After the Civil War there was some reorganization of the police forces. The Asaltos were abolished and the policing of urban areas was handed over to the new Policía Armada y de Tráfico. Rural, coastal and frontier zones continued to be policed by the Civil Guard. This remains a para-military body dependent for disciplinary matters upon the Army Ministry but otherwise at the disposal of the Interior Ministry. There are also special forces for combating crime and political opposition activities. There are municipal police forces but they are primarily concerned with traffic direction and the enforcement of local "by-laws". Otherwise, they are regarded simply as auxiliaries of the state security forces. The Civil Guard is a particularly efficient force, not least in repressing opposition political activities. Sometimes there is rivalry and friction between this body and other forces, notably the political police, or Brigada Social. The latter body was organized with the assistance of advisers from Nazi Germany.

THE COUNCIL OF MINISTERS[17]

The Council of Ministers is the formal centre for taking important policy decisions. Its meetings are convoked by Franco (or his deputy) usually once a fortnight, though more often in emergencies. Ministers are notified of them through the Council's Secretariat which was created within the Presidency as one of its measures for improving the management of official business. This body also drafts the formal agenda. Franco helps to shape it by indicating the current problems he wishes to discuss or any measures he personally plans to initiate. These are given priority, along with initiatives from other quarters behind which he is prepared to throw his weight. At this stage he may summon individual ministers to obtain their advice and sound out opinion. They may also seek interviews with him to discuss their problems and, if possible, to win his backing for departmental initiatives—a necessary step if these are controversial or represent significant policy changes. In the give and take of these interviews Franco can directly exert his influence by modifying plans that are put to him or by putting them aside as subjects for further study or informal interministerial consultation, especially if he anticipates considerable hostility. Such audiences also provide ministers with one of their chief opportunities for determining the general course of governmental discussion. Indeed, the frequency with which ministers obtain interviews is an indicator of the confidence Franco currently places in them and hence of their capacity for shaping policy.

The Secretariat's location within the Presidency gives the latter particular influence over the agenda's preparation. This has been used, most notably, to give priority to discussions of economic problems.

Franco's style of leadership has left all ministers fairly free, however, to bring problems of a more routine, detailed or technical nature directly to the Council's attention. In fact prior to a law of 1958 ministers could place items on the agenda without previously notifying their colleagues. The practice was only to submit proposals to the examination of allies or to associates whose co-operation it was expedient to obtain. This often meant, particularly when complex technical questions were involved,

[17]The formal powers and structure of the Council of Ministers are discussed in A. Guaita, *El Consejo de Ministros, op. cit.* The following account of its day-to-day operations is largely based on interviews with former ministers and senior officials.

that a measure's proponent was the only minister properly equipped to discuss it. Thus his plans could be approved without adequate scrutiny. To deal with this problem it was established that eight days notice had to be given of proposals requiring the Council's attention, unless the Council itself decided that it was an urgent matter requiring immediate attention. Plans are now usually circulated in advance of meetings, either through direct ministerial contacts or via the Secretariat. This gives the chance to send back observations or to raise preliminary objections. This may lead to amendments, which relieve the Council of unnecessary discussion, but remaining disagreements can be raised in formal session. This procedure has not completely remedied the situation it was designed to meet. Old habits persist, albeit in modified forms. Sometimes the formalities are observed but plans are circulated unaccompanied by data necessary for evaluating them properly. This is particularly serious as most ministers lack staff qualified to advise on matters outside their immediate juris-diction. On other occasions the "eight-day rule" is not strictly observed and time for proper study is wholly lacking. The amount of business that the Government now handles means eight days is in any case often too short a period for adequate preparation. Finally, the Council has freely interpreted the meaning of an "emergency". Emergency procedures are often invoked simply as a device for slipping matters on to the agenda at the last minute. Objections are not raised for all ministers wish to retain this procedural device for themselves. Thus ministers often remain inadequately briefed with results that will become apparent.

After the preliminary exchanges the Secretariat drafts the final agenda which is invariably congested. There are several reasons for this. Partly it results from the extended scale of governmental activity. Such a growth can be seen as part of a universal tendency. It must also be seen in the context of an authoritarian régime which regulates matters largely beyond the control of "representative" governments. The Council, for example, is the final court of appeal in the case of politically contentious trials conducted before military courts—a function it performed during the crisis of Christmas 1970.[18]

The régime's authoritarian character also partly explains a tendency for formal decision-making to be very centralized. Not only does the Council

---

[18]Legally appeals are addressed to the Head of State but the Council of Ministers is called on to advise him.

discuss the broad outlines of national policy, it also ratifies all matters requiring legislation, all ministerial decrees and most public appointments. Formally, at least, this makes provision for Franco to check on all important ministerial decisions and for ministers to watch each other. But such centralization is also partly explicable in historical terms. In many particulars Franco's governments have followed traditional practices. These formed an adequate basis for the management of affairs when the State's responsibilities were limited, but once they grew the Council found itself burdened by too many routine administrative decisions better handled elsewhere. For a long time few steps were taken to deal with this situation and, for example, it was left until the reforms of 1957 to provide for a system of government committees to which routine responsibilities could be delegated.

A firm dividing line cannot of course be drawn between the policy-making and administrative processes; the two constantly interact. However, Spain's government undoubtedly tends to be overloaded with relatively minor administrative matters. Thus it is hard to find time for careful discussion of long-term problems and harder to agree upon clear and consistent lines of collective action. Major problems tend, instead, to be examined as they arise and their resolution is determined by the current balance of forces within the Government. This will be made clearer by examining procedures within the Council itself.

Until recently, at least, Franco has almost invariably presided over the Council's sessions. He begins meetings with a general survey of current problems that enables him to set the tone of subsequent discussions. He chiefly reports on the state of international relations but sometimes covers internal problems, particularly those affecting public order. Then ministers, in a prescribed order, explain their departments' current problems and present matters that are awaiting a decision.

Their treatment varies with the nature of the business. The many routine matters consume time but individually are dealt with fairly quickly. In the case of appointments this is because of a convention that each minister should enjoy considerable freedom of choice. But in other cases it is because ministers are inadequately briefed to challenge their colleagues' many and often technical measures. Some important matters are also decided without difficulty. The same factors partly account for this but there is also a process which could be described as a form of "log

rolling". Provided ministers consider their departments' vital interests
are not involved, they permit quite drastic measures to pass on the tacit
understanding that they can enjoy similar freedom in their own spheres.
In particular they guard their freedom to use decree-laws which enable
them to override special interests in the event of conflict or obstruction.[19]

In this situation able and determined ministers operating in fields which
involve relatively little political controversy have achieved significant
results, for example, in housing and the promotion of tourism. But the
same procedures have also led to the approval of quite unco-ordinated
proposals from ministers with overlapping responsibilities. This has
resulted in inconsistent policies or a failure to complement each other's
efforts. Thus economic problems, in the 1950s, were exacerbated by a
lack of co-ordination between the Labour Ministry, responsible for approving wage rises, and the ministers responsible for managing official price
controls. Similarly, there were delays in building roads to bear Spain's
increased tourist traffic. Lack of co-ordination can also waste resources.
Many ministries, for example, have undertaken building programmes
which could have been better handled in co-operation with the Public
Works department.

Controversial questions are handled differently. In these cases Franco
permits discussion to roam freely and, given the Government's composition, it can be long and fierce. Such discussions are frequent for in
practice no issues are totally excluded, not even military matters. This
accords with Franco's conception of the Council as a "miniature parliament". It provides a forum where the conflicts of the major interests
which must be accommodated and kept in harness can be resolved under
Franco's supervision and without encouraging public debates that might
endanger the régime's stability.

Franco stands aloof from these discussions. He listens to the views
expressed and confines himself to general guidance of the debate. The
proponent of a measure who has mastered his case can retain the initiative
in the face of opposition from less prepared colleagues, particularly if he
is known to have Franco's support or has powerful allies. But as the usual
practice is not to terminate discussions at a given point with the taking of
formal majority decisions and is rather to continue until some form of

---

[19]This power, of course, cannot be used so freely in dealing with questions or
groups of major significance to the régime.

agreement has emerged, determined opponents can prolong talks until they have extracted important concessions as the price of their consent.[20] A minister with limited political weight, however, may be unable to override opposition. Deadlock may also be reached if groups of ministers or a particularly powerful individual remains obdurate. At such a point Franco may directly intervene by bringing his prestige and experience to bear in the formulation of a compromise that offers an escape from the impasse. If this proves impossible he does not ride rough-shod over opposition but defers the matter for further study and consultation at the departmental level or deliberately allows time for tempers to cool. Yet even if an agreement is reached powerful ministers can reopen the question and have the means later to modify decisions on terms more acceptable to themselves. They may initiate fresh legislation of their own or remain obstructive when applying policy. In particular the Finance Ministry, as has been already observed, may withhold the necessary funds.

These procedures help to explain the nature of decisions taken on controversial subjects. They are essentially of two kinds: major policy changes and conflicts of departmental interests. In practice the two cannot be divorced as ministers attempt to enlarge their prerogatives as part of the struggle for political influence and political rivalries exacerbate battles for administrative control. For example, the Presidency's increased administrative importance is, in large measure, both a cause and an effect of the expansion of Opus Dei's political influence. Opposition to extensions of this influence also partly explains hostility to the Presidency's administrative reforms. But for convenience the two can be examined separately.

In areas of mainly political controversy the circumstances in which decisions are taken provide the opponents of innovation with many opportunities for obstruction or fighting back. This can lead to a state of drift in which problems are indecisively tackled or solutions to them are deferred indefinitely. It also produces serious inconsistencies in governmental policy.

Three examples will be used to illustrate this. A long-standing problem is that of agrarian reform. The régime's conservative basis precludes

[20]It may be that procedures are more formalized now that Franco has released his grip on the day-to-day management of affairs, but this is a matter of conjecture. The above evidence refers to pre-1969 governments.

drastic[21] solutions but the Government has been timid in using the means it does have at its disposal. The most determined efforts to deal with the problem were perhaps made between 1951 and 1956 by a Falangist Minister of Agriculture, Señor Cavestany. His measures included legislation providing for the expropriation of under-used estates. However, such attempts at reform aroused the hostility of landowners, and their allies in the Government, who saw a potential threat to their interests. Eventually the Minister was dismissed and had less active successors who were generally more acceptable to agrarian interests.

Great difficulties also faced Castiella in his attempts to pass a law granting religious toleration. It was first mooted in 1957 and initially caused trouble with Church leaders. They were instructed by the Vatican to negotiate with the Government and an agreement was reached. But then a prominent minister led a revolt within the Government which delayed the measure until rulings from the Vatican Council destroyed the opposition's case.[22] The law did not reach the Cortes until 1967 and was only approved after a debate of unprecedented bitterness.[23]

Finally, there is the case of recent legislation governing the press. In 1961 a new Minister of Information and Tourism promised a relaxation of press censorship but only in 1966 was a law presented for the Cortes' approval. Subsequently, revisions of the penal code, a new Statute for the Profession of Journalism and a new "Official Secrets Act" have enabled more conservative elements to limit the value of earlier concessions.[24]

Departmental rivalries also raise difficulties. A classic case has been the struggle of the Interior and Housing Ministries. The former's responsibility for local government once subsumed town planning but in 1957 this became the Housing Ministry's concern. The two functions are clearly complementary yet co-operation has been impeded by a prolonged "demarcation dispute". There has been a running battle for control over areas of unclearly demarcated territory and each department has tried to encroach upon the other's jurisdiction.

The frequent resort to compromise solutions for patching up similar

[21]Cf. Chapter 7 for a further discussion of this theme.
[22]The minister in question is believed to have been Admiral Carrero Blanco.
[23]Cf. *B.O.E.*, 1 July 1967, for the contents of this law.
[24]It is significant, for example, that the Official Secrets Act emanated from Carrero Blanco's department.

disputes produces some irrational situations. The Ministries of Agriculture and Public Works, for example, have a divided responsibility for irrigation projects which has resulted in duplicated effort and unco-ordinated schemes.

The problem of co-ordination also arises from each department's determination to keep its "empire" intact. Thus the Interior Ministry, which has a general responsibility for health matters, initiated a law to co-ordinate all hospital services but the measure finally emerged with several departments left in control of their own virtually independent hospitals.[25] The same department's efforts to redistribute responsibility for the regulation of road traffic ran into similar difficulties.[26] Consequently departments tend to remain as largely autonomous entities and therefore able to keep up the battle on behalf of their separate interests.

In all these circumstances there is a continuing tendency for the Government to find itself deadlocked, and therefore inactive, or for it to devise policies on the basis of unstable compromises patched up by interests capable of finding only limited areas of agreement: policies which often lack coherence in their formulation and consistency in their application.

ADMINISTRATIVE REFORMS

Administrative reforms initiated from the Presidency have sought to tackle these problems. One reform was the creation of a government

[25]It should be indicated that the Ministry of the Interior ran the first state-administered hospitals. These still exist but can perhaps be best compared with "Poor Law" institutions. The Ministry of Labour now runs well-equipped hospitals and dispensaries as part of its social security programme but particularly in rural areas there are many not covered by its provisions. In addition there are military hospitals (administered by the service departments), prison hospitals (administered by the Ministry of Justice) and a small number of hospitals run by local authorities. Finally, there is a significant private sector usually providing above average service but at prices only prosperous middle- and upper-class groups can afford. The net result of this division of responsibility is a lack of overall planning and services which vary greatly in quantity and quality according to the region of the country and the socio-economic status of the recipient. The Interior Ministry's attempted reform did little to alter this situation.

[26]A major problem in this sphere is a long-standing dispute between the Ministry of the Interior, with its policing functions, and the Ministry of Public Works which builds roads and claims a corresponding right to make traffic regulations.

Secretariat, which has already been mentioned. Before its foundation the Government's problems were aggravated by the lack of a proper record of its decisions which made it easier to reopen controversies.[27] Now formal minutes are circulated and after their approval the Presidency sends general policy statements to departments as guides for action. Continuing divisions within the Government still leave room for dispute but some pretexts for initiating controversy have been eliminated.

Another significant step was provision for a system of government committees designed to relieve the Council of Ministers of routine business and to produce better interdepartmental co-ordination. Previously the only permanent body of this kind was the National Defence Council.[28] This was established in 1939, under Franco's chairmanship, to co-ordinate defence planning. It included the service ministers and the chiefs of staff of the armed forces: significantly civilian ministers could only participate by special invitation. The international crisis in 1939 made the establishment of this body advisable but its powers and composition underlined the régime's nature and sense of priorities. In practice, however, it seems that even this body met infrequently and usually to deal with pressing problems. It met during the World War, for example, to prepare for a possible allied invasion and a joint Spanish–German attack upon Gibraltar. It was later convened to formulate Spain's negotiating position in the talks which preceded the installation of American bases. But in all cases the wider policy questions were debated in full council and were ultimately decided by Franco himself.

In 1957 provision was made for four more committees, to which another was later added, composed of ministers with a specialized interest in a given field and all under Franco's chairmanship.* Provision was also made for committees of "junior ministers" or departmental "under-secretaries". It was hoped that these bodies would facilitate formal consultations at a lower level, which had been lacking, and prepare the ground more thoroughly for ministerial discussions.

The practical results of these reforms have not matched up to expectations. Traditional practices persisted and only one committee of under-

[27]Previously a member of the Council had acted as its Secretary. From 1951 to 1957 this was amongst Carrero Blanco's functions.

[28]One seeming exception to this was the establishment of a special interministerial committee to handle the distribution of American aid.

*In 1971 a ministerial committee was created to tackle environmental problems.

secretaries (for transport and communication) was established. The ministerial committees have, at best, functioned intermittently and have had difficulty in achieving the objectives for which they were created. A partial exception has been the economic affairs committee. This of course reflects the priority given to economic problems since 1957 and the growing power of those ministers charged with economic management.

This development improved the handling of economic affairs in two important respects. Firstly, the committee's preparatory work enabled the Government to make major decisions on the basis of more informed judgements. Secondly, for a time at least, it relieved the Council of Ministers of much routine business. Its ability to develop building and investment programmes, for example, gave it considerable responsibility for the implementation of policy. But it has had only limited success in the co-ordination of economic policy. One reason for this has been its size. Its membership has fluctuated according to the problems under discussion but it can include up to half of the full Council. This has made it too unwieldy when it has come to the detailed examination of technical problems.

Since October 1969 a question-mark seems to have appeared over even this body's future. Some observers maintain that the committee was chiefly designed as a formal meeting ground for the economic ministers sympathetic to Opus Dei and as a means of withdrawing problems of interest to them from the purview of the Council of Ministers itself. Now that adherents of Opus Dei have secured control of all the important economic ministries they may feel more disposed to develop their policies at plenary sessions of the Council. Thus advantages secured by the use of a committee may have been partially lost.

Another problem confronting the Government's economic managers has been the absence of an executive body capable of exercising decisive leadership and of laying down lines of action that individual departments are bound to follow.[29] However, a series of steps have been taken which have provided some answer to this problem. Firstly, in 1957, an "Office of Economic Coordination and Programming" was established within the Presidency. This had a board bringing together technical experts from

[29]For a discussion of the problems of economic management cf. R. Tamames, *La Estructura Económica de España*, 2nd ed., Madrid, 1963, pp. 763–92, and Charles W. Anderson, *The Political Economy of Modern Spain*, Wisconsin, 1970.

the "spending departments", and the Finance Ministry, to draw up co-ordinated investment programmes for the economic committee's subsequent approval. But at the planning and decision-making stages departmental representatives continued to act in the light of their particular interests. The investment plans they produced were therefore the sum of individual departmental programmes and did not represent a coherent whole. There was also no machinery for implementing the plans in accordance with any carefully selected priorities. Nevertheless, the habit of co-operation at the technical level was established and this proved useful when the Government adopted its first major "Stabilization Plan" for its execution demanded at least a minimum of co-ordination.

The Stabilization Plan achieved its immediate objectives. Then, inspired by French experiments with "indicative planning", machinery was created to provide for controlled expansion. A planning "Commissariat" was established under López Rodó, once again within the Presidency, to draft national plans. Their results will be scrutinized elsewhere but there is a need here to look briefly at the Commissariat's relationship with ministerial departments and the latter's part in the execution of plans.[30]

The Commissariat was equipped with a staff of technical advisers who draft plans on the basis of evidence and proposals submitted by "horizontal" and "vertical" commissions modelled on the French pattern. The former, eight in number, examine such general problems as finance, labour and commerce, whilst there are twenty of the latter to study different sectors of the economy—energy and housing for example. In both cases they are staffed by businessmen, union leaders and representatives of ministries concerned with a particular problem or sector.

The Commissariat's draft plans have been submitted for study to the ministerial committee for economic affairs and after final government approval have taken the form of laws ratified by the Cortes. The aim of the two plans so far drafted has been to promote expansion through public and private investment. Only government agencies are officially obliged to invest at prescribed rates; private concerns are simply encouraged to fulfil the plan through special incentives which the Government has been empowered to deploy. The Commissariat was charged with implementing this, under the Government's general supervision.

[30]Cf. Chapter 7 for a fuller discussion.

In practice there have been problems in the formulation and execution of plans, including problems posed by the behaviour of government departments. Firstly, their original projects have been inadequately co-ordinated. The first plan, for example, incorporated housing and road-building programmes drawn up at an earlier time and on separate assumptions. Also, the plans have not always proved to be binding on the departments. They have shown a continuing tendency to function independently and at their own speed, quite frequently making decisions without reference to the plans. It is therefore clear that departments have been slow in abandoning their old habits. To some extent the explanation lies in the nature of the planning machinery itself. It was in its general principles a faithful reproduction of the French system but some of the factors accounting for the relative success of the French experiment have not been present in Spain.

French planning has owed much of its success to a fairly compact and highly qualified Commissariat which has been largely independent of sectional interests and enjoyed considerable autonomy. These things gave it prestige and the position of an independent arbiter often able to achieve significant results simply by the use of persuasion. Spain's Commissariat includes competent administrators but it lacks some of the necessary technical means and political independence. At the technical level insufficient attention was paid, at the outset at least, to the construction of a forceful team capable of debating on equal terms with the powerful public and private interests involved in the planning process. In addition it has lacked adequate tools, particularly reliable statistical information. The Commissariat also started without the prestige and authority needed to impose its will upon those responsible for approving and implementing the plans. The final formulation of the plans and their execution have largely depended upon a dialogue between the Commissariat and the Government's economic committee. The precise nature of the relationship remains obscure but the Commissariat has clearly tended to be a junior partner. This has meant that the ministerial committee (or even the Council of Ministers) has assumed responsibility for decisions of a technical nature which would have been better left to the planning authority.

Two more deep-seated factors have complicated the planners' task. Firstly, belief in the efficacy of state planning is less firmly rooted in the

Spanish administration than in the French bureaucracy. The stress of the planners themselves on the role of private as opposed to state activity in promoting economic growth helps to confirm this view. The planners are heirs to a lengthy tradition of state intervention in the nation's economic life but the concept of long-term planning is relatively new. Secondly, the planning apparatus has been largely in the hands of people identified with one political tendency and suspected of "empire building" by other groups represented within the régime. The Commissariat's permanent staff and a significant proportion of the officials and business-men on the planning commissions appear to be associated with Opus Dei. This has reinforced the reluctance of their opponents to co-operate in the planning process.

In such circumstances major decisions governing the drafting and fulfil-ment of the plans have tended to be taken in the ministerial committee or in the Council of Ministers on the basis of compromises reached between departments with conflicting interests and subject to differing pressures rather than as part of a concerted attack upon developmental problems.

López Rodó's appointment to the Government was an attempt to tackle this problem. By giving him ministerial rank it was hoped to grant him the authority needed to deal on equal terms with his colleagues and so to enforce stricter observance of the plans. The Government changes of 1969 could, in part, be regarded as a logical sequence to this move. The appointment of two new ministers from amongst López Rodó's lieuten-ants must be viewed as both effect and cause of the Commissariat's growing influence and as an indicator of its determination to create a new ministerial team more unified than its predecessors in its attacks upon economic problems.

It is too early to comment upon the outcome of these developments. Spectacular results, however, seem unlikely. Opus Dei's leaders have pursued their objectives through administrative reforms and considerable improvements in the Government's functioning have been brought about in this way. The difficulty is the extent to which administrative and political interests have become entangled. Administrative reforms have been, in part, a vehicle for extending the political influence of one group and are partly resisted for that very reason. Until 1969, at least, opponents of the reformers were entrenched in the Council of Ministers itself. This was an almost inevitable outcome of maintaining a system of coalition government. The present more homogeneous "Cabinet" should facilitate greater co-operation at the ministerial level but many of the difficulties confronting the administrative reformers seem likely to persist. They are inherent in the present structure of Spanish politics. Firstly, Franco's régime (despite recent developments) necessarily continues to rest on a coalition of interests and embraces factions that remain sceptical about, or indifferent to, the aims of the technocrats associated with Opus Dei. Such groups still have some representatives in the Government and have sympathizers at strategic points throughout the bureaucracy. Moreover, there is always the possibility of further government reshuffles should the ministers recruited from Opus Dei encounter grave economic problems or should they overplay their hand and unite other elements in opposition to their policies. Secondly, in the absence of effective political parties the reformers themselves must to a considerable extent depend upon administrative structures that are manned by officials with their own interests which, as later chapters demonstrate, they strongly defend. In the long run these administrative interests are only likely to be subjected to firm control by political leaders willing and able to mobilize public opinion in support of a radical reform programme. This would demand basic changes of attitude amongst the middle-class groups who have traditionally supplied the bulk of Spain's political and bureaucratic leaders. It would also presuppose extensive public debate and widespread political participation both of which are alien to the political style of the technocrats of Opus Dei and quite unacceptable to other groups with whom they must coexist within the Nationalist régime.

CHAPTER 5

The Civil Service

INTRODUCTION

In Spain, the absence of effective political parties leaves government members particularly dependent upon civil servants for information and advice concerning the formulation or execution of policy. Consequently, ministers and their deputies are constrained to identify closely with long-established departmental traditions that naturally tend to be transmitted or defined by permanent officials.

Similarly, the Nationalist Régime has been compelled to renew its political élite from within the administration. Attitudes and loyalties developed whilst working in the civil service are therefore well represented at "Cabinet level" and serve to blur the always uncertain dividing line between political and administrative activity or interests. Spain's politics cannot be understood without reference to the organization of its bureaucracy. This bureaucracy was inherited by Franco's régime and is the product of a lengthy evolutionary process.

The machinery of the modern Spanish State owes something to the Napoleonic model of post-revolutionary France. Its nineteenth-century creators were impressed by the possibilities of a proficient professional administration for holding together a politically divided nation and promoting the prosperity of an economically backward society.[1] One lasting reminder of this French influence is the distribution of central government employees throughout the country, with approximately 14 per cent in Madrid and the rest acting as visible representatives of the state in provincial centres. But the effort to transplant administrative organs into an alien historical and social environment led Spain's civil service to develop along unintended lines. The early nineteenth century's

[1]For an understanding of this cf. A. Olivan, *De la Administración Pública con relación a España*. First published Madrid, 1843.

chronic political instability provided only rare opportunities for constructive change. The majority of those involved in public life devoted their energies to factional disputes and only small groups were concerned with the creation of modern instruments of government. Reforms were piecemeal and given little time to take root or were politically contentious and so liable to amendment or deformation in the course of implementation.

The first reform proposals came during the War of Independence. But the subsequent period of political reaction led to a restoration of the institutions of the Ancien Régime and the traditional practice of selling public offices. This practice did not wholly disappear until 1872. It was largely superseded by a "spoils system" which, at bottom, was a continuation of favouritism and particularism in a new guise. The spoils system characterized the early period of experiment with constitutional government and was a major factor in the experiment's failure. The awarding of posts to unemployed political hangers-on and the constant reshuffling of state employees inevitably reduced administrative efficiency and fostered scepticism about the bureaucracy's probity and effectiveness.[2] Also, political conflict was exacerbated by the existence of a permanent pool of office-seekers with a vested interest in the fall of governments.

These problems were first seriously tackled in 1852 during the brief premiership of Don Juan Bravo Murillo who, unlike most of his contemporaries, grasped the long-term advantages of a professional administration.[3] Confronted by parliamentary opposition he enacted his reform through a "provisional decree". However, apart from substantial modifications made in 1918, it remained the formal basis of the civil service's organization until 1963. The decree provided for recruitment and promotion based upon merit and outlined a hierarchical career structure. Since it was provisional no machinery was created for enforcing changes and in practice the "spoils system" survived. The decree was also vague about the functions of officials at each level of the hierarchy. Thus in this, as in other matters, departments went their own way and there was no semblance of a unified career structure.

[2]The fate of a functionary caught in the toils of this system is well described in the novel, *Miau,* by Pérez Galdos. It is available in the Penguin Classics series.

[3]Cf. *Discursos leídos para conmemorar el primar centengario de Don Juan Bravo Murillo,* Madrid, 1952.

Nevertheless, the principles established in 1852 were never entirely ignored. Middle-class administrators anxious for security increasingly appreciated the value of a professional status whilst politicians grasped the value of security of tenure, if only as a means of entrenching their own appointees.

These views gained ground, particularly after the Bourbon Restoration of 1874. Economic and social changes then made new demands upon the administration and led to its expansion. Simultaneously a need for greater specialization was met by recruiting engineers and other technical experts. They began to vie for influence with the lawyers who had traditionally supplied most of the administration's better qualified personnel. They also helped to give public service a new prestige amongst Spain's traditional middle and upper middle classes, which it has never completely lost.

THE EMERGENCE OF THE CORPS[4]

In these circumstances politicians responded to the demands of particular groups of officials who because of their professional competence, the importance of their functions, their group solidarity or their political affiliations were well placed to obtain special treatment. In this *ad hoc* way the notion of the administrative corps gained acceptance in Spain. The concept survived, in some cases from the Ancien Régime, but it now obtained greater significance as several groups, almost always dependent on a single department, were recognized as special corps with their own rules exempting them from the customary hazards of civil service employment.

The membership of some special corps was confined to the holders of specific professional qualifications, but most sought to protect career interests and only then tried to justify a separate existence in terms of some administrative speciality. Thus doubts remained about the precise functions of any group and the corps was primarily a device for giving particular sets of officials security of tenure and protection against obviously partisan appointments or promotions. These special corps proliferated in response to specific pressures and without reference to any

[4]On the development of the corps cf. "Los Cuerpos de Funcionarios" by A. De La Oliva de Castro and A. Gutiérrez Reñon in *Anales de Moral Social y Económica*, Vol. 17, Madrid, 1968, pp. 87–157.

clear design. It was apparent, however, that the pace setters were technical experts, principally engineers and highly qualified legal advisers. They came to form an administrative élite occupying policy-making posts as well as performing specialized technical tasks.

Early this century some departments created general corps. These were only partly composed of non-specialists performing general administrative tasks. They were principally conceived as devices for extending security of tenure and other guarantees to officials excluded from the already established special corps. Thus steps were taken toward an entirely professional administration.

The final step came only in 1918 and was in response to threats of a breakdown in order. The mass of poorly paid and insecure officials had their claims taken up by the military "Juntas" which were exerting pressure upon the Government at that time. This pressure succeeded (where orthodox trade union activity had failed) in extracting major concessions. One was a general pay rise, but of more lasting consequence was the civil service's final conversion into a wholly professional body and some recognition of the corps as the basic organizational unit.

Two "general" corps were established in every department. The senior "technical–administrative corps" were recruited from graduates, principally in law, to fill the rough equivalents of "administrative" and "executive" class posts. "Auxiliaries", recruited from secondary school-leavers, formed a "clerical grade".[5]

These measures might have given the administration greater cohesion, particularly as members of the general corps were expected to occupy leading positions in each department. But departments continued to recruit and organize their own general corps and no statutory organization had an overall responsibility for enforcing change. Also, the new law failed to clarify the exact functions of the general corps. Entrenched special corps exploited the opportunity this gave them to resist encroachments upon their strongholds. After 1918, in fact, most departments saw a period of competition between general and special corps. In departments whose responsibilities had not encouraged the formation of powerful specialist groups, the Interior Ministry for example, the general corps established their supremacy. Elsewhere unstable and frequently irrational com-

[5] A third category of *subalternos* was later devised. They depend upon the Presidency and supply porters and other largely unskilled personnel to all ministerial departments.

promises were reached. Some special corps concentrated upon the domination of one section of a department by annexing posts for which its members were unqualified whilst abandoning positions elsewhere to less-qualified competitors. Likewise, some general corps initially asserted themselves by filling as many posts as possible. Usually they overreached themselves and subsequently sustained losses of prestige and authority. Indeed, the special corps in some departments, Agriculture and Public Works for example, retained such control that university-trained members of general corps were relegated to clerical positions.

In these circumstances the élite corps inevitably recruited the cream of civil servants whilst the general corps were, paradoxically, weakened by an excess of well-qualified manpower. In a country with the problem of intellectual unemployment public service of any kind frequently offered greater security than comparable careers elsewhere, and so a high percentage of graduates continued to enter the latter groups. The price was a large number of educated people in frustrating and minor posts and hence a serious lowering of morale and efficiency.

Finally, the general corps suffered from the limitations of the formalistic legal training given to most of their members by the universities. This produced officials who tended to adhere to well-tried routine procedures. They lacked the expertise and dynamism necessary for assuming the growing responsibilities of a modern state. The tendency for technicians to occupy policy-making and senior advisory posts was consequently increased.

The general picture was therefore of a bureaucracy almost entirely recruited and organized upon a departmental basis and with an unofficial hierarchy in which an official's position or access to particular jobs depended as much on membership of a particular corps as upon his personal rank.[6]

THE TRIUMPH OF THE CORPS

The corp's acceptance as a basic organizational unit, combined with the absence of any coherent personnel policy, provoked a chain reaction with far-reaching consequences.

[6]One partial exception is the élite corps of Abogados del Estado (state lawyers) which depends upon the Finance Ministry but is at the disposal of all departments. They represent the State in litigation and occupy high-level advisory posts.

Amongst compact specialist groups an especially strong sense of corporate identity developed, with loyalty to the corps taking precendence over all other administrative obligations (in other words the traditional spirit of particularism in yet another guise). The authoritarian attitudes of successive governments who refused to recognize civil service unions or to establish consultative machinery for reviewing pay and conditions encouraged this development: officials naturally turned to the corps as the only alternative instrument for defending their interests.[7] The corps consequently became involved in a free for all, pursuing their own aims with little regard for the administration's general welfare or efficiency. In particular, the relatively small and homogeneous élite corps were well placed to use pressure group tactics with a view to converting themselves as far as possible into self-regulating bodies. Political circumstances after 1918 favoured this development.

Primo de Rivera tried to curb the independence and privileges of powerful corps but his government had to abandon the attempt and ratify demands for further privileges. His régime's narrowing popular base meant that its continued viability depended upon retaining the active co-operation of at least some administrative groupings who extracted a price for their support. Similarly, republican governments were too shortlived and unstable to tackle the problem effectively.[8] During the Civil War there was some crumbling of the lower reaches of the civil service and many minor officials were identified with the republican cause, but members of the élite corps tended to be Nationalist supporters. Indeed, high-ranking officials from these latter groups played a vital role in reconstructing the bureaucracy on behalf of the "New State". Thus despite the upheaval of the Civil War and the purges of officials which it entailed, Franco's régime inherited an unreformed civil service.

RECRUITMENT

There are several yardsticks for gauging the progress of the corps in their drive for autonomy: for example the degree of control that they

[7] Cf. J. R. Parada, *Vázquez-Sindicatos y Asociaciones de Funcionarios Públicos*, Madrid, 1963.

[8] An attempt was made in the "Ley de Restricciones" of 1 Aug. 1935 but it was never properly enforced.

could win over the recruitment and promotion of their own members. The success of certain groups, and particularly of élite bodies, in achieving the first objective can be gauged by the extent to which the staff of some departments, through a process of co-option, became self-perpetuating groups. One indicator of this is the frequent reappearance of the same family names in particular ministries. Similar factors may also partly account for the disproportionate numbers of senior officials who have continued to be drawn from the traditional middle and upper middle classes of such regions as Castile.

Co-option is facilitated by the essentially medieval system of *oposiciones*. Though the public nature of these examinations may preclude gross abuses, the custom of packing examining tribunals with senior members of the relevant corps gives these groups a large say in the selection of their own members.[9]

The surest guarantees of control lie, however, with those departments and influential corps who have created their own specialized training schools. These include the Foreign Ministry's diplomatic school, which recruits from the universities, and prestigious technical schools which give the equivalent of degree courses to candidates for the membership of various engineering corps. The latter, in particular, are noted for the production of well-qualified specialists but the corps have allegedly used their control over courses to restrict, by artificial means, the flow of recruits. The value to a corps of such "restrictive practices" probably explains the long and frequently successful resistance to efforts to integrate the specialized schools more effectively into the general state educational system. In the past decade these schools have responded more satisfactorily to demands for larger numbers of well-qualified graduates, but they still remain a hallmark of the autonomy enjoyed by the élite corps.

Recruitment and examination systems are liable to criticism on other grounds. Examinations have often placed a premium on rote learning which tests memory rather than intellectual capacity or administrative aptitude. Also, the lengthy periods of preparation (which are often at the post-

---

[9]In most *oposiciones*, apart from those for university chairs, examinations are written rather than oral but, in the past, this has not necessarily ruled out the possibilities of co-option. For example, members of civil service families will be much better acquainted with the examination procedure than their rivals with different backgrounds.

graduate level), the frequent need to contest several *oposiciones* before obtaining a post, the centralization in Madrid of training facilities and the examinations themselves, all tend to discriminate further against candidates from lower income groups.[10] Efforts to deal with such difficulties have, moreover, been restricted, partly because of attachments to tradition but also because the corps uses the existing system as one essential guarantee of their independence.

PROMOTION

The degree of control won by the corps over the promotion of their members is shown by the widespread acceptance of variants on the principle of promotion according to seniority. Striving after this objective came as an understandable reaction against the favouritism of the past. Some special corps owed their entire existence to a search for guarantees against arbitrary or politically motivated promotions. Indeed, in some corps, reminders of traditional practices still remain. Their rules governing promotion are sufficiently vague to leave the way open to political interference. A fairly clear-cut case is provided by the Ministry of Information and Tourism's employees responsible for broadcasting. They are not even recruited by way of the customary examination procedure.

The seniority system, however, obviously cannot ensure that responsible jobs go to the appropriate candidates. In certain departments this was recognized for (prior to 1963 at least) officials were to be found whose seniority was notionally less than that of their subordinates. Similarly, the system provided few incentives to special effort as nearly all officials had in practice to begin their careers at the very bottom of the ladder and climb slowly upwards. The 1918 law did provide for some direct recruitment to fairly senior posts but this part of the reform was only enforced in the Education Ministry—and very belatedly at that. Such conditions adversely affected morale. Morale particularly suffered from the widely differing prospects for promotion which existed within corps of different sizes. Officials in some corps could be promoted very quickly to quite senior

[10]The very high percentage of officials born in Madrid itself is most significant. Evidence of the tendency appears in Chapter V of *Informe Sociológico Sobre la Situación Social de España 1970*, Fundación Foessa, Madrid, 1970. This chapter did not appear in the final published edition because of problems with the censor.

positions whilst colleagues in other corps waited for years before obtaining similar posts. Indeed, in some corps promotion blockages encouraged members to hive off and establish new groups.

Experience suggests that a pure seniority system is perhaps only defensible in the case of compact élite groups, like the Abogados del Estado, composed of officials with almost identical qualifications and performing similar functions. It is perhaps significant that such groups remain amongst the most efficient and have not been dispersed.

PAY[11]

Even more important in fostering the creation of new corps has been the civil service pay structure which, after 1918, replaced the search for security of tenure as the chief preoccupation of public employees.

The reform of 1918 left senior officials, at least, as one of the best paid groups in the country and in 1924 a system of retirement pensions was added which was superior to anything available in the private sector. But civil servants soon suffered a sharp decline in living standards. Earlier gains were cancelled out by inflation. Moreover, in the absence of negotiating machinery or pressure from unions, there were no new general salary increases. Each corps was consequently driven to fend for itself as best it could.

One response to this general economic crisis, particularly in the middle ranks of the civil service, was for breakaway groups to seek a separate existence with their own improved salary scales. Frequently these administrative corps met no real administrative need. The Interior Ministry, for example, had four medical corps distinguished by little apart from distinct pay structures. There were extreme cases of corps with only four members. The net effect was an inflated bureaucracy composed of well over 200 separate entities.

The freezing of official salaries also led to an extension of the phenomenon of multiple job-holding. Until about 1930 most officials had only one post but thereafter civil servants were driven to seek additional work in both the public and private sectors. Eventually officials with a single job were the exception and many had more than two. Frequent attempts to legislate against this have proved ineffective. One reason is that some of

[11]The whole subject of pay and efforts to reform it is dealt with in A. Nieto, *La Retribución de los funcionarios en España*, Madrid, 1967.

the most important groups, simultaneously employed in the public and private sectors, engineers for example, have used their political influence to gain exemption from the relevant legal provisions. A breakdown in discipline has been another factor. In principle penalties for breaches of disciplinary codes are severe, but in practice group loyalties are such that senior officials join with their subordinates in evading provisions. This has been particularly true of bans on multiple job-holding.

Multiple job-holding has inevitably led to a further decline in efficiency. Faced with many conflicting demands most officials have tended to confine themselves to a minimum of routine administration. This has necessarily impaired the administration's capacity for tackling new tasks with speed and vigour and has not been least amongst the difficulties experienced by the Government in its efforts to implement programmes of planned economic development. The nature and quality of many administrative decisions can also be partly explained by the extensive "traffic in influence" created by multiple job-holding. This is perhaps particularly true in the realm of economic policy. Since 1940 (though not before) high-ranking officials have not infrequently combined their posts with seats on the boards of private concerns. Thus senior civil servants might be called to sit in judgement upon the claims of enterprises in which they have some interest.

The crisis in civil service pay also helped to destroy the official hierarchy, as first established in 1852. Many corps resolved the financial problems of their members by the simple expedient of abolishing the lower rungs of the career ladder and granting everybody "artificial promotions". The result was, for example, many officials with the rank and pay of departmental heads filling no more than clerical posts. There were considerably more departmental chiefs than departments. In one commentator's words, Spain's bureaucracy became "like an army largely composed of generals".[12]

But even these devices failed to resolve completely the problem of inadequate pay. The corps therefore used their influence to establish a multitude of sometimes spurious bonus and incentive schemes. Ultimately these were so commonplace that for most officials the basic salary

---

[12]T. R. Fernández Rodríguez, "El aspecto orgánico de la reforma administrativa: evolución y perspectivas" in *Revista de Administración Pública*, No. 48, Sept.–Dec. 1965.

became only a fraction of the net income. Similarly, the corps established their own (very varied) social security systems. The resort to such expedients betrays the survival of traditional attitudes (traceable back to the Ancien Régime) which held that an official post was virtually the private property of the occupant, to be used for his personal benefit.[13]

Similar attitudes underlay the élite corps' response to the pay crisis. It was their response which had the most profound consequences. Whilst the less prestigious corps concentrated on modifying career structures, more influential groups became almost completely self-governing bodies. They laid claim to most senior positions within their particular sector of the administration and pressed their demands until they had obtained a virtually monopolistic position. Some corps obtained sufficient bargaining power to gain access to posts of a technically "political" nature. In the Ministry of Public Works, for example, most posts were for a long time monopolized by members of the corps of road, canal and port engineers. In the most extreme cases certain corps successfully laid claim to specific ministerial posts. In recent times Finance Ministers have been recruited from one of three élite corps and Education Ministers have invariably been members of the Corps of University Professors.

More will be said about these developments later on. It is already abundantly clear, however, that the élite corps secured sufficient vantage-points to exercise a major and sometimes decisive influence upon policy-making within their spheres of competence. Furthermore, this influence was used to secure material advantages for corps members. Thus there was, particularly after 1940, a large-scale revival of practices which, in isolated cases, had survived from the Ancien Régime. These involved collecting extra-budgetary sources of income for which officials were not publicly accountable. Amongst them were *tasas*, or surcharges levied for services rendered, and shares in incoming revenues. A particularly criticized instance of the latter was provided by Financial Inspectors who claimed a percentage of the taxes whose collection they supervised.[14]

[13]This attitude is evident in the terminology used to describe civil service appointments. Thus an official is deemed to hold his post *en propiedad* and by virtue of his post he has certain "acquired rights". The notion of acquired rights has often been used (with success) to defend special privileges.

[14]*Tasas* and their consequences were the subject of comment in *The Economic Development of Spain—report of a mission organized by the International Bank for Reconstruction and Development*, Baltimore, 1963 (Chapters 3–10).

THE FRAGMENTATION OF THE ADMINISTRATION

These developments had important implications. Firstly, the system of *tasas* gave corps powerful material incentives to defend their spheres of competence against any outside interference and to extend their jurisdiction. At best this has tended to reduce the administration to a series of water-tight compartments lacking in effective co-ordination. At worst it has led to competition or duplicated effort in areas of overlapping jurisdiction. The ambitions and rivalries of administrative corps in fact frequently underlie much of the interdepartmental conflict which has already been described.[15] They also partly account for the strong pressures upon ministers to defend established departmental interests and the accompanying tendency (to be noted below) for each branch of a ministry to resist the control of its political head.[16]

Similarly, some important policy decisions are only explicable in terms of a particular élite corps' conception of its own self-interest. Investment priorities in the realm of irrigation, for example, sometimes seem to have been influenced by the size of the reward which interested corps could earn in the form of *tasas*. Or again, the creation of new high-level administrative organs in some departments seems to have little *raison d'être* apart from enlarging civil service career opportunities. Thus the corps which began as a device for the classification of administrative personnel has become a means of transforming administrative structures to serve private ends.

THE DEPLOYMENT OF PERSONNEL

This situation also stands in the way of a rational deployment of administrative personnel. Mobility between ministries is rare and between corps it is still rarer. State legal and economic advisers are found in all (civilian) departments and the promotion of élite corps' members to political posts may involve moving to another administrative sector. These are, however, exceptions to the rule and even in these cases basic loyalties are not necessarily changed. Abogados del Estado are still regarded as

[15]Chapter 4 for the effects of this on decision-making at the ministerial level.
[16]Chapter 6 on Ministerial Departments.

employees of the Finance Ministry whatever branch of the administration they may be temporarily advising and the State's corps of
economists has a similar relationship with the Presidency. Likewise,
political appointees may be regarded by their corps as being on leave of
absence. There is certainly nothing to parallel the use of the French *grands
corps* as sources of talented recruits for senior posts throughout the civil
service. Staff at all levels is recruited and deployed by a number of competing agencies without reference to the administration's overall requirements. Indeed, not even the Government itself is quite sure how many
persons it has in its employ. Thus some vital parts of the administration
are understaffed whilst others may be overmanned. The Finance Ministry,
for example, is handicapped by a shortage of manpower and reforms of
the State's educational system are similarly held back by the Education
Ministry's inability to attract sufficient teachers. On the other hand, the
State has kept officials in jobs created to administer economic controls
long after many of the controls had been relaxed. In extreme cases
experienced officials of one department have been compulsorily retired
whilst newly created departments have simultaneously had to establish
new corps largely composed of fresh recruits. Frequently departments
have been driven to resolve staff problems on a purely *ad hoc* basis. A
customary expedient has been to recruit unqualified temporary staff who
de facto obtain security of tenure. This solves the short-term problem but
in the long term lowers standards of competence and undermines the
morale of properly qualified officials.

The entire system is in fact shot through with anomalies and inequities.

Officials of comparable age and qualifications and with similar responsibilities have pay and prospects which vary widely according to the
size, traditions and political influence of their respective corps. Above all
there are huge discrepancies between the pay and conditions of élite
corps, at one extreme, and the mass of ordinary public employees with
little bargaining power and no private sources of income, at the other.
Primary school teachers and postal workers, for example, are amongst the
largest and (according to some observers) most efficient groups of functionaries. They are, however, subject to relatively harsh discipline and have
relatively low incomes. The highest-paid officials are estimated to earn
about forty times more than the lowest paid which is probably the
largest gap of its kind in Western Europe.

ATTEMPTS TO REFORM THE SYSTEM[17]

Such a system clearly required reform and, particularly after 1950, there was renewed interest amongst some academics and officials in the possibility of change. Subsequently the group of reformers associated with Opus Dei got their foothold in the Presidency and began to implement a reform programme. A first step was the creation of a special school dependent upon the Presidency, to provide post-entry training for general administrators. In this way it was hoped to give entrants to the "technical–administrative" corps more adequate preparation for handling modern administrative problems (by stressing organizational rather than formal legal questions) and to promote a greater sense of unity. But as each department retained its own general corps, organized on traditional lines, this development had a very limited effect. In 1964, however, new legislation set in motion an overhaul of the entire civil service.[18] This law entailed the abolition of all existing general corps and the creation of three new ones organized on interdepartmental lines under the Presidency's auspices. The "technical–administrative" corps were replaced by one "technical" and one "administrative" corps. The former was to be recruited from graduates with the aim of forming a compact group of all-rounders capable of occupying senior policy-making and advisory posts. The highest policy-making posts were to be reserved for a special category of technical corps members who had received advanced training at the Presidency's school. The administrative corps was conceived as a larger but well-qualified group, similar to the British executive class, underpinning the technical corps and aiding it in the preparation or execution of policy decisions. Finally, clerical posts were to be occupied by a single corps of auxiliaries. Thus it was hoped to achieve a better use of manpower and to impose a higher degree of unity upon the civil service.

At the same time, the Government was empowered to reduce the number of special corps and to impede the creation of new ones. The remaining special corps were to conform as far as possible to general rules

---

[17]There is a large literature on administrative reform, for example, the three volumes *Primera, Segunda and Tercera Semana de Estudios Sobre la Reforma Adminis- trativa.* Published by the Secretería General Técnica de la Presidencia del Gobierno.

[18]Cf. Ley de Funcionarios Civiles del Estado (*B.O.E.*, 15 Feb. 1964).

for recruitment, promotion and pay. These new rules abolished the out-
moded chain of command (created in 1852) and provided for its replacement by a new ranking system based upon a study of the tasks actually
performed by each official. Finally, a new body, dependent upon the
Presidency, was established to supervise the implementation of these
reforms. It contained civil service representatives and was known as "la
Comisión Superior de Personal".

The Comisión had also to implement the reform of the official pay
structure, set out in a law of 1965.[19] This law provided a basic minimum
salary for all officials together with regular increments. Individual variations were to be calculated according to a complex formula based upon
an official's personal degree of importance and the importance of his
corps. Also, the establishment of some centralized control over extra-
budgetary sources of income was foreshadowed.

These reforms seem promising and definitive judgements would be
premature, yet present trends indicate a lack of fundamental change. The
new general corps show signs of traditional attitudes and practices. Thus
few members of the technical corps have been given or have taken the
opportunity of the advanced training needed to qualify them for the
highest posts. Many departments have not distributed personnel between
the technical and administrative corps in the prescribed way. Special
provision has been made to retain non-graduate members of the former
technical–administrative corps in the new technical corps, even though
they may continue to do work intended for lower-grade officials. The
new category of general administrators has consequently lost prestige—
"administrative" corps members frequently find themselves forced to
remain in clerical posts. Thus the new corps of general administrators have
not established their authority nor notably increased interdepartmental
co-operation.

The administration has been streamlined by the abolition or amalgam-
ation of many special corps, but the remainder, and particularly élite
groups, retain most of their traditional powers and privileges. The corps'
lack of co-operation appears to have delayed progress toward the creation
of a more rational career structure. Corps seem to be classified in four
groups, based on the educational level expected of entrants, but access to

[19]"Ley de Retribuciones de los Funcionarios de la Administración Civil del
Estado" (*B.O.E.*, 5 May 1965).

the best paid and most influential job is still reserved for members of a few élite groups. But it is perhaps the question of pay which best illustrates the continuance of traditional practices. Some corps seized upon ambiguities in the new law on pay structures in order to wrest maximum advantage for themselves. In this way they set in motion another free for all which has done little to remove old anomalies.

Increases in basic pay rates have proved insufficient to keep abreast of inflation whilst differentials, in practice, have continued to reflect the bargaining power of each corps rather than any more rational criterion. Changes in the system for administering extra budgetary sources of income are also more apparent than real. They are now paid into a central fund in the Finance Ministry but each department is compensated by grants from the fund. Their distribution is supervised by senior officials of the department concerned. Though secrecy continues to surround these operations it seems safe to assume that the grants are principally used to benefit the élite corps.

THE ACHIEVEMENTS OF THE CORPS

This account has been critical, yet Spain's administrative corps have, within their own distinctive context, performed some useful functions. First, the corps have given most officials a minimum of protection against arbitrary treatment which the absence of civil service unions might otherwise have encouraged. Second, the protection of their members' interests has moderated the more obvious forms of corruption. Third, *esprit de corps* and pride in corporate traditions have given important sections of the administration incentives to uphold quite high standards of competence and only to recruit members of proven ability. Finally, the corps, by helping to maintain the prestige traditionally attached to a civil service career, have retained the services of senior and able people who might, with a rapidly expanding economy, have been attracted elsewhere. There is evidence suggesting that in some portions of the *clases medias*, at least, civil service careers continue to be more highly regarded than business careers even though the latter may offer greater material rewards.

Nevertheless, the system remains badly in need of change and it now remains to account for the inadequacy of recent reforms. In large part this is a matter which has already been explained. As already indicated the leaders of the reform movement lack the authority to impose their will upon the administration. In present political circumstances they are likely to remain a minority dependent for success upon the active co-operation of officials with a vested interest in the *status quo*.[20] They must rely upon persuasion or upon reform from within. Such tactics necessarily run into two major difficulties. Firstly (as has been previously stressed), there is suspicion of the reformers' motives. It seems likely, for example, that the new corps of general administrators are resented partly because their training school is controlled by members of Opus Dei. Secondly, though widespread lip-service is paid to the idea of reform it has in fact got little positive support. Some officials are actively hostile to present reform schemes and many more appear to be ignorant of, or indifferent to, their aims.

The composition of the Comisión Superior de Personal indicates what lies at the heart of these difficulties. It contains civil service representatives drawn largely from élite groups and political appointees also identified with established departmental traditions. Such a body is bound to preserve the gulf currently separating a privileged minority of élite corps from the great mass of officials. As long as these élite corps retain their present bargaining power the administration is likely to be a largely self-regulating body whose interests and rivalries will continue to have a profound effect upon the formulation of national policy.

[20]Such problems are discussed by Juan J. Linz and Amando de Miguel in "La Elite Funcionarial Española ante la Reforma Administrativa" published in *Anales de Moral Social y Económica*, vol. 17, *op. cit.*, pp. 199–249.

CHAPTER 6

The Ministerial Departments

INTRODUCTION

Ministerial departments have always occupied a dominant position within the modern Spanish administrative system. The essential features of their organization were established long before the Civil War and have survived many political upheavals.

The present system of departments can trace its origins back to the Ancien Régime.[1] The monarch was then helped in the exercise of his powers by specialized councils organized upon territorial or functional lines. These bodies had secretariats staffed by permanent officials who were used by successive monarchs to reduce the authority of the traditional councils.

In 1834 the secretariats, or Secretarías de Despacho, after much experimentation, were definitively reconstituted as ministerial departments. They included the Ministries of Foreign Affairs, War and Finance. Also there was a Ministry of Justice, responsible for maintaining and staffing the law courts, regulating the legal profession and administering prisons. Finally, a Ministry for internal affairs was given responsibility for maintaining law and order, controlling the police, supervising local administration and a variety of functions affecting the country's economic and social development which, as will be seen, have since become the concerns of other departments.[2]

The first departments were small in number and size, for they were created during a period when the State had a strictly limited role. But the subsequent growth of state activity has produced a more complex administration. Its growth cannot be traced in detail for there have been so

---

[1] Cf. A. Guaita, *El Consejo de Ministros, op. cit.*

[2] This department is known, significantly enough, as the "Ministerio de la Gobernación".

119

many reorganizations. During the Second Republic, for example, governmental changes frequently involved the restructuring of departments. But general trends are perceptible. In particular, the Ministry of the Interior has progressively shed functions in favour of more specialized departments.[3] Originally this department had responsibility for all matters not clearly falling within another Ministry's jurisdiction but these residual functions grew too large and complex for one department to handle. The present Ministries of Public Works, Agriculture, Industry, Commerce, Education and Science, and the Ministry of Labour can all trace their origins back to this common source. Since the Civil War similar developments have given rise to the Ministry of Information and Tourism, and a Housing Ministry. During the early days of the present régime the Interior Ministry was responsible for censorship and controlling the mass media, but these functions were for a time transferred to the Falangist party and then to a branch of the Ministry of Education. Finally, in 1951, a specialized department was established. Simultaneously, the importance of tourism to the national economy was recognized by transferring the responsibility for its promotion from the Interior Ministry to the new "double-barrelled" department. Similarly, the Housing Ministry, created in 1957, combined functions once performed by the Ministry of Labour, with a concern for town planning which had been another of the Interior Ministry's responsibilities.[4] The latter therefore now remains a department primarily concerned with such sensitive political questions as the maintenance of law and order, the control of police and the supervision of local administration. But its continued responsibility for such miscellaneous activities as public health, postal services and telecommunications, is a reminder of the Ministry's earlier all-purpose nature.

Since the Civil War it is the Presidency which has assumed the responsibility for functions which cannot easily be allocated to one of the traditional departments. This development has, however, been examined already and requires no further comment.[5]

The three service departments also enjoy a special status under the present régime and merit special mention. They are the product of a

[3] Cf. the article by A. Guaita in *Documentación Administrativa*, No. 53, Madrid, 1962.

[4] As noted in Chapter 3, political tactics played their part in the Housing Ministry's creation but administrative considerations were also present.

[5] Cf. Chapter 4.

tripartite division of the traditional War Ministry.[6] During the Second Republic this department was subject to civilian control but its three successors are dominated by serving officers. Consequently the service ministries are not covered by any of the generalizations which may be made about the operation of ministerial departments.[7]

The number and diversity of the departments make any generalization difficult to make. There are now seventeen of them ranging from the Foreign Ministry which has just over 700 employees, to the Ministry of the Interior with over 48,000 officials.[8] The absence of an effectively unified civil service has also permitted each department to develop very distinct traditions and practices. There is, for example, a distinction between departments performing functions which give their employees ready access to extra-budgetary sources of income and those ministries which lack these means of bolstering their independence and prestige. Above all there is a difference between technical departments dominated by powerful specialist corps and those ministries where similar groups have not developed. In the first category are the Ministries of Public Works and Agriculture, whilst such departments as the Interior and Education fall into the second category.[9]

[6]Cf. Chapter 4.

[7]Cf. Chapter 2 for a reference to military organization.

[8]These figures do not include employees of local authorities under the Ministry's supervision, but they do include members of the police forces dependent upon the department. In any case, the figures quoted can only be taken as very rough guides, for quite apart from periodic fluctuations in the numbers of state employees, there are also problems over the reliability of statistics. It is doubtful if even the Spanish Government knows the exact number of its employees at any given moment. For this problem cf. Beltran Villalva, "Datos para el estudio de los funcionarios públicos en España" in *Documentación Administrativa*, No. 83, Madrid, 1964, pp. 9–48. A. Gutierrez Reñon, "Estructura de la burocracia española"—*Revista Española de Opinión Pública*, No. 3, Madrid, 1966, pp. 23–50. Julio Feo & José Luis Romero, "La Administración Pública Comparada en tres paises continentales", *Anales de Moral Social y Economica*, vol. 17, *op. cit.*, pp. 315–76.

[9]Since 31 May 1966 the latter department has been described as the Ministry of Education and Science. The change of title signified a decision to give the promotion and encouragement of scientific research greater importance within the department's programme of activities. This is an attempt to meet a need made plain during the execution of the national plan of economic development and modernization. It is possible that resemblances to changes in Britain were not purely coincidental but were influenced by the British example.

The system of corps also creates marked diversities of interest and custom within departments. Organizational patterns, for example, vary from branch to branch of the same Ministry.

THE FRENCH LEGACY

All this causes confusion, but some general observations are possible for the whole system ultimately rests upon the same principles which guided its founders. They consciously tried to copy French institutions and so conceived the State as a centralized entity with ultimate responsibility for all public services. The ministerial departments therefore had great authority which has been increased by the subsequent extension of state activities. The establishment of decentralized bodies on both functional and territorial lines has had significant repercussions but, in principle, has done nothing to change the system.[10] The drive for regional autonomy in the Basque and Catalan provinces did for a time produce fundamental changes but the present régime has of course strongly reaffirmed the concept of the "unity of the State".

Spain's ministerial departments therefore perform many functions which in Britain are entrusted to local authorities or even remain the responsibility of private bodies. There are, for example, national police forces dependent upon the Ministry of the Interior. The State education system is also centralized and like its French counterpart includes the universities.

The ministries administer their services with the aid of field agencies (collectively known as the "Administración Periférica"—Perepheric Administration), which are also modelled on the French pattern. Thus every civilian department, except the Foreign Ministry, has "external services" responsible for implementing policies in each of the nation's provinces.[11]

Finally, the French distinction between the "active" and the "consultative" administration has been accepted. Thus the active administration

[10]Cf. Chapters 7 and 8.
[11]The idea of the State's local administrative agencies being on the "periphery" is most significant. It points to the highly centralized nature of government and betrays the attitude of Castilians in general and Madrid-based governments in particular to the rest of Spain.

has executive powers and is conceived as a hierarchically structured chain of command extending from the Minister to the lowest provincial official. On the other hand, the consultative administration is composed of collegiate bodies which in theory can do no more than advise.

Spain's ministries have, however, developed their own distinctive characteristics during the course of their history. Some departments, for example, have so many and varied responsibilities that the control and co-ordination of their activities have become particularly difficult. The growth of the administrative corps created similar problems and placed obstacles in the way of attempts to modernize traditional structures. In the rest of this chapter it is hoped to show the nature of these problems by a more detailed examination of the internal workings of departments.

THE ACTIVE ADMINISTRATION

The "Subsecretaría"

The first sign of growing administrative complexity was the creation in 1834 of the office of departmental "Subsecretario" or under-secretary. Under-secretaries were appointed to relieve ministers of responsibility for less important political questions and for routine administrative decisions. But as no other department has a unified civil service under a unified command, the under-secretary is not to be mistaken for a permanent departmental head. On the contrary, under-secretaries have always been political appointees and are still regarded as ministerial "understudies".[12]

The significance of the office has, however, undergone changes as a result of the administration's growth. The situation was particularly transformed by the splitting of departments into specialized divisions or "Direcciones Generales". These are headed by Directors-General who are directly responsible to the Minister for administering the services under their charge. The growth in the size of public services and their impact on society tended therefore to give the post of Director-General great political significance. This development frequently occurred at the expense of under-secretaries who were not supported by equally large

[12]This subject is discussed by L. de la Morena y de la Morena, "Las Subsecretarías en el Derecho Organico Español", *Documentación Administrativa*, No. 101–2, Madrid, 1966, pp. 41–67.

administrative organs and lacked any precisely defined functions. The under-secretary's authority became particularly circumscribed within those departments dominated by special corps who have, of course, been resistant to any form of "interference" from outside. The under-secretary's office (or Subsecretaría) therefore became largely confined to the handling of such internal departmental questions as personnel management. But the authority of some under-secretaries has even been challenged in this sphere, for Directors-General are closer to the officials serving under them and therefore can exercise a more effective control.

There are indications, however, of an attempt to restore under-secretaries to something like their original importance and so to make departments more responsive to the direction of their political heads. This was first clearly observable in the tendency, in some departments, to create special "Direcciones Generales" to handle managerial affairs thus leaving under-secretaries freer to assist their superiors in the resolution of political problems. From 1957 onwards it was increasingly common for ministers to delegate some of their functions to their under-secretaries.[13] In the Ministry of the Interior, for example, the under-secretary has been expressly empowered to decide on some important matters affecting local administration. Under-secretaries may also act as the chairmen of advisory bodies or, in some cases, preside over the boards of autonomous agencies. The attempt to establish interdepartmental commissions composed of under-secretaries is another indicator of the same trend. Even more recently, in November 1967, there was a reaffirmation of the under-secretary's role in internal departmental affairs. A decree law at that time insisted that all matters affecting the employment and pay of departmental personnel, as well as all appeals against departmental decisions, should be handled by special offices to be established within the Subsecretaría. Likewise, it was laid down that inspectorates concerned with purely internal departmental affairs should be answerable to the under-secretary.

For a time the traditional Subsecretarías co-existed with other organisms possessing the same name but charged with different functions. In such cases one under-secretary remained the deputy departmental head whilst the other acted as a "super Director General" responsible for co-ordinating

[13]Impetus was given to this development by the Ley de Régimen Jurídico de la Administración del Estado, *op. cit.*, which provided for a greater delegation of ministerial authority.

one portion of the department's activities. The Ministry of Information and Tourism, for example, had a sub-secretary for tourism. The importance of such officials could be gauged by the fact that, in practice, the creation of a second Subsecretaría was frequently a prelude to the establishment of a wholly new ministry. The Ministry of Industry and Commerce, for example, had two Subsecretarías prior to its division into two separate departments. In 1967, however, there was an administrative overhaul which involved the abolition of the "Super Directors-General". The only exception was in the Ministry of Commerce which retained a special Subsecretaría for merchant shipping.[14] Thus a challenge to the traditional under-secretary's special position was removed. The immediate aim of the 1967 reform was a reduction in administrative costs, but it played its part in a process aimed at giving the official deputy-departmental head a more positive role in the formulation of policy and at tightening his grip on the administrative machine.[15]

The value of the under-secretary as an agent for helping ministers to control their departments naturally depends upon the relationship between the two parties concerned. It is therefore important to note the practice, which has sometimes been followed, of balancing a minister from one political group with an under-secretary representative of another tendency. This has been one of the tactics employed in the attempt to maintain a form of coalition rule. But the price has been the creation of friction at the highest levels of a department and important inconsistencies in departmental policies. Thus during the Second World War, foreign observers sometimes noted intradepartmental conflicts on significant policy issues. Even now, when one (civilian) political group appears to have won a more or less pre-eminent position, vestiges of the practice survive. Thus a Carlist Minister of Justice is balanced by an under-secretary identified with Opus Dei.

[14]This Subsecretaría enjoys a special status for it has organic links with the Navy Ministry.

[15]This reform was part of a more general effort to cut administrative costs in the wake of the devaluation of the peseta in Nov. 1967. The immediate financial crisis gave a weapon to government members who had long been aware of the inflationary costs of the Spanish bureaucracy, but who had met with strong resistance to change. Cf. below for other changes made following the same financial crisis. The reform was announced in a Decree Law of 27 Nov. 1967.

The "*Dirección General*"[16]

Despite recent changes the Dirección General, in most departments, remains the major administrative unit; there is usually no intermediary between ministers and their Directors-General. The latter are also political appointees. Their appointments are confirmed by decree but they are usually made on the recommendation of the relevant minister. But ministerial freedom of choice is rarely complete for the capacity of the administrative corps for obstruction makes it prudent to make appointments acceptable to corps members. The majority of the Directors-General are therefore drawn from the civil service and some are promoted from within the branch of the administration they are expected to control. It is only a minority who are drawn from other sections of society; from the business community for example.

Ministers must also consider factors of a more clearly political nature. Thus they may seek to increase their department's bargaining power within the Government by appointing officials acceptable to more than one political group. They may also have to take account of varying political tendencies represented amongst their own senior officials, or amongst the interest groups with whom they must deal. These factors perhaps explain why in one department at least the key posts have been distributed amongst representatives of several political groups. The appointment of a member of Opus Dei as Director-General of Ecclesiastical Affairs by a Carlist Minister of Justice is also partly to be explained in these terms.

The discretionary appointment of the Directors-General helps ministers to retain control over their departments. But their effectiveness as instruments of control is naturally diminished by the identification of many Directors-General with established administrative interests and attitudes. Above all there is some compulsion to identify with the special interests of the Dirección General as defined by its senior officials. This is particularly true where senior posts are monopolized by members of a single (special) corps. But the tendency also exists where specialists share control with general administrators or even where the latter predominate. Thus even a Director-General who comes into office as the close ally of a

[16]For a guide to the major divisions within departments cf. *Guía de la Administración del Estado*, Madrid, 1965.

minister is likely to develop separate and sometimes conflicting interests.

These problems of control have been aggravated by the growth in size of departments. Thus until 1968 the Ministry of Finance had seventeen Direcciones Generales, or organs of equivalent rank. In January of that year this number was cut by half, but departmental organization necessarily remains complex.[17] The Interior Ministry, to take another example, still has seven major divisions.[18] Only the Ministry of Justice retains a relatively simple structure and has not significantly expanded in the post-Civil-war period.[19] Therefore departmental problems have become far too large and complex for ministers to keep abreast of all significant developments. At most they can take a special interest in certain of their department's responsibilities. Ministers of the Interior, for example, tend to concentrate on questions directly affecting public order. Therefore all services enjoy varying degrees of discretion in the making and application of policy. In these circumstances departmental activities must be co-ordinated on a largely *ad hoc* basis and as a result of intermittent contact with the minister's office.

One measure of the autonomy of many of the Direcciones Generales and of the influence wielded by the administrative corps which staff them is the lack of unity in their internal organization.[20] Initially they were all divided into "Secciones" and these were divided into "Negociados" (departments). This relatively simple pattern disappeared and more intermediate organs appeared. Secciones were grouped to form organs known variously as Servicios or Divisiones. The latter were also frequently grouped to form a "Subdirección General". The administrative reform initiated in 1967 made a new attempt at simplification by adopting the Division as a standard unit. In many parts of the administration, however, new Subdirecciónes Generales have continued to proliferate and to complicate the picture.[21]

Recent changes have been made as part of a reform programme whose

[17]Cf. Decree 151 of 25 Jan. 1968 (*B.O.E.*, 30 Jan. 1968).

[18]For the organization of the Interior Ministry cf. Decree 246 of 15 Feb. 1968 (*B.O.E.*, 17 Feb. 1968).

[19]Cf. Decree 1530 of 12 June 1968 (*B.O.E.*, 15 July 1968).

[20]Cf. T. R. Fernandez Rodriguez, *op. cit.*

[21]Cf. L. Fernando Crespo Montes, "El Subdirector general en la Administración española", *Documentación Administrativa* No. 75, Madrid, 1964, pp. 41–49.

ostensible aims include the production of a more effective division of labour and the speedier handling of official business. In some cases administrative corps have established new organs with the intention of creating greater career opportunities for their members. This explains a recent tendency to upgrade the status of existing bodies or to create new high-level organs which perform relatively unimportant functions. Thus many units meriting a relatively low status are now described as a Sección or even as a Subdirección General.[22]

As the Sub-Directors-General are also ministerial appointees, fears have been expressed about the dangers of political partisanship in the administration's lower reaches. There are indeed cases of purely political appointments, but those nominated are usually permanent officials promoted from within the department. In addition the large numbers of new organs make intradepartmental communication particularly defective. The net effect of the change is therefore some increase in the autonomy of the corps occupying "medium"-level posts.

The "Administración Periférica"[23]

The administrative corps' drive for independence also led to a proliferation of the central administration's field services. Initially, the only external services were supervised by provincial governors and dependent upon the Ministry of the Interior. But other ministries subsequently established their own agencies. The first was the Finance Ministry. In this and some other departments, founded much later, there were unified field services under a single head known variously as a *delegado provincial* or a *Jefe provincial*. The Labour Ministry, for example, had *delegados* in each provincial capital. In these cases provincial representatives reported directly to the Minister or his deputy. But elsewhere, and especially where élite corps had gained control over entire branches of the administration, there was a tendency for each corps to establish its own field services

---

[22]L. Saavedra, "El peligro de una inflación en la organización administrativa" *Documentación Administrativa*, No. 95, Nov. 1965.

[23]For a general discussion of the problems of the "Administración Periférica" cf. E. García de Enterria, *La Administración Española*, Madrid, 1964, pp. 85–118, and J. L. Vallina, "Problemática actual de la Administración Periférica," *Documentación Administrativa*, No. 100, Apr. 1966.

which then received their orders directly from the relevant Dirección General. Liaison between such services tended only to take place on an informal basis.

Liaison was made still more difficult by a growing tendency for services to operate outside the traditional provincial framework, and to create their own special regional divisions. Such supra-provincial units have been made possible by improved communications and have provided more adequate frameworks for dealing with many contemporary economic and social problems. But most of them were created on an *ad hoc* basis and without proper study of existing units. Thus there has been much overlapping of territorial boundaries.

The possible confusion has been aggravated by the number of special regional divisions. Initially these were few in number. The Ministry of Education's university districts were one early example. But eventually there were over 100 different patterns of territorial organization. The Ministry of Public Works, for example, established regionally based building services and divided the country into special regions for the purpose of road building and maintenance. The Ministry of Agriculture also had a variety of external services, not all of which were created within the provincial framework.

The absence of a co-ordinating agent at the local level left a vacuum which was sometimes filled by initiatives from a local agency, but more often by instructions from a Dirección General in Madrid. In other words, the same autonomy which permitted the élite corps to establish independent field services enabled them to retain strict control over their own provincial and regional dependencies. Thus decision-making has traditionally tended to be controlled in the capital. The relatively low percentage of senior élite corps members out in the field continues to be a reminder of this.

The absence, from most departments, of a single chain of command and the centralization of authority combined to affect the quality of decisions. Both factors impeded a free two-way flow of information between officials in the field and those ultimately responsible for departmental policy. It became difficult for the latter to obtain a clear overall view of a ministry's activities or to get information necessary for drawing up coherent plans.

The diffusion of responsibility amongst several and sometimes competing groups has also made it difficult to apply consistent policies. "Demarcation disputes" between the administrative corps have made possible the evasion of responsibility and have impeded the co-operation necessary for solving many problems. The existence of so many points at which pressure could be applied has also made it easier for important social or economic groups to obstruct the implementation of policies threatening to their interests.[24]

In large part these factors explain why, for example, the Ministry of Agriculture's attempts to improve the standard of life in rural areas have not always lived up to expectations. The department has teams of well-qualified technical experts but they have not been well deployed. There has been a tendency to concentrate too many technicians at the centre and to put too few of the best qualified officials in close contact with local problems. Also, the department's field agencies have often failed to co-operate in the tackling of common problems or in the wearing down of resistance to land reforms.[25]

The nation's first development plan acknowledged these problems and urged each ministry to unify its "external services". But the administrative corps were, until 1967, able to oppose the implementation of this reform which was viewed as a threat to their independence. The financial crisis of 1967, however, gave a chance for reform to be pushed through on the grounds of economy. It was then decreed that each department's field services should be unified under one provincial chieftain with the title of "Delegado". In the case of supra-provisional services it was decided that each one should be placed under the direction of the Delegado located in that provincial capital which had previously served as the regional service's headquarters.

The lengthy period of reorganization demanded by this reform means that it is still too early to evaluate its effects. In the short run, it seems likely that there will continue to be some friction between members of previously independent services. In the long run, however, the reform should simplify administrative processes and promote greater intra-departmental efficiency. On the other hand, the reform does not get to the root of the

[24]Cf. the reference in Chapter 4 to the tendency to apply pressure on an *ad hoc* basis and in a diffuse manner.

[25]The organization of the Ministry of Agriculture's field services is discussed by D. Alvarez Pastor in *Documentación Administrativa*, No. 82, Oct. 1964, pp. 9–35.

problems caused by creating a multitude of *ad hoc* regional services. Also, it provides no guarantee of greater co-operation between field services dependent upon different ministries. As will be seen, this is a problem that, in the immediate future at least, is likely to remain.[26]

One factor which helps to account for this last difficulty is the continuing reluctance of senior officials to delegate more authority to subordinates. This is partly to be explained by the desire to guard the administrative corps against all possibility of outside interference. But it is also explicable in terms of long-established authoritarian attitudes within the administration. These traditions have fostered a marked lack of confidence in subordinates who are in their turn reluctant to take responsibility for anything apart from the most routine decisions.[27]

This pattern of authority was perhaps defensible when the administration had relatively few responsibilities but is poorly adjusted to the demands made by an increasingly interventionist state. Those charged with formulating policy are now distracted by too many minor administrative matters. They must deal, for example, with many problems which could be more appropriately handled at the provincial level.[28] Consequently inadequate attention tends to be paid to long-term planning and the routine decisions are likely to be delayed.

The administrative reformers have recognized this problem and have tried to tackle it. But they have had relatively little success. Only a few departments have taken any action and they have generally confined themselves to a limited transfer of functions amongst high ranking officials. Officials in the field have certainly received no significant increase in their authority. The chief exception is in the Ministry of Industry which has reorganized its services in the attempt to distinguish more clearly between policy making and managerial functions.[29]

The need to decentralize decision-making therefore remains. But this and other reforms must await fundamental changes of attitude within the administration which cannot be expected in present political

[26]Cf. Chapter 8.

[27]Cf. the article "La Desconcentración Administrativa" in *Revista de Administración Pública*, No. 35, Madrid, 1963, pp. 110–36.

[28]Just to cite one of the many possible examples, municipalities wishing to create new municipal slaughter-houses have to seek the approval of the Ministry of Agriculture in Madrid.

[29]This reorganization occurred when Sr. López Bravo was Minister of Industry.

circumstances. The reliance which present political leaders must place on established bureaucratic interests necessarily limits their capacity for recasting administrative institutions and for fostering new attitudes.

THE "CONSULTATIVE ADMINISTRATION"

This account has so far been confined to the active administration. There **are,** however, a variety of organs which in principle do not form part of the active administration and upon which ministers can call for help in the managing of their departments.

Ministerial "Gabinetes" and the "Secretaría General Técnica"

In some departments, bodies have been created which resemble the French ministerial "Cabinets" and are generally described as "Gabinetes Técnicos". They are normally composed of officials, but they are allies of the minister upon whom he can personally rely for information and advice. Their precise functions vary. The Minister of Finance, for example, has a Gabinete for the study of any economic or financial problem which he may refer to it. The Minister of Information and Tourism, on the other hand, has a specialized Gabinete to help him to co-ordinate the activities of those organs responsible to him for the dissemination or control of information.

A law of 1957 attempted to create institutions with similar functions, in all departments. Thus every civilian department now has a special planning office known as a "Secretaría General Técnica".[30] Some departments had organs with this name for several years but the administrative reformers of the Presidency encouraged all ministers to establish similar agencies and to use them for the study and planning of departmental activities. In particular it was hoped that they would promote greater intra-departmental co-operation, encourage the better use of personnel and speed up administrative procedures.

Though not part of the "active administration", these bodies do not have the collegiate structure of the traditional consultative organs. They are staffed by planners who are hierarchically subordinate to a Secretary-General who is appointed by the Minister and usually has direct access to him.

[30]For details cf. J. Dietta, *Las Secretarías Generales Técnicas*, Madrid, 1961.

The high level status of the Secretarías Generales Técnicas reflects the degree of importance attached to their functions but in practice their impact has been limited. This is largely to be explained by the "active administration's" resistance to any form of direction but it is also due to a traditional scepticism about the value of planning.[31] This second factor means that the new planning organs often lack the prestige necessary for effecting significant changes or for attracting staff of high calibre. Some Secretarías have tried to compensate for this lack of prestige by assuming responsibilities which properly belong to the active administration. But this has only increased hostility toward them. Finally, the continued existence, in certain departments, of specialized Gabinetes either deprives the Secretaría General Técnica of responsibility for some important matters technically within their jurisdiction or tends toward a duplication of effort.

It is only fair, however, to indicate that in some departments these new organs have attracted professional civil servants of a high calibre and exercised considerable influence. In the Ministries of the Interior and of Commerce, for example, they have had some success in ensuring the fulfilment of their department's obligations under the national development plan.

Inspectorates

Some of these difficulties have confronted the inspectorates which are to be found in every department. They have been established to supervise the operation of public services and are essentially of two kinds. There are, firstly, inspectorates which are responsible for enforcing legislation that directly affects private citizens. The Inspectors of the Ministry of Labour are in this category. The remainder supervise and report upon the administration's internal workings. They may also be used by ministers or senior officials to make special studies of administrative problems.

The inspectoral function is not always performed by specialized bodies. In many of the services run by one of the special corps the job of inspector automatically belongs to the corps' most senior members. The Ministry

---

[31] Cf. Chapter 4 for a reference to traditional administrative attitudes to planning. It is also important to note that the association of these new agencies with the administrative reformers of Opus Dei has awakened suspicions of their intentions.

of Agriculture's veterinary services, for example, are liable to inspection by senior members of the National Veterinary Corps.

This kind of check is a guard against administrative incompetence but the inspectors are too closely associated with the administrative corps to make them very effective instruments of political control. As the senior members of a corp they may indeed be the principal defenders of its special interests.

There are, however, specialized bodies specifically assigned the task of supervising departmental services. The Ministry of Information and Tourism, for example, has a "general" inspectorate of this type. But the most prestigious group is La Inspección de Servicios of the Ministry of Finance.[32] It is recruited by special examination from the Ministry's chief corps and therefore constitutes a departmental élite similar to the French Inspections des Finances. But it does not play the same creative role as its French counterpart. Its terms of reference are narrower and it takes a more restricted view of its responsibilities. In other words the emphasis is placed more on identifying breaches of legality or administrative errors than on encouraging administrative reforms or the adoption of new techniques.

This negative view of the inspectoral function is common. It may be partly due to the formalistic legal training of many officials. Until recently, at least, the same attitudes were reinforced by the system of *tasas* which gave inspectorates a material stake in the *status quo*.[33]

Amongst most officials this negative approach has engendered suspicion of inspectoral bodies. Thus there is a tendency to withhold co-operation and to conceal information from them which makes the problem of control still more difficult.

Advisory councils[34]

The advisory bodies so far discussed are closely concerned with the routine operations of ministerial departments. But the earliest consultative organs were further removed from the daily work of the active administration.

[32]Cf. F. Benzo Mestre, *La Organización de la Hacienda Española*, Bilbao, 1967.
[33]Cf. Chapter 5 on the "Civil Service" for the case of Tax Inspectors.
[34]The best introduction to this subject is in E. García de Enterria, *op. cit.*, pp. 54–81.

These bodies were collegiate in nature and were required to reach collective decisions about questions referred to them for advice. Advisory councils of this sort still exist. The oldest and most prestigious is the Consejo de Estado (the Council of State), but because of its special importance it will be examined separately.[35] A more recent creation is the Consejo de Economía National which was founded by Primo de Rivera to advise the Government on economic matters. It fell into abeyance during the Republic but it was revived by the present régime as an adjunct of the Presidency. Its members are all appointed by decree. Most of them are prominent representatives of important political groups, though some are eminent economists. On paper they are a significant body, for legislation requires the Government to seek the Council's advice on a wide range of issues. In practice, however, it carries little weight and appointments are of an essentially honorific nature. Attempts were made in 1957 to give the Council real influence by appointing its chairman to the Council of Ministers, but the opportunity was not seized and the real responsibility for economic policy remained firmly in the hands of ministerial departments.

All the civilian ministerial departments have their own advisory councils. Some of them, like the Ministry of the Interior's Consejo Nacional de Sanidad,[36] are ascribed to a particular Dirección General. Others advise on a whole range of activities. Thus the Ministry of Education and Science has a Council concerned with all branches of the state educational system.

Until 1968 it was the rule for all departments to have a multiplicity of advisory councils. In some ministries, however, the post-devaluation efforts to simplify bureaucratic machinery have included measures to simplify the structure of the consultative administration. The Ministry of Agriculture, for example, has established a single Consejo Superior Agrario in place of four separate and specialized organs. Specialized groups, or sections, continue to operate within the framework of multipurpose advisory bodies. For example, the Ministry of Industry's former advisory council on naval engineering retains its identity as a section of the Consejo Superior del Ministerio de Industria. But in principle at least such bodies no longer function as wholly distinct entities. On the other hand, departments like the Interior, and Information and Tourism, which have

[35]Cf. Chapter 9.   [36]National Health Council.

very diverse responsibilities, continue to receive advice from a variety of separately constituted bodies.

The composition of advisory councils varies considerably. Thus some are presided over by members of the administration whilst others are chaired by ministerial appointees drawn from outside the administration. Likewise, there are considerable variations in the composition of rank and file membership. Two general categories, however, are discernible. In ministries with long-established advisory bodies these have tended to be staffed almost entirely by civil servants. In principle they have been freely appointed by the minister but in practice some élite administrative corps have successfully asserted the right to supply the members of a council in whose activities they have an interest. This is the case, for example, in the Ministry of Agriculture. In such instances the original distinction between the "active" and "consultative" administration has of course tended to be blurred. Indeed some councils obtained the right to make decisions about the pay or discipline of civil servants and so became instruments for defending the career interests of the administrative corps. This was true, for example, of the former advisory council on marine engineering. The recent streamlining process may have been partly aimed at weakening the influence wielded in this sphere on behalf of special bureaucratic interests. It is perhaps premature to judge the success of such efforts. Nevertheless, the continued presence of senior members of the élite corps on advisory councils, and the tendency for traditional organs to preserve their identity as specialized sections of new enlarged advisory bodies suggests that, in some cases, the dividing line between the active and the consultative administration will remain indistinct. Pending more drastic administrative reforms it is possible that some branches of the consultative administration will continue to be instruments for buttressing special administrative interests. The control of advisory bodies by élite corps will provide the latter with additional opportunities for regulating the flow of information to their political chiefs and for defending privileged positions.

In ministries with more recently created councils, however, representatives of interest groups from outside the administration are sometimes appointed to advisory bodies. Normally these representatives are chosen by ministers in consultation with the affected interests. But there are exceptions. The *Sindicatos*, for example, have the right to nominate their own representatives to the Labour Ministry's advisory council. This broadens the basis of the consultative process but does not, of course, imply consulting with declared opponents of the existing political system. The spokesmen for the *Sindicatos*, and other bodies, are chosen from the official leadership.

In practice the precise nature of each council's functions also varies. Until 1968 there was a tendency for every council to be covered by a large and complex body of legislation defining the circumstances in which its advice should be sought. Recent reforms have included an attempt to simplify and consolidate this legislation. Thus some general principles have emerged. Nevertheless departments remain free in reality to determine the exact nature and scope of the consultative process. All this makes it difficult to generalize about the influence advisory bodies can exercise.

Undoubtedly they do perform certain useful if limited functions. In particular they may keep open formal channels of communication with groups which are directly affected by governmental policy. The National Press Council, for example, provides a forum within which representatives of proprietors and journalists can try to impress their point of view upon the Government. Members of the Government may also have formal links with bodies whose assistance is useful in drafting legislation. Thus members of the Press Council had some influence on details of the law of 1966 which relaxed press censorship.

There are instances in which legislation demands that the active administration should not only seek but also follow the recommendations of advisory councils. For example, a law of 1962 requires that modifications of existing urban development plans, which involve eating into green belts, must be sanctioned by an organ of the Housing Ministry and by the Consejo de Estado. Decisions given in such cases help to determine public policy. But the initiative almost invariably has to come from the active administration. Partial exceptions are only to be found in the case of those bodies which have been used to defend the interests of the administrative corps and have become adjuncts of the active administration. Such bodies, as already noted, have assumed a limited rule-making authority.

CONCLUSION

This account has stressed the limitations placed upon the exercise of ministerial control. But in conclusion it must be emphasized that the vast legal powers at the disposal of ministers make it possible for able and energetic departmental heads to take important initiatives and even to enforce their own policies in the face of opposition from within the administration. The majority of ministers have tended to administer their departments along already established lines but others have initiated significant changes of direction.[37]

The precise extent of a minister's authority is likely to depend, however, upon the traditions and structure of his department. Relatively small departments, like the Ministry of Justice, can be more easily controlled than departments which are as complex as the Ministry of Finance. It is also easier for ministers to assert their authority within newly created departments which lack the firmly fixed traditions and the strongly entrenched administrative corps of older ministries. For example, it is in the Ministry of Housing, created only in 1957, that resistance to staff reductions appears to have been most successfully overridden. Finally, there is a distinction between departments dominated by élite corps and those ministries where groups of technical specialists do not monopolize the administration's higher reaches. Thus the Ministry of Education and Science has no groups capable of permanently obstructing important ministerial initiatives. It is significant, for example, that a new minister appointed in 1968, was able to initiate a re-examination of the state education system with relatively little delay. In the Ministry of Public Works, on the other hand, the corps of road engineers for long successfully resisted efforts to curb their decisive influence upon departmental policy. But even in this special case recent departmental history reveals the existence of limits to the power of entrenched interests. A minister appointed (in 1965) from outside the road engineers corps made strenuous and partly successful efforts to neutralize the corps' stranglehold upon departmental policy-making.

It is therefore apparent that no minister need be simply the spokesman for special bureaucratic groups and in some departments, at least, there is great scope for ministerial action. But in all departments permanent officials have considerable influence and some ministers have their freedom of action seriously curtailed by the need to come to terms with established administrative interests.

[37]Cf. Chapter 4 for examples of this.

CHAPTER 7

The State as the Promoter of Economic and Social Change

INTRODUCTION

Until as late as 1923 the Spanish State's responsibilities were mainly confined to such traditional activities as national defence, the maintenance of public order and the administration of justice. Public services were largely limited to road building, education and elementary welfare services. The State's impact on national economic development owed comparatively little to its own expenditure or commercial activities.

During this century, however, and especially since Primo de Rivera's régime, direct state intervention in Spain's economic and social life has grown fairly steadily. Its new responsibilities have frequently been assumed by "functionally decentralized units" rather than by the traditional ministries. These agencies are now numerous and manage economically, socially and politically important activities. This chapter traces the growth of state responsibility for social and economic affairs and discusses the position of the new autonomous agencies within the Spanish administrative system. It concludes with a critical look at recent experiments in economic planning.

THE PRE-CIVIL-WAR SITUATION

Extensive state responsibility for economic and social matters is relatively recent, but reminders still exist of a tradition of government economic activity reaching back to the Ancien Régime.[1] The State continues to control

[1] A brief account of the growth of the "Public Sector" from the earliest days appears in *Información Comercial Española*, Mar. 1964.

mercury mines which Spanish monarchs possessed in the sixteenth century. Also, under the Ancien Régime, the right to exploit commercial monopolies was sold to private concerns who, in return, collected taxes levied on their products and surrendered fixed shares of the profits to the Government. Such a "fiscal monopoly" still controls cigarette production.

Doctrinaire liberalism, prevalent during much of the nineteenth century, induced the State to beat a partial retreat from involvement in economic activities. This was evident in the State's espousal (in 1869) of free trade. It was also apparent from the part played by the State in facilitating transfers of land ownership from public, or quasi public bodies, to privileged private interests. Not only did it place on the market land which had belonged to traditional religious and economic corporations, it also allowed some of its own property to fall into private hands. Tracts of forest land fell into this category. Thus, for a time, the State's impact on national economic life was largely indirect in nature. It chiefly made itself felt through taxation (which was levied for revenue-raising purpose only) and monetary policy.

These tendencies, coupled with Spain's economic and social backwardness, ensured the absence of an effective demand for extensive state intervention in economic and social matters. Nevertheless, older traditions survived and even when the liberal tide was running at its strongest, some developments occurred. Thus official concessionaires developed the railways and the State developed new mining interests.

A particularly important reversion to more traditional practices came when, from 1891 onwards, the State progressively abandoned its free-trade policy. A coalition of interests, spearheaded by Catalan textile manufacturers and reinforced by Basque industrialists and Catilian wheat-growers, turned to the State for protection against foreign rivals. By 1906 their pressure had made Spain's tariff barriers the highest in Europe. After 1907 the State further increased official protection by compelling concerns linked to the State, such as the railways and contractors engaged upon public works, to purchase domestic products.

The sharpness of this reversal of policies was, in part, testimony to the power of tradition. It indicated the repudiation of policies regarded by many as alien importations and a reassertion of that ". . . traditional paternalism of the Catilian State (which) had never been eroded".[2] It also

[2]Cf. R. Carr, *op. cit.*, p. 395.

indicated a backward nation's efforts to secure a measure of self-sufficiency. Such efforts were a particularly important feature of Primo de Rivera's rule and, under him, they entailed unprecedented amounts of direct state intervention in the nation's economic life. He pursued the logic inherent in existing policies, and to that extent cannot be regarded as an innovator, but the range of commitments he encouraged the State to assume was something new.[3]

The details of Primo de Rivera's policies were worked out by non-political technocrats who were given a chance to encourage some modernization. Their experiments can be grouped under two main headings. Firstly, there were ambitious programmes of public works designed to create employment and, ultimately, to add to the nation's productive capacity. In the case of the régime's road-building programme there was no new commitment on the part of the State and no new administrative agencies were created. The assumption of direct state responsibility for promoting major irrigation projects did, however, signify a new departure. The irrigation and colonization of arid land had already been proposed as a method of raising agrarian productivity and lowering rural unemployment but the State's role had hitherto been largely confined to unsuccessful attempts to encourage investment by private landowners. In an effort to remedy this situation Primo de Rivera's régime undertook the construction of hydraulic works designed to serve entire river basins. Administrative organs known as Confederaciones Hidrográficas were established for the purpose.[4] Secondly, the State, as part of a "grand design" for strengthening the Spanish economy, greatly extended its financial and commercial activities. To this end three types of institution were created: semi-official banks, new "fiscal monopolies" and special regulative committees. The new banks were founded in the face of stiff opposition from established financiers. Their aim was to make loans readily available for projects deemed to be of national interest. They included institutions to finance local authorities, to relieve Spanish overseas trade from dependence upon foreign credit and to promote new industries. A similar mixture of financial prudence and economic national-

---

[3]Cf. *ibid.*, pp. 577–81 for mention of his work.
[4]Cf. the section below on regional planning for further references to these bodies.

ism underlay the creation of new fiscal monopolies. The most important of these was the body created to control the distribution of petroleum—C.A.M.P.S.A.[5] It was established in 1927 as a state concessionaire with two avowed aims. In the first place it was intended to divert the profits of distribution from the two foreign companies then dominating the market and to halt the fiscal evasion for which they had been allegedly responsible. It was also intended that C.A.M.P.S.A., by prospecting for and acquiring oil deposits, by constructing a tanker fleet and by building refineries, should eventually reduce Spain's dependence upon foreign oil suppliers. Economic nationalism also largely accounted for the creation of Primo de Rivera's system of regulative committees. They were created to regulate each major sector of the economy with a view to protecting established concerns and to encouraging import substitution.[6]

These measures were accompanied by extensions of state activity in the realm of public transport. In 1927 Spain's first international air lines were fused to form a single company (later called Iberia) with the State as its majority shareholder.[7] State support was needed to make civil aviation viable. Similarly, renovation of the national railway network (often created on the cheap by speculative foreign investors) demanded such extensive public assistance that the State was induced to tighten its control over concessionaires. Special bodies were created to supervise investment policies and to regulate such questions as railway tariffs.

Mention must finally be made of Primo de Rivera's innovations in the realm of social policy. As early as 1908 an unofficial body (el Instituto Nacional de Previsión) had been established to administer a voluntary social security scheme and in 1919 this had been made the basis of a compulsory state scheme providing retirement insurance. In 1929 Primo de Rivera's régime extended social insurance to expectant mothers.

[5]The full title is la Compañía Arrendataria del Monopolio de Petróleos S.A. It is a private monopoly in which the State has an approximately 30 per cent interest. But the decisions of its board can be vetoed by a *delegado* of the Ministry of Finance.

[6]It should also be noted that Primo de Rivera's régime was the first to envisage (on any scale) the possibilities of tourism as an earner of foreign currency and hence as a factor in Spain's balance of payments. A start was made during his period in office on the chain of official hotels or *paradores*, which has since been much extended under the auspices of Franco's régime.

[7]There is now a separate state-controlled air line operating on domestic routes.

Similar developments occurred in the field of labour relations. Thus a private Instituto de Reforma Social established to advise governments on labour relations was taken over by the State and in 1924 its machinery was used as the basis of an institutionalized system of wage negotiations. Committees of workers and employers met under state auspices to settle disputes.

Primo de Rivera's fall coincided with the world depression. The relative paucity of Spain's economic links with the outside world cushioned her against some of the worst effects of this disaster. Nevertheless, the impact (in terms of reduced economic activity and increased unemployment) was considerable and, in accordance with contemporary orthodoxy, the Republic's leaders made considerable cuts in public expenditure. These entailed the abolition of much of Primo de Rivera's machinery for regulating industry. During the Republic little attention was paid to the modernization of Spain's industrial sector. On the other hand, the new credit institutions and fiscal monopolies survived albeit without realizing all their original aims. C.A.M.P.S.A., for example, outlived both Primo de Rivera and the Republic, but it tended in practice to give a relatively low priority to the creation of a viable Spanish petroleum industry.[8]

Primo de Rivera's system for regulating labour relations was also, in effect, taken over by the Republic and, for a time, was used to bolster Labour's bargaining position. Potentially more radical were efforts to grapple with fundamental agrarian problems. In 1932 an Instituto de Reforma Agraria (I.R.A.) was created with the power to expropriate large under-productive estates. It was intended to weaken the political power of large landowners and to appease traditional demands for land redistribution. The execution of its plans was impeded, however, by political instability and inadequate technical preparation. The biggest landowners seem to have been little affected by its activities. Extensive land redistribution only came with the unofficial seizure of estates during

---

[8]C.A.M.P.S.A. in conjunction with foreign companies has, especially since 1958, invested considerable sums in prospecting for oil but generally with disappointing results. Recently the Spanish government has expressed hopes of finding up to 10 per cent of its oil supplies from domestic sources but this remains to be seen. Meanwhile oil imports have a considerable adverse effect on Spain's balance of payments. Cf. R. Tamames, *op. cit.*, pp. 283–91.

the period of Popular Front government. The same period also witnessed
the socialization of industry in many areas.

THE POST-CIVIL-WAR SITUATION

Experiments with "workers control" were reversed by the Republic's
own war-time governments and the Nationalist Régime naturally repudiated them. It relied heavily on the economic expertise, financial
backing and political support of Spain's traditionally important economic
interests. Militant Falangists advocated nationalization of the banks and
further land reforms but their demands were ignored. Concessions were
made to their viewpoint in the field of social policy but even there the
party's goals were far from being reached.

When it came to economic policy the New State leaned most heavily
on groups who questioned the legitimacy of public enterprise. They continued to expect state assistance but rejected the idea of public ownership.
They frequently got favourable responses from Franco and his economic
advisers for they counted on established economic interests to assist in the
reconstruction of Spain's badly damaged post-war economy and the
latter used to good effect the bargaining power that this gave them. Thus
existing protective measures were maintained and were in several ways
strengthened. First, industries declared to be of special national interest
received tariff protection, tax concessions and guaranteed returns on
capital.[9] Second, the new *Sindicatos* helped to contain labour costs and a
regressive tax system left large enterprises shouldering a relatively small
proportion of the nation's total tax burden. Third, price controls, conceived mainly as guards against inflation, tended in practice to become
officially approved price fixing arrangements geared to the interests of
the least efficient firms. Fourth, import licences and licences required for
the creation of new industrial plant were frequently used to guard established concerns against competition. Fifth, official banks made credits
freely available to leading private companies. Private banks, for their
part, were protected by a law preventing the creation of rivals. Finally,
the practice of selling exclusive manufacturing rights to private concerns
was revived. In particular the processing of certain agricultural products,
sugar for example, was restricted to a few privileged companies who

[9] Cf. Laws of 24 Oct. 1939 and 24 Nov. 1939.

profited considerably at the expense of small producers and most consumers.

Nevertheless, the post-Civil-war period saw unprecedented extensions of state intervention in economic life. Several factors underlay this trend. First, the régime's nationalist temper and its trading difficulties impelled it to pursue the policy of "autarchy". The Second World War and the subsequent economic blockade of Spain reduced supplies of raw materials and capital equipment from her traditional trading partners. Thus the State sought to mobilize the nation's own resources and adopted a battery of controls designed to regulate exports, imports and production levels. Trade was conducted on a bilateral basis, foreign exchange dealings were rigidly controlled and imports were subject to a strict licencing system. Second, post-war shortages compelled the adoption of rationing and official price fixing. The internal market was subject to the intervention of many official entities each of which regulated a particular sector. Third, only the State could marshall sufficient resources to tackle many of the post-war reconstruction problems. Finally, many new state activities simply represented the logical development of tendencies discernible before the war. The new and essentially conservative régime sought solutions to its problems by exploring some of the implications of established traditions.

In each case force of economic circumstance was probably the chief factor. Ideological considerations, though not absent, were usually of secondary importance. Autarchy, for example, could be presented in ideological terms, appealing to both conservative nationalists and militant Falangists, but official arguments were largely rationalizations of measures forced on the régime by Spain's international isolation. Indeed, some of the régime's constituent groups had to accept measures at odds with their traditional ideological positions. On the other hand, the formulation and execution of new policies revealed the continuing influence of established economic interests. A closer examination of post-Civil-war developments should clarify this picture.

AGRICULTURAL POLICY[10]

In the agricultural sector attempts to transform property relations were

[10]For a general discussion of agrarian problems cf. Juan Anlló, *Estructura y Problemas del Campo Español*, Madrid, 1967. Cf. also R. Tamames, *op. cit.*, pp. 29–202.

naturally abandoned and most expropriated land was returned to its original owners. But it was apparent that state action would be necessary to encourage increased food production and the better use of land. Initially food production was not a major problem for the New State. The chief producing areas quickly fell into nationalist hands and, at the outset, they had no large industrial populations to supply. The absorption of republican territories, however, presented major supply problems which were aggravated by a war-time decline in yields and by difficulties in importing foodstuffs. The magnitude of the difficulty can be gauged by the fact that pre-war production levels were not reached again until the 1950s.

Long-term remedies required state action. Also, the latent social tensions in many rural areas made it politically prudent to make gestures, at least, toward the idea of agrarian reform. Thus the I.R.A. was replaced by the Instituto Nacional de Colonización (I.N.C.) which was given responsibility for irrigation and land settlement schemes aimed at expanding Spain's total area of cultivatable land. The wider distribution of land ownership was a secondary consideration. The accent was switched from social to economic objectives.

The I.N.C.'s policies were not wholly new. They represented the latest step in a lengthy process of increasing state responsibility for irrigation. Primo de Rivera's hydraulic works had been a previous step in this process but their objectives had not been wholly achieved. Private landowners remained reluctant to construct the additional irrigation works and the complementary infrastructure needed to make state investments productive. Much potentially fertile land stayed neglected. The I.N.C. assured responsibility for constructing necessary irrigation schemes and for making productive use of the land thus made cultivatable.

During the 1940s and 1950s the scope of the I.N.C.'s powers and operations progressively increased. Extensive tracts of land were acquired and eventually the Institute took almost complete responsibility for irrigating the areas under its jurisdiction. Ultimately it became the nation's largest landowner whilst handing over considerable areas of newly cultivatable land to private ownership. But the administration of its programme has been criticized on several grounds. In some areas, for example, much new land has been sold to companies already controlling the production and marketing of staple crops. Also, the number of landless labourers to have been settled is relatively small. Lastly, the I.N.C. has been attacked for undertaking too many costly prestige projects and for not concentrating on those of maximum economic benefit.

The last objection has, in part, been met by steps taken under the aegis of the first national development plan. This provided for a more careful costing of projected irrigation schemes and for a better ordering of priorities. In other respects, however, the I.N.C.'s policies have not been substantially modified.

In 1953 the State also assumed responsibility for land consolidation in those areas characterized by *minifundia*. The Servicio de Concentración Parcelaria was created to encourage the formation of more productive units and greater mechanization. In 1964 it was renamed El Servicio de Concentración Parcelaria y de la Ordenación Rural and the provision of general social amenities was added to its responsibilities. This body has also helped to transform significant areas and to increase productivity. The national plans have laid special emphasis on this particular aspect of official thinking. But the general tendency has been to pursue cautious policies. Investments have not been on the scale needed to produce spectacular results. Thus newly consolidated units have generally been small and mechanization has proceeded at moderate rates. The first development plan's declared aim of giving landless labourers access to holdings virtually remained a dead letter. Lastly, limited encouragement has been given to the formation of co-operatives which, in some areas, could perhaps offer efficient and equitable methods of working consolidated units. The official *Sindicatos'* claim to regulate the formation of all co-operatives, combined with state inertia, has impeded movement in this direction. The second development plan promises more adventurous land consolidation programmes but their results remain to be seen.

Official responsibility for land consolidation is recent, but State interest in reafforestation can be traced back to 1833. The foundation of a corps of "forestry engineers", in 1867, increased this activity's importance. Lastly, in 1935, an autonomous body, El Patrimonio Forestal del Estado, was created with the intention of replacing depleted stocks of public woodland. This body had only a legal existence under the Republic but the new régime pressed it into service for the conduct of extensive reafforestation programmes. Commencing in 1940, it has added considerably to national wood stocks and has done much to check soil erosion. Most woodland, however, remains in private or municipal hands. Also, still more public investment is probably necessary for a wholly successful fight against soil erosion.[11]

After the war special agencies were also created to foster and regulate supplies of basic foodstuffs. They have constituted another arm of the Nationalist régime's agricultural policy. The most important is the Servicio Nacional de Cereales (S.N.C.). This is another body whose conception is not wholly attributable to the present régime. The administrative machinery is of post-war creation but the original concept was formulated during the Republic. The idea was to give the corporation exclusive rights to purchase wheat from primary producers. In this way it was intended to peg wheat prices and to protect farmers against market fluctuations of the sort experienced in the 1930s. The importance of guaranteeing domestic supplies, the unemployment likely to result from dislocations of the market and the political influence of major wheat-growers, all indicated the desirability of such a device.

The service's original objectives have been satisfactorily achieved. The problem now, is that it perhaps encourages an over-production of wheat. Economic growth has created a market for a greater variety of agricultural products which domestic producers cannot, at present, supply. A solution to this problem could be to encourage important landowners to diversify their output. The S.N.C.'s assistance to wheat-growers offers little incentive to do this. A guaranteed sale for their wheat discourages the making of new investments. The two national development plans have not broached this problem. The short-term interests of influential landowners and the S.N.C.'s attachment to traditional policies make it politically difficult for the present régime fundamentally to revise its attitudes.

Some critics argue that the effectiveness of agricultural policy, as a whole, is limited by what the régime considers politically desirable or feasible. Production increases have been fostered but they have not always kept pace with population rises. The economic planners have deliberately emphasized industrial growth as the key to national economic development and have tended to dismiss massive investment in agriculture as economically wasteful or politically unfeasible. There are reasons for supposing, however, that balanced and healthy economic growth

[11]R. Tamames, *op. cit.*, pp. 203–24.

requires a more aggressive approach to agrarian problems. At present Spain's trading position is adversely affected by the importing of food-stuffs which could be produced internally. A greater and more diversified output would also increase foreign exchange earnings and so facilitate the purchase of capital equipment necessary for sustaining industrial growth. Industrial growth is also retarded by the low purchasing power of the still significant rural population. Migrations to urban centres continue, but without marked rises in the living standards of those left behind. Thus the social costs of urban growth mount whilst many rural areas tend to stagnate. Existing policies ameliorate this situation but administrative inertia and the resistance of powerful agrarian interests limit their impact.

The same interests, and the Nationalist Régime's generally conservative temper, have impeded any significant attack upon the problem of the *latifundia*.[12] This has perhaps been the chief weakness inherent in official policies. The preservation of huge under-productive estates, frequently producing only one crop, has inevitably retarded rural development. Landowners have lacked incentives to reinvest profits or to raise the living standards of labourers and tenants. The Ministry of Agriculture has often proved responsive to their demands or has been unwilling to override their resistance to change. The rural *Sindicatos*, for their part, have generally been the least able to challenge the interests of employers. Thus legislation, enacted in 1953, which envisaged the expropriation and re-distribution of patently inefficient estates, has not been effectively imple-mented. New legislation of a similar kind is now being enacted, within the framework of the second development plan, but a question mark must hang over its success. The new legislation's appearance demon-strates that the Government's economic managers are aware of the difficulties. It remains to be seen, however, whether they possess the political will and authority needed to implement their proposals. On the other hand, they have forged policy instruments which others might sub-sequently be able to use to greater effect. By indicating alternatives to the break up of great estates, which once proved politically so contentious and which many economists now agree could be an economically retrograde step, they have perhaps opened the way for a later more energetic, yet politically viable attack upon rural problems.

[12]*Latifundia* are the subject of special comment in Juan Martinez/Alier *La Esta-bilidad del Latifundismo*, Ediciones Ruedo Ibérico, Paris, 1968.

Spain — a ~~fascist~~ state ? (handwritten)

COMMUNICATIONS

State control of radio TV (handwritten)

The Nationalist Régime also extended official responsibility for the maintenance of communications of all kinds. In the case of the mass media the desire to regulate flows of information was obviously the motive. Thus all radio stations became liable to supervision from the Ministry of Information and Tourism.[13] The State, however, does not monopolize broadcasting, for its stations coexist with those of such semi-official entities as "the Movement" and private stations holding official concessions. Television, by contrast, was created as a state monopoly and is directly controlled by a Dirección General of the Information Ministry.[14]

telephone service (handwritten)

Political factors may also explain the New State's purchase of a majority shareholding in the American-owned national telephone service. Thus the service is now operated by the Compañía Telefónica Nacional de España, which runs as a private concern and draws on private capital, but in which the Government has a controlling interest. It was probably considered necessary to have such vital concern under national ownership.

Railways (handwritten)

State control of the railways, by contrast, was the result of economic factors, and was asserted through a wholly public body. War damage to the national network was so great that reconstruction was inevitably beyond the means of private concerns. Also, the Government, faced with an acute shortage of road transport, decided, in the first instance, to use the railways rather than the roads as an aid to national economic recovery.[15] Thus the New State pushed the policies of Primo de Rivera's régime

[13]Earlier censorship had been the responsibility, in turn, of the Falange, the Interior Ministry and the Education Ministry. The creation of a specialized ministry was a measure of the importance attached by the régime to the control of information.

[14]Particularly in the past decade the Government appears to have made increasing use of television as a means of putting across its case. This was true, for example, during the referendum of 1966. Opposition groups, of course, have no access to this medium. It is also worth observing that no provision is made, on television, for minority language groups. It is a measure of the vitality of the Basque and Catalan languages and cultures that they continue to survive after being denied expression, via the mass media, for over thirty years.

[15]Until the initiation in 1962 of a fifteen-year national road-building and reconstruction programme the national road network remained in a largely run-down state. The number and quality of highways has now been considerably improved though there are outlying rural and mountainous areas which remain poorly served by roads.

through to their logical conclusion by revoking all its concessions (except those of some narrow-gauge railways) and, in 1941, establishing an official monopoly: La Red Española Nacional de Ferrocarriles (R.E.N.F.E.).[16]

INDUSTRIAL POLICY

Rationing and the policy of autarchy necessarily involved the imposition of controls over the production, distribution and importation of raw materials. For this purpose many new administrative organs were created. To cite only two examples, a Comisión para la Distribución del Carbon was founded to administer coal rationing and the cement market was regulated by La Delegación del Gobierno en la Industria del Cemento. Such bodies, above all, accounted for the massive post-war proliferation of special government agencies. The administrative problems this unwielding system created will be discussed later. At this juncture two points can be noted. First, the system encouraged that illicit use of political influence for commercial profit which characterized the period of post-war shortages and had such demoralizing effects upon political life. Secondly, it fostered a huge black market that enriched some entrepreneurs but had inflationary effects that weighed on lower-income groups.[17]

It soon became apparent that such controls, even when supplemented by attractive incentives, could not ensure that the goal of autarchy would be reached.[18] It was evident that private concerns could not be induced to increase or diversify their production at the necessary rates. Indeed, those companies in a position to dominate their particular sector frequently persisted in the traditional practice of artificially restricting production. Thus, in 1941, the Government was persuaded to create its own holding company modelled upon the Italian Instituto per la Riconstruzion Industriale.[19] The new body, the Instituto Nacional de Industria (I.N.I.),

[16]It was created by the Ley de Ordenación Ferroviaria y de los Transportes por Carretera of 24 Jan. 1941.

[17]Cf. D. Ridruejo, *Escrito en España, op. cit.,* pp. 98–104.

[18]For an official view of autarchy cf. M. Capella, *La Autarquía Económica en España,* Madrid, 1945. For an appraisal cf. M. Torres, *Juicio de la actual política económica español,* Madrid, 1955, and R. Tamames, *op. cit.,* pp. 251–67.

[19]Cf. Law 25, Sept. 1941.

was launched as an organ for supplementing or encouraging development within the private sector. It was empowered to take over existing concerns or, if necessary, to create new ones in industries considered vital to Spain's economy but unattractive to private investors. It was also expected to compete with private monopolies that were curtailing production. Only in the field of armaments was I.N.I. intended to occupy a pre-eminent position. It was specifically charged with the creation of a viable Spanish armaments industry. For these purposes I.N.I. received substantial founding capital and such executive powers as the right of compulsory purchase. Also, its dependent companies were guaranteed the privileges earlier granted to private concerns considered to be of "national interest". These privileges came, in fact, to be conceded more often to I.N.I.'s dependencies than to private companies.

Initially I.N.I.'s holdings were confined to the relatively few industrial or commercial undertakings already under state control. But as the result of takeovers or new creations it came to participate in over sixty companies. In most of these it had a controlling interest and generally did not rest content with minority holdings. The companies were engaged in such diverse activities as electricity supply, shipbuilding, steel-making, aluminium smelting, and the production of cars, chemicals and cement. In no case, however, has it wholly controlled basic sectors of the economy and it ". . . did not pre-empt much industrial terrain from the private sector".[20] Moreover, its holdings in any given field of activity have generally been scattered. Thus it has several companies supplying, between them, approximately 30 per cent of Spain's electricity. Likewise, figures available in 1967 showed that I.N.I.'s companies then produced about 40 per cent of the nation's steel and about 50 per cent of its chemical fertilizers. A look at the sum of I.N.I.'s investments points to similar conclusions. Between 1943 and 1960 its annual investments, on average, amounted to about 15 per cent of all Spain's industrial investments. This contrasts with France where, during roughly the same period, the State's industrial investments represented about 31 per cent of the country's investments in industry.

This situation can be partly explained by the lack of any well-defined strategy and by the subsequent piecemeal nature of I.N.I.'s growth. It concentrated its efforts in vital sectors of the economy and to that extent

[20]Cf. Charles W. Anderson, *The Political Economy of Modern Spain, op. cit.*, p. 40.

contributed significantly to national economic development. I.N.I.'s
activities were of signal importance to the economic growth of the
1950s. But frequently it has seemed concerned to extend its influence in
the maximum number of directions and to embark upon any potentially
lucrative enterprise rather than to invest in a few carefully selected
projects likely to promote quick yet well-balanced expansion. Its assets
have been too widely and thinly spread for it to provide the Government
with an instrument capable of decisively affecting the overall speed and
direction of development. On the contrary, it did not satisfactorily fulfil
the tasks it was originally given and it may even have aggravated some of
the economy's structural problems.

Autarchy was never a realistic goal but I.N.I. did not always help to
reach it. Indeed, its imports of capital equipment were not paid for by
later import savings and they frequently prevented adequate supplies
going to private concerns. It fostered new industries but these were
sometimes inefficient and frequently created at great cost. Their products
competed with difficulty in international markets. Except for the construction of warships I.N.I. also failed to build an effective armaments
industry and the armed forces, once dependent upon German assistance,
now largely rely on the U.S.A. for modern equipment. Another difficulty
has been the lack of an effective policy for dealing with monopolies.
Enterprises were created to compete with established concerns in such
fields as steel production, electricity supply and textiles, but in practice
there has been some tendency to co-operate with private competitors in
maintaining restrictive practices. I.N.I.'s electrical supply companies, for
example, belong to a trade association which has successfully lobbied
the Government for higher tariffs. At the other extreme, in the textile
industry, I.N.I.'s participation has perhaps exacerbated a problem of
excessive capacity. In 1963 the Ministry of Commerce created a special
tribunal for investigating restrictive practices but it received no cases in
its first year of life and I.N.I. certainly made no effort to set its machinery
in motion.[21]

I.N.I.'s contribution to the modernization of Spanish industry has undoubtedly been limited by the low priority which it has given to basic
research and industrial training. Similar criticisms can be levelled against
most official research and technical training activities. These have been

[21]Cf. R. Tamames, *La Lucha Contra Los Monopolios*, 2nd ed., Madrid, 1966.

undertaken by a multiplicity of agencies (mostly of post-Civil-war creation) which have been poorly endowed and whose activities have been insufficiently co-ordinated. Agricultural research and extension programmes, for example, have been hampered by these factors. I.N.I., however, must accept a considerable share of responsibility for the general situation for its large resources could have enabled it to take significant initiatives with benefits for the whole economy.

The liberalization of commerce which occurred at the time of the "Stabilization Plan" (1959) presented I.N.I. with new opportunities for promoting the overhaul of inefficient and poorly equipped industries. The Government certainly intended that increased overseas competition should act as a spur to Spanish industrialists and relaxed domestic controls in the hope that this would facilitate a positive response. Thus this might have provided the psychological moment for I.N.I. to have launched a modernization campaign. The opportunity, however, was not properly seized. Indeed, I.N.I. appears to have offered little resistance to private lobbying for special new protective measures. For example, it did not discourage the iron and steel industry's efforts to get special protection. Partly because of this Spain's revised tariff structure, published in 1960 in the wake of the Stabilization Plan, left its industry more protected than most of its competitors. Moreover, the structure seemed to represent *ad hoc* responses to specific pressures as much as it did a coherent strategy. The Government did not appear to be very selective in its choice of industries warranting special protection. Consequently trade liberalization, though perhaps salutary for some industries, did not encourage a wholesale abandonment of traditional attitudes and modes of organization.

I.N.I.'s policies have also had adverse repercussions on Spain's finances. It was calculated, in 1960, that nearly 90 per cent of its investments had been financed by direct grants from the State or (more importantly) by credits conceded by the Bank of Spain. Resort to credit on this scale implied large increases in the monetary supply which, being quite unmatched by rises in productivity, had serious inflationary effects. I.N.I.'s expansion therefore contributed to the difficulties that made the Stabilization Plan necessary. It also helped to erode business confidence in the private sector.

The Stabilization Plan included measures designed to tighten financial discipline within the public sector. These will be discussed later. Here it is simply appropriate to note that post-war experiences led to the assertion of direct state control over the nation's chief financial institutions. Thus in 1962 the Bank of Spain and several official credit banks were nationalized. They had been established under state auspices (the Bank of Spain in the mid-nineteenth century and all but one of the credit institutions during this century), but with the participation of private capital. During this century the State's grip has progressively tightened. The Governor of the Bank of Spain, for example, became firmly established as a governmental appointee with the power of veto. The Bank's board continued, however, to be mainly constituted by representatives of private banking and business interests who probably exercised considerable influence on monetary policy. For a long time the conservative nature of Franco's régime stopped the Government at a point short of nationalization. This move was finally initiated by the Government's economic managers, associated with Opus Dei, in the hope of exercising more effective control over supplies of money and credit during the national development plans.[22]

SOCIAL POLICY

Besides taking measures designed to promote economic growth the Nationalist régime has also taken steps designed, in principle at least, to protect or improve the living standards of socially underprivileged groups. They include initiatives in the field of housing, social security, and the regulation of prices and wages. Efforts to regulate prices and wages were partly conceived as instruments of economic policy but they are mentioned here because they were also regarded as guards against inflation and had a bearing on the purchasing power of lower income groups.

In most of these cases official policy entailed concessions to Falangists. As already indicated, these were the only policy-making fields in which Falangists made a significant impact. Their goals, however, were far from being completely reached. The original Falangists envisaged a recasting of social structures which, given the régime's nature, was out of the question. The measures taken have been attempts to aid underprivileged groups within the framework of existing institutions. In some cases they have also been extensions of pre-Civil-war measures.

[22]The Bank of Spain was nationalized by Decree-Law 18 of 7 June 1962.

Housing

State intervention in this field can be traced back to legislation of 1917, designed to encourage the construction of cheap housing. It was a rather belated response to the problems of urban growth. This legislation, complemented by measures introduced by Primo de Rivera, remained the basis of state action until 1936.[23] Action, however, was extremely limited, chiefly because insufficient resources were made available. The other aim of official policy was rent control. This began in 1920, in large urban areas, and was extended in 1931 to the whole country.

After the Civil War several factors induced the State to take much more interest in housing.[24] War damage, a war-time halt to building and accelerated migrations from countryside to town all created a large housing deficit which only state action could remedy. Also, construction traditionally absorbed such a high proportion of the labour force in Spain's underdeveloped economy, and had such significant effects upon activity in other sectors, that the Government encouraged house building to combat unemployment. Thus several agencies, mainly under the auspices of the Labour Ministry and the *Sindicatos*, were established to construct houses or to encourage private building. In addition new rent-control legislation was introduced in order to protect poorer tenants.

Between 1939 and 1954 there were essentially two types of official sponsored housing programmes. One directed by the Instituto Nacional de la Vivienda (I.N.V.) was geared to produce low-cost dwellings with fixed rents. The other managed by the Comisaría Nacional del Paro — or National Unemployment Commissariat—was to stimulate the production of houses for sale or renting on the open market. Both programmes were assisted by tax relief, loans and privileged access to raw materials, but the second programme received particularly beneficial treatment. Priority consequently tended to be given to relatively expensive dwellings. These

[23]Responsibility for enforcing this legislation was largely given to municipal authorities. Cf. Chapter 8 for their general attitudes to such problems, and why the central government has subsequently assumed the major share of responsibility for such services as housing.

[24]Housing policy and the relevant legislation are reviewed in R. Tamames, *op. cit.*, pp. 409–25. Brief references in English occur in D. V. Donnison, *The Government of Housing*, Pelican, 1967.

were built by private contractors who profited considerably from official assistance.

Neither programme, however, had sufficient resources to eliminate the housing deficit (which was accentuated by population increases).[25] In practice rent controls also tended to aggravate this situation. They protected poor tenants but also deterred private interests from supplying cheap rented accommodation. Inflation quickly eroded the value of fixed rents. In 1954, therefore, the I.N.V. was charged with the execution of an ambitious programme for providing cheap houses and was simultaneously endowed with greater resources. This measure was complemented, in 1957, by the creation of a Housing Ministry able to develop better co-ordinated policies. It was, significantly enough, put in charge of a Falangist (Sr. Arrese). Under him the emphasis was switched to providing cheap state-constructed dwellings.

The revised policy has been pursued energetically and with marked success. On the other hand, the Stabilization Plan fell particularly heavily on the State's housing programme (which led to Sr. Arrese's resignation). Also, a large and often inefficient private sector remains which, in the 1960s, was involved in a boom in speculative building that necessarily diverted resources from other more economically productive ventures. During the first national plan, house building made a very large contribution to increases in the general level of economic activity. Houses were built far faster than the plan anticipated. The associated land speculation had serious inflationary effects.

Social security

The pre-Civil-war history of state intervention in this field has already been traced. During the war, as a gesture to the Falangists and in an effort to rally working-class support, a Workers Charter was published promising a more comprehensive social security system than anything previously known. The programme sketched by the Charter was subsequently developed by the Instituto Nacional de Previsión which provided compulsory insurance for sickness, maternity, old age, unemployment,

[25]Between 1940 and 1960 (when the last official census was held) Spain's population grew from 25,877,971 to 30,430,698. In 1967, it was estimated to be about 33,295,000.

industrial accidents and diseases. Insurance against unemployment, especially, represented a significant departure.[26]

These measures gave workers (particularly in the industrial sector) a significant degree of protection and probably blunted opposition to the new régime. Nevertheless, they have been subjected to several criticisms. Administrative costs have been high whilst benefits have remained low in proportion to contributions. The State's promotion of *Mutualidades Laborales* (Workers mutual aid associations), providing parallel and sometimes overlapping services, was a tacit admission of these inadequacies. These latter bodies, moreover, owed nothing to working-class initiatives and entailed a second set of compulsory contributions, which were used to finance I.N.I.'s investments. They constituted, in other words, a form of compulsory saving.

It was only in 1966 that a unified social security system was re-established. Prior to that, in 1963, all accident and sickness insurance was removed from the private sector thus depriving private insurance companies of two particularly lucrative activities. This signified a Falangist success and showed that Falangist pressures for more radical social policies had not been completely relaxed. The general state of official social security services illustrates, however, how far short they have fallen from their original aims. Welfare benefits have clearly not produced a significant redistribution of income.[27]

The control of prices and incomes

Until 1958 both prices and incomes were officially controlled. Responsibility for price controls was shared amongst the multiplicity of organs regulating supplies. Incomes were regulated by the Labour Ministry. In principle this provided instruments for protecting economically weak groups. In practice no very coherent policy was pursued. So many bodies were involved in controlling prices that co-ordination was difficult and

[26]In practice little over half the unemployed benefit—in 1969 an estimated figure was 53·19 per cent. According to official figures unemployment, during the 1960s, never exceeded 1·6 per cent of the working population. Such figures, however, have more propaganda than scientific value. They do not allow for administrative error, seasonal variations, under-employment and hidden unemployment.

[27]Cf. R. Tamames, *op. cit.*, pp. 703–6, and M. Martínez Cuadrado, *Anuario Político Español*, 1970, *op. cit.*, pp. 410–17.

the evasion of controls easy. Also, as noted, price fixing tended to become a way of protecting the inefficient. The net effect tended to be inflationary. Wage controls also did not always operate as intended. Employers, in practice, forced up the wages of scarce skilled workers by offering unofficial bonuses. Equally, the Labour Ministry sometimes approved a general wage increase which bore little relation to rises in productivity. The net effect was an accentuation of the inflationary pressures which, naturally, hit hardest at the lowest paid.

The latter's living standards were also affected by a regressive tax system. Its essential features had been fixed by the end of the last century and had not been greatly altered. A reform was initiated in 1940 but this was designed to increase and spread the incidence of taxation rather than to change the basic tax structure. Moreover, the revised system tended, in reality, to aggravate the long-standing problem of evasion.

The Stabilization Plan entailed the relaxation of price controls and was accompanied by the introduction of a form of collective bargaining. Also, a major tax reform in 1957 had, as one of its aims, a more equitable distribution of the tax burden. In the short run these measures brought little relief to lower-income groups. These were most affected by the Government's severe deflationary measures.[28] The later period of growth offered the prospect of improvements in their position. The use made of these opportunities will be mentioned later, when examining economic planning.

The organization of the public sector

Given the multiplicity of the activities mentioned and their piecemeal growth, it is understandable that they should have been undertaken by very varied types of administrative organization and frequently improvised or inadequately considered institutions.

The earliest official enterprises were operated by the central administration or by private concessionaires. The former might have limited financial independence and some discretion in the handling of routine business but otherwise operated in the same way as traditional government agencies. Spain's postal services still function in this way—under the

[28]On this whole subject cf. R. Tamames, *op. cit.*, pp. 701–3 and 714–23. For Spain's Tax System cf. *Los Impuestos en España 1967*, Ministerio de la Hacienda, Madrid, 1967.

Interior Ministry's control. Few organs of this type have been recently created, however, because conventional managerial, budgetary and accounting methods generally proved unsuitable for commercial or quasi-commercial undertakings.

Concessions may permit flexibility but prevent adequate state control over policy-making. For example, C.A.M.P.S.A.'s investment decisions may partly reflect the influence of foreign investors, with a stake in the concern, who do not want an independent Spanish petroleum industry. Nevertheless, administrative conservatism and pressure from interested parties have combined to perpetuate this device.

The State's first (and most common) answer to these problems was the creation of "autonomous administrative entities". They are in principle dependent upon a "supervising" ministry and normally work within a framework of administrative law, but they have a separate legal existence and considerable financial independence. They are, in other words, half-way between the traditional administrative organs and the French style public enterprise—run on commercial lines.[29]

The first important autonomous entity was the Instituto Nacional de Previsión, which now depends upon the Labour Ministry. Primo de Rivera created several more to administer his public works programmes. During the Republic efforts were made to check the spread of such potentially significant sources of administrative power. Since 1939, however, they have multiplied. Several factors explain this. First, the traditional administrative organs were suddenly faced with many new responsibilities for which they were inadequately equipped. The only well-tried alternative was therefore adopted. Similarly, official inertia induced some departments to shed immediate responsibility for new tasks. Lack of co-ordination also played its part for bodies with overlapping responsibilities were frequently created by separate departments. This helps to explain the multiplicity of house building and research agencies.

In every case this expansion was facilitated by the ease with which specialized entities could be founded. Until 1958 a ministerial order was sufficient. Thus many were created as the result of pressure from administrative corps seeking increased autonomy. Corps members could be

[29]The development, organization and problems of autonomous entities are reviewed in *Documentación Administrativa*, No. 78–79, June–July 1964, pp. 59–75; and No. 89, May 1965, pp. 27–40.

transferred to senior posts in new agencies where they could more easily escape central direction. They were particularly attracted by the financial independence of autonomous entities and their power to collect *tasas*.

In these circumstances institutions with a similar legal status were established to perform widely varying functions. The autonomous entity was often an appropriate device but some tasks could have been assigned to other institutions. The activities of some bodies, for example, could be better handled by institutions operating under commercial rather than administrative law. The National Cereal Corporation's extensive credit operations perhaps put it in this category.

Some bodies called autonomous entities do in fact have their relationships with the general public regulated by commercial law. Also, their employees are not classified as civil servants but are covered by the labour legislation applicable in the private sector. The chief examples are R.E.N.F.E. and the official banks. These bodies, however, have essentially the same relationship with the Government as other entities. Indeed, it was argued in R.E.N.F.E.'s case that the commercial nature of its operations should involve a complete change of status and much more autonomy.

I.N.I. is also described as an autonomous entity and was, until recently, nominally dependent upon the Presidency. The companies which it controls are described, however, as *empresas nacionales* (national enterprises).

In principle *empresas nacionales* are organized and run in the same way as private commercial undertakings. This organizational form was first employed on any scale by Primo de Rivera's régime but I.N.I. firmly established it as a vehicle for extending the State's business interests.

I.N.I. controls them in several ways. Iberia, for example, is wholly state owned, but most companies are "mixed enterprises" created with the aid of private capital or into which the State has bought its way. The State normally has majority holdings in these but some are controlled through preference shares. Thus I.N.I.'s representatives have a majority of seats on most company boards and a veto power within the remainder. I.N.I.'s record indicates, however, that representatives of private concerns have been able to use public funds for their own rather than the State's purposes.

This raises the general problem of controlling autonomous entities and *empresas nacionales.* But an examination of this question first requires a look at their internal organization.[30]

Autonomous entities are normally administered by a board, a permanent executive committee and a senior executive official or Director. The boards meet periodically to make or review important policy decisions. They are frequently chaired by the heads of supervising ministries or officials of their departments. Other members are usually appointed by decree or ministerial order. They invariably include the Director and functionaries of the "parent ministry". The boards of major entities contain representatives of other administrative interests. I.N.I.'s board, for example, contains representatives of several ministries and of the armed forces. Similarly, the planning commissariat is represented on the boards of the official banks. Affected private interests may also be included. Thus private bankers sit on the boards of state credit institutions.

The executive committees meet more often to handle routine business and to do preliminary work for the boards. Their composition varies but they invariably contain the Director. Directors are ministerial or government appointees and are normally senior officials of the supervising ministry. The Directors of major institutions may be outstanding political figures. Until 1961, for example, I.N.I.'s Director was the former minister chiefly responsible for the policy of autarchy.

Most Directors enjoy considerable discretion in the handling of day-to-day affairs. For example, they appoint subordinate officials and prepare the budget. In principle, however, they remain responsible to their boards and ultimately to their supervising departments.

This picture suggests that relationships between autonomous entities and the central administration are so intimate that it is meaningless to discuss controls. Indeed, the composition of boards and the background of senior officials do preclude fundamental conflicts of interest. Also, the common background of many policy-makers facilitates the establishment of informal mechanisms for harmonizing policies. For example, the official machinery for determining monetary and credit supplies is supplemented by frequent informal meetings between the heads of official banks and the Finance Ministry (who are now commonly drawn from Opus Dei).

[30]Formal organization is mentioned in A. Guaita, *Derecho Administrativo Especial, op. cit.,* Tomo III.

In practice, however, the extent and effectiveness of central direction varies considerably. Thus experience suggested that modernization of the railways was hampered by excessive interference from a board which contained the representatives of several competing ministries and gave too little scope to technical experts. In 1961, therefore, prior to launching ambitious modernization schemes, R.E.N.F.E. was reorganized and its management given greater autonomy. Most agencies, however, have always had considerable freedom in the making and implementation of policy. This is chiefly because the number and size of governmental agencies make thorough supervision difficult. The Agricultural Ministry, for example, has over twenty dependencies whose total expenditure exceeds that of the supervising department. Supervision and co-ordination is intermittent and real decision-making power tends to be with senior officials of the entities themselves. The latter are well placed to protect their interests and to maintain programmes in which they have a stake. In extreme cases this means preserving redundant institutions. Thus institutions made redundant by economic liberalization found new pretexts for exercising their customary right to collect *tasas*.

It is in financial matters that effective controls have been most obviously lacking. In principle a quite thorough system exists for budgets require government approval, major items of expenditure need the Finance Ministry's clearance and accounts must be submitted to the Tribunal de Cuentas.[31] There are, however, serious practical difficulties. First, the system is designed to secure the observance of legality rather than the most productive use of public funds and therefore, when applied, it tends to impede speedy and efficient management. But usually the Government lacks the will and means needed to make the system effective. Thus the estimates of some major entities are inadequately scrutinized. Moreover, *tasas* and earnings on capital have sometimes freed entities from total dependence on the Treasury or official credit. *Post hoc* controls also tend to be ineffective. At worst accounts are not presented and at best they are uninformative.[32]

Such problems have been most serious in the case of I.N.I. Its size, huge

---

[31] Chapter 9 for references to the Tribunal de Cuentas.

[32] Such problems were a frequent cause of comment in *The Economic Development of Spain*—report of a mission organized by the International Bank for Reconstruction and Development, *op. cit.*

budgets and complexity make supervision difficult. Also, its leadership is recruited from politically influential groups with significant private interests to defend. The régime has, for example, rewarded the services of politicians and soldiers with seats on the boards of I.N.I.'s companies. The same figures are frequently directors of private banking and industrial concerns with holdings in I.N.I. Similarly, many managerial posts are occupied by industrial engineers with an interest in the growth of the I.N.I. bureaucracy and with access to decision-makers in the economic ministries. The distinction between public and private interests is consequently blurred and many decisions reflect informal understandings rather than official government policy.

These factors help to explain the failure of I.N.I.'s investment programmes to stimulate the type of expansion produced by its Italian counterpart—the I.R.I. They help to explain, for example, the State's willingness, prior to 1958, automatically to underwrite I.N.I.'s debts.

Since 1958 the Government, as part of the campaign for more effective economic management, has attempted to tighten up controls over autonomous agencies. Liberalization in the private sector has been accompanied by greater centralization in the public sector. Thus the relaxation of physical controls entailed the fusion or suppression of many organs and new creations were drastically reduced by requiring sponsoring ministries to obtain the sanction of a special law. Greater financial discipline was also attempted for autonomous agencies were denied automatic credit from the Bank of Spain. Subsequently there have been efforts to make entities adhere more closely to official plans. The success of these efforts will be examined in the next section.[33]

INDICATIVE PLANNING*

The first national plan was presented as a radical new departure but in fact it represented a reordering of priorities and an attempt to use existing administrative machinery to better effect.[34] A certain underlying contin-

---

[33]The basic legislation is a law of 26 Dec. 1958 (*B.O.E.*, 29 Dec. 1958).

[34]There is an English version of the plan, cf. *Economic and Social Development Program for Spain, 1964–1967*, Johns Hopkins University Press, Baltimore, 1965. For a critical view cf. R. Tamames. *España ante un segundo plan de desarrollo*, Barcelona, 1968.

*In 1972 a third national plan was launched. It has been impossible to discuss it in this study.

uity was maintained. In the public sector this entailed efforts to make autonomous entities fulfil previously published investment programmes. These programmes, in fact, accounted for over half the State's proposed expenditure under the terms of the first national plan.

The publication of projected investments sometimes clarified the State's intentions and so increased confidence in the private sector. It helped to create an atmosphere in which some important private interests were prepared to adopt more competitive and expansionist investment policies. Nevertheless, several factors limited the effectiveness of these measures. Firstly, the autonomous entities (like their parent ministries) still tended to draw up their investment programmes in isolation rather than as part of a coherent overall strategy. In 1965, for example, R.E.N.F.E. initiated a ten-year railway modernization scheme whose aims were not directly linked to those of the national plan. Secondly, investment programmes were not always implemented with reference to the plan. Some entities underfulfilled their obligations by as much as 30 per cent. Likewise, caution and some lack of selectivity in the credit policies of the official banks suggests that nationalization has not produced all its expected benefits nor wholly neutralized the influence, within them, of private financial interests. Indeed, some observers maintain that, in practice, the plan was "indicative" for the public as well as the private sector.

Continued resistance to external controls was most apparent and serious in the case of I.N.I. Its published investment programmes were uninformative on such basic questions as anticipated growth rates in different industrial sectors. In practice it, and its dependent companies, tended to be almost as autonomous as before.

In 1968, as a preliminary to the second plan, responsibility for supervising I.N.I. was switched to the Ministry of Industry.[35] This does seem a victory for those economic ministers of Opus Dei who have been battling to curb this institution's independence, especially as efforts to rationalize its structure soon followed. This rationalization process has been characterized by the return of some important undertakings to private enterprise. Thus I.N.I. is no longer a majority shareholder in the S.E.A.T. car firm and has sold important electrical installations to a private company. The second plan underwrites this situation. It contains no general scheme for reorganizing what remains of the "public sector" and certainly does

[35]Cf. Decree 480, 14 Mar. 1968.

not envisage giving I.N.I. complete control over any of the basic sectors of the economy in which it is involved.

This policy is consistent with the attitudes of Spain's economic managers to the entire question of public enterprise. At their first plan's outset they indicated that private concerns should take the lead in modernizing basic sectors of the economy and that public undertakings should be confined to activities clearly beyond the means of private investors. In place of direct state intervention emphasis was laid on providing incentives to private enterprise. Thus the long-standing legislation on industries of national interest was in effect updated with new provisions for agreements between the State and individual firms (or groups of firms). The latter can undertake to rationalize themselves in return for loans, tax concessions and other benefits. Several agreements of this sort affecting the steel industry, for example, have been concluded.

These measures have not gone unchallenged. This is partly a question of resistance from orthodox Falangists still attracted by the notion of autarchy, and of groups (in I.N.I. for example) with vested interests at stake. But it is also a matter of new dissident Falangist groups, and of opposition elements, proposing new alternatives. They subscribe to the "structuralist school" of economics which maintains that monetary and fiscal weapons provide the State with inadequate control over the planning process and sees the root of Spain's economic problems in deep-seated structural deficiencies that can only be tackled through a radical reform programme. They argue that, in Spain, some private sectors are too fragmented for the Government adequately to supervise the implementation of voluntary structural reforms. Likewise, they maintain that in other sectors ownership is so concentrated and restrictive practices so firmly rooted that state assistance is simply used to reinforce established monopolies. They contend that wrong conclusions have been drawn from past experiences of public enterprise and that the public sector should be extended rather than reduced. Thus it is asserted that some basic industries (and the big banks) should be wholly nationalized and run by more efficient public corporations that would be more responsibe to state control and less to private interests. The same groups also advocate the conversion of such autonomous entities as R.E.N.F.E. and such official concessionaires as C.A.M.P.S.A. into fully fledged nationalized undertakings. This, it is suggested, is the only way of giving the State the leverage needed to foster and guide rapid but balanced economic growth.[36]

It may be that these groups overestimate the likely impact of their reform proposals. But the first plan's execution certainly suggests that, at present, the State has a strictly limited degree of control over the process of economic development. It induced some important business leaders to adopt more adventurous investment policies, but the nature and extent of economic growth appears to have owed rather little to direct state intervention. Much growth appeared to occur in spite of rather than because of the plan. Thus the plan was least "indicative" for those activities— construction and tourism—which contributed most to expansion. Equally, Spain's satisfactory balance of payments was due, in large part, to tourist earnings, the remittances of Spanish workers employed abroad and foreign investments in Spain.[37] In none of these cases had the planners accurately gauged the part they were to play in economic recovery. By the same token, the planners left themselves vulnerable to possible future developments over which they could have little control. This appears to remain the case during the second plan.[38]

The plans and social change

The first national plan was officially described as a plan of "Economic and Social Development". Initially, however, the planners seemed to regard planning largely in terms of providing incentives to industrial growth. Their advocacy of planned social change appeared to represent an exercise in public relations as much as a firm policy commitment. Several things support this view. Firstly, the term "Social" was almost a last-minute inclusion in the plan's title and early drafts paid little heed to social problems. Secondly, the planning commission concerned with "Human and Social Factors" reported back well after the plan's initiation. Thirdly, little information was published on the implementation of this aspect of the plan. Finally, where figures were available they indicated

[36]Alternatives to official policies are discussed in Charles W. Anderson, *The Political Economy of Modern Spain, op cit.*

[37]Cf. During the 1960s the Labour Ministry had a policy of encouraging emigration. As for foreign investment, critics of official policies fear that Spain's economy will become excessively dependent on borrowed technology.

[38]Cf. "II Plan de desarrollo económico y social", Madrid (*B.O.E.*, 1969).

that the underfulfilment of public investment programmes was greatest in such fields as education, professional training, public health and welfare services. The official targets of the second plan, on the other hand, indicate rather more determination to tackle social problems. This shift in emphasis comes partly as a response to criticisms of the first plan, constantly voiced by Falangist and opposition groups. But it is also probably due to a change of perspective on the part of the planners themselves. Experience gathered during the first plan probably confirmed the existence of obstacles to development lying outside the planners' immediate area of concern. They were impelled during and after the first plan to pay greater heed to matters conventionally classified under the heading of "social policy". This was perhaps most apparent in the educational sphere.

Education[39]

Until very recently, at least, Spain's educational system was essentially based on principles laid down in 1857. As will be seen there are now plans for transforming the system, but traditional patterns seem likely to remain strongly resistant to change.

The traditional system has been markedly élitist in nature. The great bulk of the urban and rural working classes did not normally progress beyond the primary level and considerable numbers dropped out before reaching the age at which compulsory education legally ends. Thus illiteracy has been a considerable problem. Secondary education and preparation for the *bachillerato*—which is necessary for access to higher education— has largely been the preserve of the middle and upper classes. The educational system has both reflected and reinforced Spain's established social patterns.

Another significant feature of the traditional educational system has been the division between the public and private sectors. The bulk of primary school pupils have always been found in state schools whilst something over 80 per cent of secondary education has been in private and, above all, Church hands. The general tendency has been for secondary schools, controlled by religious orders, to recruit most of their pupils from fee-paying private schools and subsequently to prepare them for

[39]Cf. *La Educación en España. Centro de Publicaciones del Valle de los Caídos*, Madrid, 1970.

entry to the universities or the higher technical schools associated with the prestigious administrative corps. This situation underlines the identification of the Church with the *status quo* noted earlier in this study.[40]

The most determined efforts to reform this system were made during the Second Republic. There was then some attempt to increase educational opportunities and an attack upon the Church schools which had been dedicated to the production of Spain's traditional élites. The Nationalist Régime reversed these trends. In 1964 there were fewer state secondary schools than in 1935 and there was a corresponding expansion of the private sector. Moreover, it was made plain during the régime's formative stages that secondary and, more especially, higher education were conceived as instruments for producing the "New Spain's" élite groups. The role officially given to the Falangist party in the universities was the clearest indication of this.

As previously noted, the educational system failed, in any positive sense, to fulfil its political role.[41] After the ministerial crisis of 1956, at least, it was apparent that the educational system was unlikely to serve as a vehicle for political indoctrination or for mobilizing support on behalf of the régime. Simultaneously, the new technocratic elements, particularly associated with Opus Dei, began to show some preoccupation with the relationship between economic development and general educational standards. Before and during the course of Spain's first two development plans there appeared to be a growing awareness in government circles of the obstacles to economic development presented by an inadequately prepared labour force, shortages of technical and managerial skills and the relatively low priority given to scientific training and research. The undertaking of various official studies, and Spain's commitment to the O.E.E.C.'s programme for promoting educational change in the Mediterranean region, were indicators of this changing climate of opinion. The creation of special funds to provide state scholarships for students from lower-income groups and to encourage a greater equality of educational opportunities were gestures of a similar sort.

Pressure for change was reinforced by a growing popular demand for at least some democratization of the educational system. It was also reinforced by the growth of dissent within the universities. Apart from a

[40]Cf. Chapter 1.
[41]Cf. Chapter 2 for the growth of a university-based opposition.

minority of private universities (mostly of recent creation) these are state bodies. They have suffered from overcrowding, inadequate teaching facilities and outdated syllabuses. Such problems have generated discontent amongst vocal minorities of students and teachers and this discontent has provided some of the motive power behind university-based political movements. It is significant that the most radical re-examination of Spain's educational system undertaken since the Civil War should have been initiated by a Minister of Education appointed in 1968 when student opposition activities were particularly intense.

The new minister (associated with Opus Dei) and his closest collaborators produced a *Libro Blanco* (a White Book)[42] in which several significant changes were proposed. Chief amongst these were plans intended to eliminate the situation in which middle-class children began working for the *bachillerato* at the age of 10 whilst the majority of their peers simply continued primary education until leaving school. There were also proposals for reorganizing university education.

The *Libro Blanco* subsequently became the basis for new educational legislation.[43] Several question marks, however, must hang over the Government's apparent change of policy. Firstly, some commentators argue that insufficient attention is being paid to the problems of primary education which will have adverse implications for education at higher levels and particularly for the majority who still do not proceed much beyond the primary stage. Secondly, doubts remain about the State's capacity to increase the number and quality of the teachers needed to implement its reforms. This is partly related to a third problem—the State's willingness to make the necessary investments. Delays experienced during the 1960s in the execution of school-building programmes and the limited number of state scholarships which were, in practice, provided suggests that the political will necessary for implementing serious reforms is not present in all sectors of the administration. Expenditure on education has been increased and, at all levels, those receiving education have grown considerably. Equally, illiteracy seems well on the way to being eliminated. Nevertheless, the State's performance has frequently failed to live up to expectations. It seems likely that major reforms would only be con-

[42]Cf. *Libro Blanco de Educacíon*, Madrid, June 1969.
[43]Cf. "la ley General de Educación y Financiación de la Reforma Educativa, 4 Aug. 1970.

sistently applied by an administration subject to pressures from an informed public opinion and, in particular, to the pressures of groups able to speak effectively for all educational interests. This raises the final and more basic question of whether Spain's present authoritarian political system is capable of fostering the democratization of the educational system now apparently desired by significant sections of the society. In practice policy-makers still have an essentially élitist approach to educational problems and have geared their reforms to the production of technically qualified minorities deemed necessary for guiding the process of economic development. They are also linked to established groups, particularly conservative groups within the Catholic Church, who have vested interests in the traditional educational system.[44]

Increases in expenditure on education indicate a significant reassessment of priorities. Nevertheless, the present structure of Spanish politics seems likely to set definite if as yet unreached limits to the extent of educational reform. More drastic changes presuppose a democratization of society and a reallocation of resources that would be unacceptable to most of the Nationalist régime's constituent groups. At present they could only come through a marked strengthening of radical Falangist elements which is an unlikely development. The same factors also probably preclude a major redistribution of the national income. Indicators of this are provided by the approach of the planners to the issue of prices and incomes.

Prices and incomes[45]

During the first plan Spain's Gross National Product and *per capita* income both grew at quite spectacular rates. Indeed, unexpected pressure from the *Sindicatos*, fighting to retain their members' loyalty, forced average wages up to quite unforeseen levels. These increases, however, contributed to large price rises that not only upset the planners' calculations but also penalized large numbers of lower-paid workers. Few of the

[44]It should be added, however, that some Churchmen wish to make their educational facilities more generally available, but this presupposes state aid on a scale that is not forthcoming. This withholding of assistance may be partly due, of course, to the Church's changing political views.

[45]Cf. R. Tamames, *España ante un Segundo Plan de Desarrollo, op. cit.*, pp. 161–66, and Charles W. Anderson, *op. cit.*, pp. 218–24. For survey data on income levels and allied issues cf. *Informe Sociológico Sobre la Situación Social de España, op. cit.*

benefits of economic expansion percolated down to them. Their situation contrasted with the growing profit margins of some major financial and industrial institutions.

The planning apparatus was not equipped to respond to this situation. The first plan affirmed the Government's responsibility for controlling wages and prices, but particularly in the case of prices it was vague about the measures to be taken. In practice fairly rapid increases in the cost of living seemed to be accepted as the price of continued expansion. This highlighted the priority given to economic growth over the redistribution of wealth.

When, in 1964 and still more in 1967, the Government felt obliged to confront this situation, it fell back on the orthodox monetary and fiscal tools which it had employed during the earlier Stabilization Plan. As before, the least privileged tended to bear a disproportionate share of the necessary burdens. Measures proposed in the second development plan indicate some sensitivity to criticism of this situation. They include an undertaking to tie incomes more closely to both the cost of living and productivity. There are also references to sindical proposals for profit sharing. In reality, however, these provisions seem more likely to represent a symbolic gesture of reassurance than a substantial policy change. The major reordering of priorities is likely to occur until labour is able to obtain much more real bargaining power than is currently possible. No *Sindicatos* have successfully pushed wage claims, sometimes to the embarrassment of their political opponents in charge of planning, but they lack the independence needed to secure a major reassessment of aims. The necessary freedom to organize, on both the industrial and political fronts, would imply the abandonment of controls that the present régime has always regarded as an indispensable feature of its system of rule. Moreover, most functionaries at present responsible for the day-to-day management of economic affairs are, by virtue of their backgrounds and general attitudes, well disposed to the business community and more accessible to its spokesmen than to the official spokesmen for labour. The latter are not only regarded as unrepresentative by many of their constituents but they also tend to be junior partners in the official policy-making process.

By the same token government planners tend to be unresponsive to the demands of the small and medium-sized firms which depended on the "economic sections" of the *Sindicatos* for putting their case across to the

State. The economic managers associated with Opus Dei, in their search for an independent power base, have been inclined to short circuit the entrenched syndical bureaucracy and to deal directly with unofficial business leaders (sympathetic to their aims) drawn from large concerns. Thus the planning process has often been a question of a dialogue between relatively small élite groups.

The net effect of this situation is the widespread lack of any positive commitment to, or understanding of, the aims of the national plans. This is reflected in opinion polls revealing considerable popular ignorance of the whole planning process.[46] Such a state of affairs raises the question of whether existing political institutions can provide a satisfactory framework for the conduct of "indicative planning". The special case of regional planning casts light on this subject.

Regional planning

Since the Civil War the State has assumed an increasing degree of responsibility for the promotion of regional development. There has been a growing awareness of discrepancies in the levels of economic and social development between the industrialized Catalan and Basque regions, at one extreme, and the agricultural provinces of Andalusia and Extremadura, at the other. Equally, it is now better appreciated that a more balanced national economy could stop backward areas putting a brake on the development of more advanced regions and prevent overcrowding in a few major urban centres. State action to encourage the development of areas of low employment, investment, productivity and grossly unequal income distributions has been accepted.

But important political and administrative difficulties have impeded the effective handling of these problems. First, planned regional development requires concerted action by several ministries. These include the Ministry of Public Works with responsibility for road building and other major engineering projects; the Ministry of Agriculture concerned with the increase of agricultural productivity; the Ministry of Industry responsible for the promotion and location of new industries; the Ministries of Education and Labour interested in combating illiteracy, offering

[46]These issues are explored in R. Tamames, *España ante un Segundo Plan de Desarrollo, op. cit.*, pp. 205–7.

chances for technical training and creating employment; the Ministry of Information and Tourism which seeks to generate economic activity through the encouragement of tourism; the Interior Ministry which supervises local administration; and finally the Finance Ministry which provides much of the necessary credit. Co-ordination has been made difficult, however, by the rivalries which are so characteristic of Spain's administration. Second, experience gathered in France, for example, indicates that effective regional planning needs to be on the basis of new supra-provincial territorial units, corresponding to economic and social realities, and requires some mobilization of local interests. In Spain both these factors have been missing. Politicians and administrators have resisted sharing their decision-making powers with representatives of local interests and they have discouraged all forms of political activity likely to threaten the present authoritarian régime. Finally, the State has generally taken a limited view of what constitutes regional development. It has tended to view it simply in terms of economic growth. Only recently has it paid much heed to relevant social questions. The overall result of this has been a very tentative and piecemeal approach. Brief references to Spain's various experiments in regional planning should clarify this picture.

Spain's first experiments in regional planning were conducted by Primo de Rivera's Confederaciones Hidrográficas.[47] They were intended to promote the planned exploitation of the resources of entire river basins. Such bodies could have established significant precedents. They were based on natural economic units, provided machinery for co-ordinated state action at the local level and envisaged the co-operation of state officials with representatives of affected local interests. But these expectations were not fulfilled. In practice local spokesmen were effectively excluded from decision-making and the Confederaciones became no more than centrally controlled administrative devices. Moreover, they did not establish themselves as the instruments of a well-co-ordinated national policy. Each Confederación tended to go its own way and individual performances varied enormously. They also had to contend with the competition of other administrative bodies. Their own parent ministry, the Public Works department, assumed some of their functions and the

[47]Cf. S. Martín, *Retortillo. De las Administraciones Autonomas de las Aguas Públicas*, Seville, 1960.

Ministry of Agriculture developed a competing interest in irrigation projects.

These two departments have taken the lead in some post-Civil-war planning experiments. Official studies, initiated in 1945, demonstrated the need for state action to remedy regional economic imbalances.[48] The necessary resources and political will were not forthcoming, however, until the 1950s. Even then the first practical steps were confined to two programmes of public works designed to develop the very depressed agricultural provinces of Badajoz and Jaén.[49]

These two plans have provided valuable infrastructure and produced some rise in income levels. But they have also been the objects of some sharp criticism. They have been seen as official showpieces, conceived within the traditional provincial framework largely as tokens of concern for depressed areas. In the case of Badajoz, at least, the desire to make a conciliatory political gesture was probably an important factor.[50] The planning machinery was created on the same *ad hoc* basis. Distinct administrative organs were established for the drafting and execution of each of these two plans and they have both retained their separate identities through all subsequent shifts of official policy. Also, little effort was made to engage the interest of local representatives. The formulation and execution of the two plans have been largely the work of officials of the central government. Finally, it has been objected that the plans have concentrated too much on the creation of material capital and not enough on the mobilization of human resources. Investments in education and technical training have not matched those in irrigation, agricultural processing, industrial and road-building projects.

The duplication of effort and the waste entailed in these arrangements has been aggravated by a lack of satisfactory departmental co-operation. The planning process is directed by interdepartmental committees nominally dependent upon the Presidency but tending in practice merely to institutionalize existing administrative conflicts. They meet too seldom to develop much *ésprit de corps* and their permanent secretariats lack the

[48]These studies were conducted under the auspices of the official *Sindicatos* which have done quite a lot to promote official interest in regional questions.

[49]Cf. Laws of 7 Apr. 1952 and 17 July 1953.

[50]The local population suffered particularly badly at Nationalist hands during the Civil War.

political weight needed to bargain on equal terms with the interested ministries. The plans have therefore tended to be a series of loosely related departmental projects each based on partial studies of local problems.[51]

From 1955 onwards there were efforts to develop similar plans for other areas. Another interdepartmental committee was established, with limited powers, to promote the development of backward rural areas throughout the country (outside of Badajoz and Jaén). These schemes have tended, however, to be starved of resources and, initially, there was no permanent machinery capable of giving a lead or providing co-ordination. In 1958 the scope of the plans was enlarged and a secretariat was established, but the basic problems were unresolved.[52] Similarly, though there was provision for supra-provincial planning and for the establishment of local consultative bodies, the provincial framework has been adhered to in most cases and the consultative organs are primarily staffed by state employees. The net result has been plans which, like the prototypes in Badajoz and Jaén, have tended to lack internal coherence and to be largely unrelated to each other. The State has begun to elaborate a general strategy for tackling the problem of rural underdevelopment but continued emigration to urban areas and disappointing agricultural yields highlight its inadequacies.

Spain's first development plan represented a further stage in planned regional development. It included new measures for helping backward rural areas and for the first time seriously broached the question of balanced regional growth. Early drafts of the plan made no special provisions for regional development. These were incorporated chiefly as the result of pressure from the *Sindicatos*.[53] Such responsiveness to the pressures of a competing group indicates some flexibility on the part of the planners and shows that conflicts within the Nationalist Régime are capable of generating some significant policy initiatives. Such a capacity for adjustment and for innovation, in the face of changing circumstances and pressures, is undoubtedly one precondition of successful "indicative planning". The formulation and execution of the new regional development

[51]Amongst many commentaries cf. M. Martin Lobo, *Realidad y Perspectiva de la Planificación Regional en España*, Madrid, 1962, pp. 85–135.
[52]Cf. Decree Law 13 Feb. 1958.
[53]Cf. Charles W. Anderson, *op. cit.*, pp. 210–18.

plans indicate, however, some of the difficulties currently involved in carrying out experiments of this type.

The chosen instruments of development have, in this case, been specially designated development areas. To these the State seeks to attract new enterprises through special tax and credit concessions. The areas are of two types, *polos de desarrollo* where special encouragement is given to established industries and *polos de promoción* for promoting entirely new ones. The latter receive the more ample concessions.[54]

In practice seven areas have been selected. Six of them seem to have been arranged in complementary pairs. Thus the existing industrial centre of Valladolid (a *polo de desarrollo*) has been paired with its less developed neighbour, Burgos (a *polo de promoción*). Zaragoza is the only area without a "twin".[55] They have all been located in areas which were once backward and have now become centres of considerable economic growth. During the first three years of the first plan, for example, over 1000 new enterprises were established and more than 107,000 new jobs created in the chosen areas. Nevertheless some analysts challenge the criteria by which they were selected and feel that better results could have been obtained. It is maintained, for example, that Valladolid had begun to grow rapidly without special help and scarcely needed state assistance—special incentives appear to have simply reinforced its attractiveness to private investors. Equally, Valladolid's industrial expansion has probably inhibited Burgos' growth. Though state assistance is more generous in Burgos it is not always sufficient to divert investors away from its neighbour which is already prosperous and has more of the infrastructure necessary for sustained growth. Thus state aid has sometimes tended to help private concerns to open branches in booming areas rather than to foster growth in less dynamic communities.

Important political factors underlie this situation. They arise, almost necessarily, out of the present structure of Spanish politics. Firstly, the planners selected the development areas without proper consultation with the relevant local authorities and hence without tapping possibly useful sources of local intelligence. The Provincial Governor of Zaragoza, for

---

[54]Cf. *Polos de Promoción y de Desarrollo Industrial*. Published by la Presidencia del Gobierno, Madrid, 1964. For a comment cf. R. Tamames, *España ante un Segundo Plan de Desarrollo, op. cit.*, pp. 118–27.

[55]Since these lines were written a *polo de desarrollo* has been created at Granada.

example, spoke against the location of a development area in his Province but his advice was neglected. This neglect of local opinion is partly explicable in terms of Spain's traditionally centralized decision-making processes. But, in this case, it is also explicable in terms of the internal politics of the Nationalist Régime. The planners, associated with Opus Dei, lack support within the traditional organs of local administration and have therefore sought to free themselves, as far as possible, from dependence upon them. It seems likely that the planners listened, instead, to allies in the business community. Some of these have certainly profited from government assistance to the designated areas. By the same token public enterprises, notably I.N.I., have not been systematically used as instruments for promoting regional development. This contrasts with the situation in France, for example. Ideological factors and the desire to curb I.N.I.'s political importance both prevent the present planners from using public enterprise to correct regional imbalances.

The desire to short-circuit local authorities also probably explains the steps the planners have taken for tackling the urban growth problems thrown up in the wake of industrial development. Specialized autonomous agencies, dependent on the Housing Ministry, have been created to provide housing and other necessary services. Their responsibilities overlap those of local corporations who are thus discouraged from providing much of the infrastructure required for development. The result has been to increase the size and, ultimately, the cost of the problems of urban growth. The second plan, in principle, addresses itself to this situation. It recognizes the part local authorities can play in the gauging and meeting of local needs. It is vague, however, about the means for doing this. Moreover, as the next chapter will show, it is doubtful if the present system of local government is capable of mobilizing and releasing local energies on the scale required. Without much more popular political participation, which the Nationalist Régime is unlikely to tolerate, local authorities are unlikely to develop the necessary political will or to command the necessary resources. Urban development problems will, meanwhile, probably become more acute.

A policy of industrial decentralization, included in the first plan, has tried to tackle difficulties of this sort, particularly around Madrid. The policy has largely consisted, however, of fiscal measures, and has had relatively little impact. Policy-makers have been cautious about the making of tax concessions and about the widespread dissemination of industry.

The recent regional development projects have also been criticized for the failure adequately to integrate them into the overall national development plans. The development areas have tended to be one more *ad hoc* administrative device to set alongside other instruments employed in the attack on underdevelopment. It is characteristic of the piecemeal approach to the problem adopted by the Spanish Government. Thus government departments concerned with industrial development have been inclined, in practice, to look at the problems of particular industries, on a national basis, and not to view them in the context of a policy for regional development. Likewise, policies for regional industrial growth have not been satisfactorily linked to agricultural, educational, road building and other developmental programmes.

The partial exception to this has been the plan for developing Gibraltar's long neglected hinterland. This, however, was drawn up in response to particular political problems. It seems designed to provide alternative employment for Spaniards now employed in Gibraltar and so to undermine the British position in that place. It was not seen as part of a general regional strategy.

Such experiences seem to confirm the view that a coherent national policy for the regions can only be elaborated and administered with the aid of a comprehensive system of socio-economic regional units. Such units could overcome the limitations imposed by working within the present provincial structure and could facilitate a more rational allocation of national resources.

No practical steps have in fact been taken in this direction. There is legal provision for special "public order" regions to be established for the purpose of confronting national emergencies, but even these have only a paper existence. The major difficulty is, again, political. The Nationalist régime has consistently opposed the creation of territorial units that could become a focus for the aspirations of local nationalists and a channel through which they could exert pressure. It is particularly feared that the Basques and Catalans might stimulate centrifugal forces within the Spanish polity. The régime is firmly opposed to fostering regional loyalties.

CONCLUSION

This evidence concerning regional development certainly seems to confirm that present political circumstances are not wholly propitious for experiments in "indicative planning". More widespread participation in the planning process seems necessary before policies can be developed that will command widespread support and so make possible a more effective mobilization of the nation's material and human resources. The necessary institutional changes, however, entail political risks unacceptable to the régime. The introduction of a form of collective bargaining, for example, indicates that policy-makers are prepared to accept some relaxation of authoritarian controls as the price to be paid for their type of planning. But the failure to implement a thorough trade-union reform and to create regional planning units exemplifies the difficulty the planners have in facing up to the logic of the trends they have themselves initiated. They cannot create institutions and foster political participation that might facilitate the planning process but which could also imperil the régime's existence. On the other hand, the régime has firmly established the legitimacy of direct state intervention amongst interests which had once seriously questioned it. Thus future debates are likely to concern the extension of present commitments and the better administration of existing programmes rather than their complete reversal. Such debates should be less disruptive than those of the pre-Civil-war era.

CHAPTER 8

Local Administration

BASIC PRINCIPLES

The origins of Spain's local government system can be traced back to the early nineteenth century. It rests on principles consciously borrowed from France. Efforts were made to copy the Napoleonic model at the local as well as the national level.

The first important development occurred in 1812. The Cortes of Cadiz then envisaged a territorial reorganization based on France's system of *departements* and *communes*. Permanent implementation of the system was deferred, however, until 1833. Political instability permitted opponents of change to fight back. Even in 1833 there was not a wholly clean sweep.[1]

In 1833 the nation was divided into legally uniform provinces (now fifty in number). They were intended to provide convenient units for the administration of state services. The provinces were subdivided into municipalities which also had a uniform legal status. No legal distinction was drawn between urban and rural areas. They too were conceived as units for the administration of state services. But, unlike provinces, they were from the start also recognized as local government units. Municipal authorities were representatives of the State but also possessed some independent rule-making powers.

These structures represented efforts to impose a rational territorial system upon the map of Spain. In practice difficulties arose. Thus legally uniform provinces and municipalities have widely differing areas, socio-economic structures and financial resources. The bulk of Spain's municipalities are in poor, thinly populated rural areas but their powers and institutions are

[1] For the foundations of the system cf. A. Mesa Segura, *Labor Administrativa de Javier de Burgos*, Madrid, 1946.

essentially the same as those of densely populated urban municipalities. Differences are of detail rather than principle. Only the municipalities of Madrid and Barcelona depart significantly from the rule. Likewise, the backward rural provinces such as those in Estremadura have the same legal status as the developed Catalan provinces.

On the other hand, relics of the Ancien Régime survive to complicate the issue. There are still instances of territory, legally belonging to one province, actually forming an enclave within the territory of another. Of greater importance is the special position of the Provinces of Navarra and Alava. They have kept traditional institutions and financial arrangements unknown elsewhere. They stand as reminders of the extent to which traditional practices survive within the Spanish administrative system.[2]

Strong local pressures have deterred governments from pushing the rationalization of territorial structures to a logical conclusion. The cases of Navarra and Alava are, however, exceptional for their provincial boundaries corresponded closely with those of former territorial units. Most provinces were largely artificial creations, established primarily for administrative convenience. The subsequent organization of political life on a provincial basis has forged some sense of communal identity and created vested interests in the survival of the present system of provinces. Nevertheless, in most regions of Spain there is still a much stronger popular attachment to the local township or village community.

The key figures in Spain's local administrative system also have their French equivalents. Thus there is a hierarchical chain of command stretching from the national capital through the province to the municipality. At each level the State is represented by an executive agent who is responsible, in principle, for translating its will into action. The State's chief provincial representative is the Provincial Governor, who corresponds to the French Prefect. Officially Governors are appointed by the Head of State though for most purposes they depend upon the Interior Ministry. They have a general responsibility for the smooth running of the *Administración Pereférica*. Above all, they are charged with maintaining public order.

The State's municipal representative is the Mayor. He is responsible, subject to the Governor's supervision, for enforcing official policies and maintaining the peace. However, the modern Spanish Mayor has always

[2]Cf. F. Gómez Anton, *El Consejo Foral Administrativo de Navarra*, Madrid, 1962.

had dual functions. He has been the State's local representative and the President and chief executive officer of a locally elected council, or *Ayuntamiento*, with its own legally defined powers. In practice the two roles are not always clearly distinguishable. Prestige accruing from activities in the first sphere can reinforce his authority in the second. Nevertheless, when acting as a local official the Mayor technically remains the *Ayuntamiento*'s servant.[3]

Initially the powers of *Ayuntamientos* were very limited, both in theory and practice. Legislation enacted in 1924 by Primo de Rivera's régime sought, however, to extend their powers.[4] "A general empowering clause" apparently conceded sweeping powers covering most matters of local interest. It was hoped that municipalities would contribute to Primo de Rivera's plans for national regeneration. This measure remains the basis of current legislation regulating municipal administration.[5] Its practical implications will be examined later. It is sufficient to observe that most *Ayuntamientos* in reality have very limited freedom of action.

Organs of local government at the provincial level have been still slower in developing. Initially provincial councils, or *Diputaciones*, were simply advisory bodies. They advised Governors on political questions and assisted them in the discharge of their administrative obligations. By 1882 *Diputaciones* had their own legal personalities and decision-making powers, but significant extensions of authority only came in 1925.[6] *Diputaciones* were then enpowered to take initiatives in all fields of general provincial concern. The Governor remained as President of the *Diputación* but, in matters of local interest, he technically became its servant. Post-Civil-war legislation embodied these principles. It even appeared to go a stage further for the office of President of the *Diputación* was created, with its own executive powers, as something quite distinct from the Governor's office. In principle Governors remained solely as "honorary Presidents".

These changes ostensibly converted *Diputaciones Provinciales* into significant political and administrative institutions. In reality principle and practice diverge more at the provincial than the municipal level. Outside

[3]For the Mayor's powers cf. *Manual de Alcaldes y Concejales*, Madrid, 1953.
[4]Cf. Estatuto Municipal, 1924.
[5]Ley de Régimen Local, 24 June 1955.
[6]Estatuto Provincial, 1925.

the Catalan and Basque Provinces, with their distinctive political traditions, *Diputaciones* have contributed little to provincial development.

The framework of administrative law within which the institutions of local government operate also owes a debt to the Napoleonic State.[7] The chief point to bear in mind is that local authorities are considered organs of the State. At all times they are conceived as part of a corpus of institutions deriving their being and authority from the State. This has two practical implications of importance. Firstly, local officials, when acting as representatives of the State, are subject to orders from superiors in the official chain of command. The former have as much discretion as their superiors permit. Equally, the State's local representatives are empowered, subject to the supervision of higher authorities, to make use of those legal powers traditionally held in reserve which have been generally regarded as falling within the executive's exclusive domain. They may, above all, invoke the State's "Police Powers". Secondly, even when local authorities act as autonomous agencies the State keeps their activities under regular supervision. "Tutelage" powers are retained to ensure authorities conform to the State's concept of the public good. Within their own spheres of competence local authorities are technically free to take initiatives of their own choosing but the State preserves controls designed to ensure that they have acted legally and in the public interest.

It is now necessary to account for the gap between precept and practice which has characterized the workings of Spanish local government. Institutions copied from the French have proved less effective than their prototypes. When set in Spain's distinctive historical, cultural and socio-economic context they developed along different lines. The factors underlying these distinctive developments need to be identified.[8]

Of outstanding importance has been the sharpness of political conflict and the "particularism" noted earlier in this study. These factors particularly affected the way in which the office of Governor developed. The development of the office had far-reaching consequences for all provincial and municipal institutions.

[7]For a discussion of basic principles cf. E. García de Enterría, *La Administración Española, op. cit.,* pp. 121–72.

[8]For historical background cf. J. Costa, *Oliquarquía y Caciquismo,* Madrid, 1902: J. Chamberlain, *El Atraso de España,* Valencia, 1902: R. W. Kern, *Caciquismo versus Self-government; The Crisis of Liberalism and Local Government in Spain,* Chicago, 1966; and H. Puget, *Le Gouvernement local en Espagne,* Paris, 1920.

The appointment of Governor was first conceived as a professional administrator to some extent removed from partisan conflicts. He was envisaged as the driving force behind provincial development and as a provider of administrative continuity and expertise. In reality Governors became strictly political appointees occupying pivotal positions in the system of *caciquismo*. They were the Government's instruments for dispensing patronage at the local level and as such were more interested in maintaining the government of the day than in resolving long-term administrative problems. They themselves received their appointments as rewards for political support rather than as opportunities for public service and, by the same token, governmental changes in Madrid entailed a wholesale change of Governors in the provinces. Equally, the staff of the Governor's headquarters (the *Gobierno Civil*) was recruited from amongst his own political hangers-on and not from trained civil servants. The administrative functions they took most seriously were those associated with maintaining order—like the handling of strikes or the licensing of public meetings—which had an obviously political content.

Partisan considerations also entered into the Governor's dealings with local authorities. He was at the centre of interdependent patronage networks that provided a link between national and local politics. A change of government at the national level would soon be reflected locally for Governors manipulated local elections in order to pack authorities with their own camp followers. Failing that, they found pretexts for invoking tutelage powers with a view to dissolving local councils and replacing their members with their own adherents. Thus Governors were the key figures in a local "spoils system". Its operations led to a pattern of local politics that reflected shifts in the national political élite rather than genuine changes in local opinion.

In such circumstances few Governors had the time, inclination or expertise to master basic administrative problems. Indeed, some commentators feel that the operations of the local "spoils system" may have been one reason for this century's disastrous events. Professional administrators might have provided some of the underlying continuity of effort needed to reduce explosive economic and social problems to more manageable proportions. As it was, the prizes at stake had the effect of exacerbating political conflicts. Equally serious, perhaps, was the tendency to breed or reinforce a popular scepticism concerning the efficacy of administrative action and a widespread indifference toward the official organs of local government. There were strong communal loyalties and considerable interest in conflicts of the parish-pump variety, but outsiders, including those identified with the State, remained suspect. In many regions indifference or hostility to innovation also remained well rooted.

Caciquismo as a system no longer exists. Growing urbanization and political awareness were in the process of undermining the basis of the system before Primo de Rivera's régime and the Republic put an end to it. The agrarian, commercial and professional interests who supplied many of the traditional *caciques* are amongst the Nationalist Régime's supporters, but *caciquismo* in its "classic" form has not been revived. Indeed, the contemporary equivalents of the traditional *caciques* are now often absent from formal positions of local political leadership. They seem to have such confidence in existing political arrangements that they remain content to exert informal pressures through personal contacts at the local, provincial and national levels. Even then they are not guaranteed a veto power in local affairs. Local authorities are now frequently in the hands of local political élites thrown up during or after the Civil War. Nevertheless, *caciquismo* has warranted some attention in this discussion of contemporary institutions for, as will become apparent, it embodied or fostered attitudes and administrative practices that have outlived the system itself. They are deeply embedded in the fabric of Spain's local political life and signify the existence of an underlying continuity in the Spanish state's approach to the management of local affairs.

Of crucial importance is the Governor's still essentially political role. Despite some recent efforts to reconvert him into a figure resembling the French Prefect, the political rather than the administrative dimensions of his job remain of greatest importance. No equivalent of the Prefectoral Corps has emerged. On the contrary, since 1940 the office of Governor has been merged with that of Provincial Head of the Movement. Governors are now *ex officio* the provincial chieftains of Spain's one legally tolerated political movement. The background of most post-war Governors underlines the continuing importance of political criteria. Many have previously occupied political posts in local government, the Movement and the official *Sindicatos* or have been recruited from the military. Only a relatively small minority has been seconded from the civil service.[9] Until 1958, at least, political criteria also remained present in appointments to the staff of the *Gobierno Civil*.

The system for appointing Governors has some bearing on their still high casualty rate. The average period in office is five years and shorter spans are common. Sometimes this can be explained by the intractability of local problems. In Catalonia, for example, labour disturbances and nationalist manifestations are likely to bring Governors into frequent clashes with local opinion. Thus they may quite frequently pay the price for failing to forewarn the Government about embarrassing crises or be sacrificed as a tacit concession to local opinion. But the high turnover is often attributable to the calibre of appointees. Given the job's present dual nature, responsibility for appointments has to be shared between the Interior Minister and the Secretary-General of the Movement. As they are generally of different political complexions they are usually forced to settle upon compromise candidates of second-class stature. These may lack the administrative skills and political finesse needed to meet the varied and possibly conflicting demands of their office. Difficulties may be encountered, for example, in attempts to mediate between state field services and local authorities. Failure to promote local interests could lower the Governor's prestige and the chances of further fruitful co-operation with local authorities. Alternatively clashes with ministerial agents could create powerful enemies in Madrid. Similar difficulties arise when seeking to reconcile responsibility for enforcing the State's policies with the need to warn superiors about obstacles to their successful implementation. Governors are not necessarily well prepared to undertake such tasks.

The development of the *Administración Periférica* has been profoundly affected by the political nature of the Governor's office.[10] Theoretically the Governor has a general responsibility for the smooth running of all state services operating within his Province. In practice lack of administrative continuity and expertise and the low priority given to administrative problems have permitted field services to escape the Governor's control. Indeed the absence of effective provincial co-ordinating agents

[9] On the Governor cf. F. Herrero Tejedor, *La Figura del Gobernador Civil en la Legislación Española. Problemas Políticos de la Vida Local*, Tomo III, 1963, pp. 9–45.

[10] Cf. E. García de Enterría, *La Administración Española*, *op. cit.*, pp. 85–118. Information supplied by the Interior Ministry has been of great help in assessing the Governor's role.

itself encouraged that fragmentation of the *Administración Periférica* noted elsewhere. Ministries, commencing with the Finance Ministry, removed their provincial dependencies from effective local control or supervision. They have tended to by-pass Governors and to communicate directly with their own provincial agents. The latter have taken their orders from officials scattered amongst competing ministries in Madrid rather than from a single locally based agency close to the local problems. The multiplication of *ad hoc* regional units has made the position of Governors still less tenable. It has been difficult for them to control field services whose headquarters may lie outside their own Provinces.

The net result of this has been an administration whose activities at the local level are poorly co-ordinated and within which decision-making is highly centralized. This has several obvious implications for provincial development. Firstly, coherent and sustained attacks upon provincial problems have either been lacking or have been hampered by administrative conflicts. Governors, for example, lost their "financial tutelage" powers to the Finance Ministry's Delegados Provinciales, thus leaving this department to vie with the Interior Ministry for control over local authorities. The outcome has necessarily been inconsistencies in official policy toward authorities. Erosion of the Governor's authority also impedes a rational processing of the demands which local authorities may make upon the State. Instead of channelling demands through Governors, authorities frequently prefer to approach leading bureaucrats, businessmen, military commanders or even Churchmen possessing direct access to the nation's political élites. The allocation of resources for projects of local interest may therefore depend as much on the influence such individuals can exercise in government circles as on any careful evaluation of local needs. By the same token no one administrative agency has been in a position to take an overall view of a province's needs. Governors have been unable to compel the representatives of central government bodies to pool their knowledge of local conditions.

Governors have also lacked the means to compel the *Administración Periférica* to co-operate with local authorities in the resolution of common problems. Indeed, the *Administración Periférica* has in practice tended to discourage authorities from assuming responsibility for local development. Ministries have employed their rule-making powers to retain or assert direct control over the administration of questions of local interest rather than delegating responsibility to those most immediately affected. Sometimes the administrative corps, in search of extended spheres of influence, have entirely removed services of local interest from local control. Local services have often been wholly superseded or are overshadowed by corresponding state services.

The attitudes of the *Administacin Periférica* explain one particularly distinctive feature of Spanish local government. It is the system adopted for associating local interests with the administration of state services. Instead of working through or consulting with locally elected authorities each field service has tended to establish its own *ad hoc Juntas* or consultative councils. They have been created at the provincial and municipal levels for such matters as education, health, welfare and town planning. *Juntas* include representatives of local authorities but these are normally state appointees and they are frequently in a minority. Provincial *Juntas* are usually dominated by members of the administrative corps. There is certainly no question of organic links existing between the *Juntas* and local authorities.

Provincial *Juntas* are usually presided over by the Governor. Technically they exist to assist him in the administration of services. In practice Governors have lacked the expertise to bargain effectively with *Junta* members drawn from the civil service. Until recently, at least, the large number of specialized *Juntas* also prevented adequate supervision. The *Juntas* consequently became instruments for defending the autonomy of specialized administrative agencies.

Municipal *Juntas* were created to assist Mayors in the administration of state services at the municipal level. They were usually appointed by, and dependent upon, the corresponding provincial *Juntas*. Though sometimes financed by *Ayuntamientos* they operated independently of them. Thus they served as instruments of central control over local affairs. They were used by government departments, often unaware of local conditions, to heap tasks upon the State's local servants. They ranged from the gathering of statistics to the administration of lotteries. Such tasks were often given to technically unprepared local personnel whose energies were consumed by the performance of routine administrative functions and who were therefore diverted from tackling pressing local problems. Provincial Governors were in no position to prevent these developments.

These generalizations about Governors require two important

qualifications. Firstly, all Governors, despite the erosion of their authority, still retain important functions. As the chief provincial guardians of public order they possess considerable discretionary powers. They are, for example, the local licensing authorities for public meetings. They also play an important part in the supervision of local authorities. As official heads of the *Administración Periférica* they retain important residual responsibilities for advising the Government, on general provincial problems. They remain the chief single source of information on provincial affairs and, in the case of energetic governors, can lobby on behalf of local interests. As "Provincial Heads of the Movement" they also have an important role to play in local political life. Secondly, there are some provinces where the Governor virtually remains a satrap. These are economically backward, thinly populated and predominantly rural provinces containing no interests capable of challenging his authority and few influential groups with direct access to government circles. The Castilian Province of Soria is one example. Here the Governor remains the chief link with the centre and there is such limited political and administrative activity that issues of more than local significance rarely arise. Such provinces, significantly enough, remain the most neglected. As long as order is maintained the Government tends to overlook their difficulties. The political incentives to take drastic action are lacking.

The present structure of local politics and the Governor's political role now require attention. Crucial to existing arrangements is the system for appointing the chief executive officers of local authorities. The Presidents of *Diputaciones* are appointed for indefinite periods by the Interior Ministry. They can be removed, on the Governor's recommendation, at any time. In practice they are usually figures of provincial rather than national importance. Their survival consequently depends upon maintaining good relations with the Governor.

Since the Civil War Mayors have also been appointed. In major urban centres appointments are made by the Interior Minister and elsewhere by Governors. In the first case national political figures may be selected but in the second appointees are strictly local leaders. In small rural municipalities, where political labels lack relevance, their allegiance to the Movement may only be nominal. This is in spite of the practice of appointing Mayors as the Movement's local chieftains. All appointments may be rescinded at any time. The State therefore has a network of local agents ultimately incapable of opposing official policies.

Periods in office depend on the nature of the area. In rural areas lengthy periods are common but in large urban centres the turnover is fairly rapid.[11] One explanatory factor is that efforts to resolve urban problems are more likely to encounter opposition from organized and influential interests, in the business community for example. Such opposition can erode the confidence of their superiors. It is in rural areas, however, that recruitment of suitable candidates is most difficult. Political apathy and fear of popular opprobrium are important factors in this situation. Appointments usually entail consultation with such local leaders as the Movement's officials, members of the *Diputación Provincial* and perhaps the Civil Guard officer or priest. This ensures that appointees have at least a minimum of local support. Nevertheless, they are generally selected from very small local political élites.

Local councils are elected but the electoral system ensures that members are also unlikely to challenge existing political institutions.[12] Representation is based on the principles of "Organic Democracy"—derived from corporatist theories. Thus *Ayuntamientos* are composed of three *tercios*, in principle representing the interests of basic social groupings, namely the family, the official *sindicatos* and professional or commercial interests. The family *tercio* is popularly elected but candidates require the sponsorship of specified local office-holders. The co-option of allies of entrenched local élites is thus assured. Elections in large urban municipalities, at least, are contested but only by rival factions within the Movement. In most rural areas uncontested elections are the norm. The other two *tercios* are indirectly elected which makes the element of co-option still more pronounced.

The Mayor is generally at the centre of this co-option process. As local Head of the Movement he can, in consultation with the Governor, regulate the dispensing of political patronage. His freedom of action is not

[11]For evidence on this point cf. the unpublished study by Juan J. Linz, "Factores Humanos en el Desarollo Económico produced for la Presidencia del Gobierno".

[12]The operations of local councils are discussed at much greater length in my own unpublished doctoral thesis, "The Legal and Political Institutions of Spanish Local Government", Manchester University, 1969.

unlimited. In urban areas with a relatively active political life prudence may dictate the co-option of elements representing all major factions within the Movement and, in elections for the family *tercio*, the Mayor's candidates may be defeated by spokesmen for rival groups. Nevertheless, the Mayor's influence is frequently decisive.

Ayuntamientos are not entirely unrepresentative of local interests. Members of the family *tercio* sometimes feel they have special mandates to press communal demands. Where the *sindicatos* have obtained some acceptance their representatives possibly speak for portions of the membership. Finally, in areas like Catalonia where the activities of interest groups are relatively intense, representatives of commercial and professional groups may speak for limited local interests. Large sectors of the population, however, are obviously prevented from obtaining effective representation.[13]

The entire membership of *Diputaciones Provinciales* is indirectly elected. Two-thirds of their members represent municipalities and the rest come, in equal proportions, from the *sindicatos* and professional or business associations. In both cases it is the Governor who is in a position to exercise a decisive influence. Particularly in the case of municipal representatives he can to a considerable extent determine the outcome. These representatives are chosen by an electoral college which, *de facto*, is normally dominated by local Mayors who owe their appointments to the Governor. His freedom of action is chiefly limited by the existence, in the electoral colleges, of a weighted voting system favouring heavily populated municipalities. Thus *Diputaciones* tend to represent the large urban rather than the small rural municipalities.

The electoral system makes it likely that executive officials will dominate the life of local corporations. The absence of formal political groupings reinforces this tendency. Theorists supposed that the *tercios* would act as cohesive units but in practice cleavages cut across these formal lines and largely depend on the issues or personalities involved. It is possible, for example, that syndical representatives will be more disposed than spokesmen for business and professional interests to accept extensions of public services, but clear patterns are not discernible. Alliances so fluctuate that

[13]Popular reaction can perhaps be measured by the fact that, despite a legal obligation to vote, there was an average national turnout of only 48·6 per cent in municipal elections held in 1970.

only the Mayor or, at the provincial level, the President of the *Diputación* is able to mobilize support for general plans of action.

Procedural devices and a battery of legal powers further strengthen the bargaining position of executive officials. For example, in all municipalities with populations of over 2000 the Mayor selects a Permanent Commission which in effect acts as an "inner cabinet". In principle it relieves the full council of responsibility for routine business but in practice leaves the formulation of policy, and responsibility for overseeing its execution, in the hands of the Mayor's chosen allies. Likewise, the Mayor is empowered to suspend the execution of decisions considered illegal or outside the sphere of competence of local authorities. In theory the Mayor uses this power as the State's local representative charged with the maintenance of legality, but in practice it can become a way of buying time in disputes with *Ayuntamientos*. Thus those excluded from the Mayor's confidence are frequently impotent and their only form of protest is to boycott council meetings. The most they can hope for is to participate in specialized committees (set up to examine particular problems or areas of policy) but these are created at the Mayor's bidding and are not an integral feature of the local government system. Opposition capable of inducing a Governor to remove his appointees normally comes from influential groups outside the *Ayuntamiento*.

At the provincial level decision-making effectively occurs within seven statutory commissions whose composition is decided by the President of the *Diputación*. He also has legal powers permitting great freedom of action. For example, contracts of less than a year's duration can be signed on his own initiative. In practice there seems nothing to prevent such contracts being perpetually renewed. Limits to the President's freedom of action are chiefly set by the Governor. His role in the electoral process makes the *Diputación* peculiarly susceptible to his influence. The initiation of policy is often traceable to the Governor and his approval is usually necessary for the success of other initiatives.

The institutions described above very strictly limit the possibilities of popular participation in the management of local affairs and, particularly at the provincial level, they seem remote from most citizens. They have not been able, therefore, to overcome the indifference or hostility towards official agencies that have traditionally characterized Spanish local government. By the same token local authorities are not subject to effective popular pressures and have few incentives to make use of their apparently considerable legal powers.

In some regions of Spain (Catalonia and the Basque Country being notable exceptions) many municipalities have not provided the most basic services of local interest even though the State officially regards them as constituting "minimal obligations".[14] Running water, drainage and street lighting fall into this category. Large urban municipalities have generally fulfilled these obligations but most of them have been cautious about the assumption of additional responsibilities. Such inertia is partly due to chronic financial shortages but it has also been due to the lack of an effective demand for action.

Another important inhibiting factor has been the State's attitude towards local initiatives. As already noted the State has assumed increasing responsibility for mounting services of local interest, using special *Juntas* as its chosen instrument. This arrangement meant bypassing locally elected bodies but initially, at least, the *ad hoc Juntas* provided for some local participation in decision-making. Local interests (including councillors) shared in the application of national policies to local conditions and could draw the State's attention to local requirements.

This century, however, has seen an increasing tendency for the State entirely to remove the administration of its services from local control and to place them into the hands of the *Administración Periférica*. The element of local participation has therefore been reduced. *Ad hoc Juntas* (at the municipal level) survive only on paper or, at best, have a marginal influence upon official policy. Such extensions of the influence of the *Administración Periférica* have ensured the presence of certain minimal standards once absent. State-employed primary-school teachers, for example, are now guaranteed regular payment. On the other hand, there are now no official channels through which local interests may be asserted and through which the State may readily identify local needs. Faced with this situation most local authorities fall back on inactivity. They could provide educational and welfare services, for example, to supplement those of the State, but in practice they contribute little to the resolution of social problems. Municipalities are similarly discouraged from creating

[14]Such minimal services are now usually provided but, as will be seen, this has frequently been the result of state and not local initiatives.

commercial undertakings.[15] Branches of the central administration, anxious to extend their spheres of influence, have used their rule-making powers to remove entire spheres of activity from local control. Local transport undertakings, for example, have been converted into concessionaires of the Ministry of Public Works. Without local control over such services municipalities have lacked the incentive to launch coherent attacks upon the problems of urban growth.

On paper deficiencies in municipal services could be supplied by forming special "inter-municipal associations".[16] Ample legal provision is made for forming such associations on either a voluntary or a compulsory basis. In reality little use has been made of these provisions. Wealthy municipalities decline to subsidize poorer neighbours, rural communities resist the embrace of urban areas and in face of intense communal loyalties the State has generally preferred not to use compulsion—even the present authoritarian régime has been reluctant to offend local susceptibilities. Since 1966 financial incentives have been available to encourage the formation of voluntary groupings, but without basic changes in local attitudes these may well prove ineffective. Likewise, the State has not pursued any consistent policy for merging municipalities. On the contrary many unviable administrative entities continue to exist and local services which could be provided by larger units remain lacking. Proposals have been made for grouping municipalities into new supra-municipal and multi-purpose territorial units, capable of supporting a wide range of services, but such suggestions remain in the realm of theory.

Most *Diputaciones Provinciales* have also been inactive. At the minimum they are expected, by law, to supply basic health and welfare services, provincial fire services and a provincial road network. In reality few *Diputaciones* have fulfilled such "minimal obligations" and health and welfare services and road construction are now largely the responsibility of central government agencies over which the *Diputaciones* have no control. Few *Diputaciones* go much beyond the legal minimum.

Following the Civil War, attempts were made to find anew role for

[15]Cf. E. García de Enterría, "La Actividad Industrial y Mercantil de los Municipios", *Revista de Administración Pública*, No. 17, Madrid, 1955, pp. 88–136.
[16]Cf. R. Martin Mateo, *La Comarcalización de los Pequeños Municipios*, Madrid, 1964.

the *Diputaciones*. Thus they were made responsible for assisting backward municipalities in the planning and creation of new services. They were required to set aside fixed sums for this purpose and were granted new sources of finance to make the idea viable. They were also required to subsidize municipalities unable to balance their budgets. In practice these schemes proved disappointing. Political pressures exercised within the *Diputaciones* frequently meant that assistance went to large municipalities least needing help. Also there were municipalities who deliberately left their budgets unbalanced in order to qualify for aid. The provincial administrators were unable or unwilling to check such abuses. Finally, the *Diputaciones*, partly as a result of their own inertia and maladministration, had to face increasing competition in this field from the State's *Administración Periférica*.

Initially it was intended that the *Administración Periférica* should help the *Diputaciones* to discharge their new responsibilities. Special *Comisiones Provinciales de Servicios Técnicos* (C.P.S.T.), composed largely of representatives of the State's field services, were established (in 1945) to act as advisory bodies and to execute provincial plans for new services of local interest.[17] The administrative corps, however, not only resisted co-operation with each other but also with the *Diputaciones*. Ultimately, in 1957, the C.P.S.T. assumed almost complete responsibility for "provincial plans of works and services". The State largely superseded local authorities in the mounting of services of the most basic kind. Only municipalities able to meet the bulk of the cost of new investments could, in practice, take independent initiatives.

Subsequently, in 1958, the C.P.S.T. became instruments designed principally to enable Provincial Governors to assert more effective control over the *Administración Periférica*. The Governor became the C.P.S.T.'s President and was empowered to veto the decisions of field agencies and to resolve "demarcation disputes". To assist him in these tasks the *Gobierno Civil* was provided with more professional staff and many of the *ad hoc* provincial *Juntas* were replaced by specialized commissions of the C.P.S.T. These measures have had some effect. Field agencies now rarely act in open defiance of Provincial Governors and the latter are generally better informed of the activities of the *Administración Periférica*. But the

[17]Cf. R. Calvo de Alcocer, *Las Comisiones Provinciales de Servicios Técnicos*, Madrid, 1966.

C.P.S.T. has not become a truly effective co-ordinating agent able to take an overall view of each Province's needs. Field agencies concentrate on their specialized activities and give a low priority to planning undertaken by the C.P.S.T. Governors, for their part, still lack the skills and the technical advisers needed to bargain on equal terms with members of the administrative corps. Thus earlier centralizing tendencies have not been reversed.

THE ADMINISTRATIVE CONTROL OF LOCAL AUTHORITIES[18]

The freedom of action of local authorities has also been reduced by a growing tendency for the central government to assume the right to lay down administrative regulations governing activities traditionally regarded as being of purely local interest. This has been particularly apparent in the case of the use municipal authorities can make of the "Police Power". When using this power to preserve public order, local officials have traditionally acted on behalf of the State and this remains the case. Thus Provincial Governors or the Minister of the Interior can completely supersede local officials when it comes to action designed to combat strikes, opposition activities and other major disturbances of the established order. Equally, Mayors may be obliged to act in accordance with instructions received from their superiors. Traditionally, however, municipal authorities have been able to use the Police Power, on their own behalf, and to deal with matters considered of purely local interest. Under this heading authorities have been able to act on their own initiative to safeguard public health, safety, morality and peace within their respective localities. For this purpose *Ayuntamientos* have passed special by-laws, which the Mayor has then been expected to enforce, or failing that, the Mayor himself has been empowered to act on his own account. In principle such responsibilities constituted one of the chief *raisons d'être* of municipal councils. In practice these responsibilities were often poorly discharged. Most small rural municipalities had no properly drafted by-laws. In many areas local safety and health regulations were no more than a series of *ad hoc* decisions taken by a series of Mayors. Partly in response to this situation (and partly because of pressure from administrative corps

[18]Cf. F. Albi, *La Crisis del Municipalismo*, Madrid, 1966, pp. 445–71.

seeking to extend their spheres of influence) the central government has increasingly expected authorities to conform to uniform minimal standards laid down at the national level. Thus the control of pollution, for example, is now a matter largely for the national government. To cite another example, local slaughterhouses have to be constructed in accordance with standards laid down and enforced in Madrid. In matters of this kind relatively little local discretion now remains. This has helped to raise technical standards but it has probably done it at the price of reinforcing the inertia and apathy frequently demonstrated by local authorities in the face of administrative problems. The referring to Madrid of decisions which could be handled at the provincial level acts as a disincentive to local initiatives.[19] It also tends to discourage local interests from actively co-operating with the central administration in the tackling of common problems.

PERSONNEL[20]

Until 1924 the recruitment and treatment of non-elected local officials was the field in which municipal and provincial authorities enjoyed the greatest freedom of action. They used this freedom to perpetuate a spoils system for some time after it had disappeared at the national level. The results of this system were low levels of administrative efficiency and little continuity of administrative effort. Officials who regarded their appointments as pieces of personal booty rather than opportunities for public service were unlikely to persuade local politicians to create effective local services and were unqualified to administer them. To deal with this problem Primo de Rivera's régime laid the foundations of a career structure for local officials which succeeding governments have built upon. Thus the three key permanent officials in the Spanish local government system (to be found at both the provincial and municipal levels) now belong to administrative corps dependent upon the Interior Ministry. The latter recruits and trains corps members and is ultimately responsible for appointing them to, or removing them from, particular posts. The

---

[19]The complexity of the relevant legal provisions is also a disincentive to action, particularly in the case of smaller and rural municipalities lacking adequate reserves of technical expertise.

[20]Cf. F. Albi, *op. cit.*, p. 473 and following pages.

Ministry may consult with the relevant local authorities but it has the last word.

The officials in question are the Secretary, who is the senior permanent official at the local level with responsibility for offering legal advice and with overall responsibility for the management of local services; the *Interventor* (or auditor) who is the principal financial adviser, and the *Depositario* who organizes the collection of local taxes. Their mode of appointment has ensured a general rise in standards of administrative competence and probity. But, for several reasons, traditional difficulties have not been entirely eliminated. Firstly, except in the most important authorities, senior officials are usually recruited from unsuccessful candidates for the central administration and so are of a lower calibre than the latter's servants. Lower financial rewards and the disadvantages of living in the provinces drive away the potentially best recruits. Secondly, there is a chronic shortage of personnel. Many small municipalities have no more than a secretary and in some cases he is an unqualified part-time functionary. Thirdly, national corps members, particularly in small towns or rural areas, may be regarded as "intruders" thus making difficult fruitful co-operation with local politicians. In most cases officials only have as much influence as the politicians permit them, so this can be a significant factor. An energetic secretary can be a major force in local affairs but this is not always the case. Finally, corps members are still paid locally and so can be subject to considerable moral pressures. The Secretary, for example, is legally obliged to advise the Provincial Governor of irregular decisions taken by a local council, but informal pressures can make difficult the discharge of this duty. Equally, officials fulfilling this obligation may find future co-operation with the politicians virtually impossible and so they may feel forced to apply for a transfer.

Such problems are perhaps more acute in the case of the great majority of more junior officials who are still recruited by the local authorities themselves, subject only to very general conditions laid down at the centre. In their case remnants of the spoils system probably survive.[21] Such officials also continue to be poorly paid and so resort to multiple job-holding.[22]

[21]The State itself has encouraged this, for in 1947 a law reserved a fixed quota of local appointments for supporters of the Nationalist cause during the Civil War.

[22]Chapter 5 for a discussion of multiple job-holding at the national level and its likely effects.

The strengthening of central controls cannot guarantee the abandonment of such practices. This is only likely to come with a radical change in the political attitudes commonly found at the local level. Such a change must entail new understandings of the nature and purpose of authority. A political system which excludes most citizens from local decision-making is unlikely to encourage this reconsideration of attitudes.

TUTELAGE

The State also seeks to control the activities of local authorities through its tutelage powers. These are of essentially two kinds: political and financial. Political tutelage is exercised by Provincial Governors and financial tutelage by the *Delegados Provinciales* of the Finance Ministry. Initially the Governor discharged both functions. The present division of responsibility indicates the extent to which the Governor's authority has been eroded. It may also be regarded as both effect and cause of a situation in which the Ministries of the Interior and Finance compete for control over local corporations. Such competition makes it hard for the central administration to pursue a consistent policy toward local authorities. The Interior Ministry may have some interest in creating viable local administrative units and so grants them certain powers and responsibilities, but the Finance Ministry, whose primary concerns are curbing public expenditure and preserving potential sources of revenue for the central government, often uses its tutelage powers to discourage local initiatives. The result is oscillations in official policy or a lack of the resources needed to give substance to the concept of local autonomy. The conflicting demands of financial prudence and local needs are more likely to be satisfactorily reconciled if tutelage powers are operated by one official who can take an informed and overall view of a Province's problems. At present the Finance Ministry and its *Delegados* take their decisions on the basis of their own rather narrowly defined technical concerns and with a partial understanding of local needs. Thus, for example, localities of quite different socio-economic structures may be compelled to draft their budgets in accordance with rigidly uniform rules or may be confronted with unrealistic financial demands.[23]

[23]Because of this municipalities have been known to draw up budgets for official inspection and then work on the basis of quite distinct provisions. This type of

Political tutelage is of two kinds: controls over the personnel of locally elected authorities and over their decisions. Under the first heading comes the power of Governors, or the Interior Ministry, to suspend or dismiss individual councillors or entire councils. Thus councillors may be removed for neglect of duty or for activities deemed prejudicial to public order. Such vaguely defined criteria, in the absence of an effective appeals procedure, obviously empowers the State to remove any serious opponents of official policies. In practice, however, such powers are now little used. They were used extensively during the last century and the early part of this. They could be used again in a political crisis. But at present Mayors and Presidents of *Diputaciones Provinciales* can be removed under the guise of a routine change of personnel. Thus the State is not compelled to admit to a lack of confidence in the officials of its own choosing. Equally, ordinary council members can normally be neutralized by informal pressures or can be prevented from standing for re-election. Opposition groups within local councils invariably find themselves in a minority and absenting themselves from meetings is about the only possible form of protest.

Three types of control are exercised over the decisions of local authorities. Most decisions are simply scrutinized to see if they are in any way illegal, exceed the powers of the local authority or constitute a threat to public order.[24] The execution of irregular decisions may be suspended by the President of the local corporation or, failing that by the Governor, pending a final decision from an administrative court.[25] The Secretary is responsible for warning the politicians against likely irregularities and if his advice is ignored he must notify the Governor. The latter is supposed to check all decisions (or at least all those which are not of a primarily financial nature) taken by authorities within his province. Such controls can guard against unduly arbitrary behaviour by locally elected bodies. There are, however, several difficulties. Firstly, Mayors can use their

---

behaviour clearly points to the possibility of corruption in the management of local affairs. It is probable that corruption is now much less prevalent than it was in the immediate post-Civil-war years, but informed observers still point to instances of misappropriated funds not only at the municipal but also at the provincial level.

[24]The last of these categories would seem to give almost unlimited scope for state intervention but in practice it seems to be rarely invoked.

[25]Cf. the next chapter for a discussion of administrative courts.

powers of suspension to buy time in conflicts with their councils rather than as a legal control. It is the last card to play in the event of *Ayuntamientos* passing decisions which they oppose. Secondly, the present Governors do not always have the expertise or staff needed adequately to scrutinize every decision. One result of this may be disparities in the way authorities are handled in different provinces. Finally, authorities may sometimes be very slow to notify superiors of their decisions. This indicates, in some regions at least, a continuing suspicion of the State. Such suspicion may well be reinforced by the strictness of the controls which the State seeks to impose.

There are also certain, usually important, decisions which either require official approval before they can become law or need clearance from superiors before they can even be formally taken. Some decisions concerning the use of public property fall into the first category and the decision to contract substantial loans falls into the second. In both cases the decision of the relevant branch of the central administration is purely discretionary. This naturally places a premium on the capacity of local authorities to lobby on behalf of their interests.[26] In the case of requests for loans, for example, the Finance Minister has to be convinced of their desirability. As such lobbying is not the subject of any effective public scrutiny, much tends to hinge on personal contacts. In practice this gives an advantage to the spokesmen for large urban as opposed to small rural localities. The former have much readier access to national political élites. Thus authorities in most need can remain the most neglected.[27]

Finally, under the heading of political tutelage brief mention must be made of the circumstances when, in principle, state officials can assume immediate responsibility for the administration of a municipality. This is legally possible when authorities fail completely to discharge their responsibilities for safeguarding public health or when they run into extremely serious and chronic financial problems. In reality such drastic

---

[26]The extent to which such lobbying goes on at the national rather than the provincial level is a measure of the extent to which decision making is effectively centralized.

[27]As will be seen in the next chapter local authorities have representatives in the Cortes but these are generally spokesmen for *Diputaciones Provinciales* or for larger urban municipalities. Thus the latter can establish contact with national policymakers.

steps are hardly ever taken. This can be partly explained by official inertia but it can also be explained by the reluctance, even of an authoritarian state, to offend local susceptibilities to the point at which there might be serious disturbances of public order. Prudence dictates to all régimes that tutelage powers be administered circumspectly.

In practice state officials, notably Provincial Governors, often prefer to rely upon persuasion rather than legal powers for raising the standards of local services. Of course the political authority vested in Governors adds weight to their powers of persuasion. On the other hand, in more traditional regions at least, suspicion of, or indifference to, innovation is such that much time and effort may be needed to prod authorities into action. Passive resistance to change remains a major political factor.

Financial tutelage has three dimensions: control over the preparation of budgets, over the use of local tax-raising powers and *post hoc* controls of local expenditure. Annual budgets must be submitted to the Finance Ministry's representatives who check them to see that they balance, that essential commitments such as the payment of local officials have been provided for and that non-essential projects have not been undertaken at the expense of basic services. In reality these powers are so extensive that they can be used to make substantial modifications in local budgets and so impose the Finance Ministry's priorities upon local corporations. The present inability of local authorities to rally public opinion in opposition to such exercises of authority means that they are, in the last resort, virtually impossible to resist. Moreover, most items of capital expenditure have to be financed through "extraordinary" budgets requiring loans or special powers of taxation that need the Finance Ministry's sanction. Few authorities can finance major projects from their ordinary current incomes. The political consequences of this situation have already been alluded to.

In principle controls over local taxation policies are limited. Authorities can levy specified taxes up to prescribed levels but within these limits technically they possess freedom of action. The one check is a system of appeals to tribunals, dependent upon the Finance Ministry, through which citizens may challenge individual decisions of the taxation authority. In reality the tribunals have gone beyond their original brief and have effectively revised the taxation policies of some authorities. This may help to iron out inequities and anomalies but it may also upset the calculations on which authorities have based their future plans.

Immediately after the Civil War the *post hoc* control of local expenditure was extremely deficient.[28] There were many reasons for this. One was a division of responsibility between the corps of *Interventores* dependent upon the Interior Ministry and the Tribunal de Cuentas dependent upon the Finance Ministry.[29] Most important was the absence of groups of councillors with a vested interest in exposing the misuse of public funds. This last difficulty can only be removed by fundamental political charges. At the technical level, however, controls have been considerably tightened. An inspectorate, dependent upon the Interior Ministry but containing officials of the Finance Ministry, has relieved an overworked Tribunal de Cuentas of the responsibility for auditing the accounts of local authorities and has promoted a previously unknown degree of co-operation between the two Ministries. However, a more truly independent controlling body would probably be a still more effective guard against the misappropriation of public funds.[30]

LOCAL FINANCES

Finally, reference must be made to local finances, for without adequate sources of income authorities obviously cannot be effective. In reality shortages of funds have been a major obstacle to vigorous local administrative activity. These shortages can by partially explained by tax evasion and by the reluctance of some authorities fully to exploit local sources of revenue. Sometimes local councils have preferred inactivity to incurring the opprobrium attached to levying taxes. At a more fundamental level the shortages could be attributable to Spain's general level of economic development. Finally, they are attributable to the State's (or Finance Ministry's) policies. It has been traditionally reluctant to give local authorities lucrative independent incomes or a significant share of its own limited resources. It has also been unable to contain inflationary pressures and so preserve the value of the funds that have been made available.

Confronted with these problems the tendency has been for the State to lurch from one expedient to another rather than to pursue any coherent

[28]This period coincided with a particularly high incidence of corruption.
[29] Cf. next chapter for mention of the Tribunal de Cuentas.
[30]For a more detailed exposition of tutelage cf. K. Medhurst, *op. cit.*, Chapter 4.

strategy for the fostering of local development.[31] The brusque changes in official policy are too complex to be charted in detail, but underlying tendencies are discernible. Most important has been the tendency for taxes of a purely local nature to be replaced by taxes collected by the State on behalf of local authorities. Thus, since 1924, and especially since the Civil War, the State (through the Finance Ministry's *Delegados Provinciales*) has increasingly tended to become the paymaster of local authorities and so be in a position to influence the speed and nature of local development. Simultaneously there have been some efforts, through state-administered funds, to redistribute revenues from the better to the less well endowed authorities. These, however, have so far been largely unsuccessful.

The effect of recent policies has been to increase the amounts, calculated in absolute terms, available for use by local authorities. On the other hand, these amounts, expressed as a percentage of all official incomes, have tended to decline. Thus, despite some improvement in their financial situation, it remains hard for authorities to keep pace with growing demands for public services. Consequently dependence upon the State is further reinforced for official loans or grants (whose use in practice entails the exercise of little local discretion) may become necessary for major projects. Most commonly the latter are undertaken by the *Comisiones Provinciales de Servicios Técnicos* with no more than a small financial contribution from the relevant local corporation. The planning and execution of projects of local interest by technocratic bodies controlled by state officials is the most extreme expression of the extent to which local authorities have become financially dependent upon the State. If the former are to contribute more positively to a resolution of the problems posed by rapid economic development they must enjoy more of the fruits of that development.[32]

CONCLUSION

The evidence suggests that growing dependence upon the State reinforces the inertia traditionally characterizing many Spanish local authorities. The centralization of authority has sometimes been in response to

[31] By creating uncertainty this has made local authorities still less willing or able to make significant investments.

[32] Cf. F. Albi, *op. cit.*, p. 480 and following pages for the evolution and structure of local finances.

inactivity at the local level but it has simultaneously deprived authorities of incentives to identify or meet local needs. The activities of the *Comisiones Provinciales de Servicios Técnicos* appear positively to discourage local initiatives. Local authorities could provide much of the infrastructure necessary for balanced economic growth and they could help to attack social problems at the grass roots. They could also provide national decision-makers with valuable local intelligence and mobilize local interests in support of official policies. In practice, however, local authorities frequently remain unwilling or unable to tackle local problems.

Some policy-makers see administrative reforms as the answer to these problems. They advocate a greater devolution of administrative authority and greater freedom in the expenditure of local funds emanating from the State. But those who resist such reforms may, ultimately, be more realistic. This is because a truly effective local government reform can probably only be conducted as part of a general political change. In the first place vigorous local authorities could generate pressures and arouse expectations that might be unacceptable to the present authoritarian régime. In the second place it is likely that municipal and provincial authorities can only be effective spokesmen for local interests when pressed or supported by an interested public. Efforts to create more effective *Diputaciones Provinciales*, for example, in part failed because of their apparent remoteness from those they ostensibly represented and because of their immunity from effective popular pressures. Thus the inertia of local authorities in some measure reflects the apathy of constituents who regard them as outposts of a remote State rather than channels for the voicing of local aspirations. Radical changes in these attitudes presuppose a local government system in which the key political figures are not primarily agents of the central administration. The Nationalist régime is unlikely to take the political risks entailed in the creation of such a system.[33]

[33]Reform proposals published in 1972 confirm this judgement. They leave the essential features of the local administrative system untouched.

CHAPTER 9

Control of the Administration

POLITICAL CONTROLS—THE CORTES

The Spanish Government is subjected to few formal controls. The principal limitations on its freedom of action are imposed by the *de facto* pressure of social, economic, and diplomatic circumstances. Nevertheless, there are institutions which do in principle, at least, exercise some control over governmental activity. Most of these are legal bodies concerned to uphold a degree of rationality and predictability in dealings between the citizen and the State or between different branches of the state machinery. These will be examined later. But first there will be an examination of the régime's legislative assembly, or Cortes, which is the only body in any position to exercise a formal political control.

The Cortes was created in 1942 and first met in 1943. Its foundation came at a time when an allied victory in the world war was becoming likely and the need was felt to give Franco's régime greater legitimacy at home and some respectability abroad. But its powers and composition contrast with those of legislative bodies in the conventional parliamentary systems.

As already indicated there is no formal separation of powers in contemporary Spain.[1] All legislative and executive powers remain concentrated in Franco's hands. The Cortes has no independent law-making power and its participation in the legislative task merely signifies a self-imposed limitation upon Franco's authority. It approves laws without prejudicing the Head of State's ultimate powers of decision. It is therefore best to talk of the sharing or co-operation of powers.

[1] Cf. Chapter 3 for the creation and powers of the Cortes. The procedures, powers and composition of the Cortes are regulated by the "Ley Constitutiva de las Cortes," 17 July 1942, and "el Reglamento de las Cortes Españolas" (*B.O.E.*, 28 Dec. 1957).

In practice, however, Franco's veto power is little used. This is partly because of the many circumstances in which the Government may legally avoid seeking the Cortes' approval for its actions. But the way in which it is constituted and its mode of functioning also explain why a formal veto power is unnecessary.

The Cortes' organization is inspired by the principles of "Organic Democracy". These assert that universal suffrage and competition between political parties are artificial devices that unnecessarily disrupt the polity. Popular participation in politics should be through such "natural" agencies as the municipality or professional organizations. Consequently law making should be in the hands of representatives of such entities.

These notions stem from the "corporativist" trends of thought that had considerable influence in Europe after the First World War when parliamentary institutions were under strain. In Spain there were tentative efforts to implement them during Primo de Rivera's régime. The Falangists borrowed some ideas from the same source. Corporativist ideas also found an echo in Renovación Española, many of whose members passed into positions of influence within the Nationalist régime. They, in conjunction with leading Falangists, provided a blueprint for the Cortes. But they had to modify traditional corporativist ideas to meet the particular contingencies of "the New State".

Thus the Cortes is divided into a number of "sectors" composed of indirectly elected, *ex officio* or appointed members. Only one sector is chosen by popular election. Moreover, members of the régime's political élite are concentrated in the appointed or *ex officio* groups.

The first sector is formed by the Council of Ministers whose members occupy *ex officio* seats.[2] All members of the Movement's National Council are also automatically entitled to seats. Initially all councillors were freely appointed by Franco but in 1955 provision was made for the Movement's adherents to elect one representative from every province. Thus there are now forty appointed and just over fifty elected councillors.[3] The first

[2]The statistics cited in this chapter concerning the composition of the Cortes come from "Quien es Quien en las Cortes" (Editorial *Cuadernos para el Díalogo, Coleción Los Suplementos*, núm. 7), Madrid, 1969. The figures refer to the session 1967–71. In 1971 a freshly elected assembly was convened but, for reasons that will become apparent, there were few substantial changes of personnel, so the original figures have been left.

[3]These include representatives of African territories.

group clearly contains the most influential figures for it includes ministers, ex-ministers and prominent military leaders known to be close associates of Franco. On the other hand, the second group is chosen by a small electorate which totalled only 26,966 during the elections of 1967. Moreover, candidates require sponsorship from officials of the Movement and need the approval of its Secretariat. This system inevitably entails a high degree of co-option. Well over one-third of the present National Council's elected members had previously been in the Cortes. Thirty-eight of them also hold appointed offices in the Sindical, Falangist or state bureaucracies.

A smaller group of *ex officio* members is composed of the Presidents of Spain's chief legal institutions and by the President of the National Economic Council. A further sector is made up of University Rectors and the Presidents of major cultural institutions. The latter also have two elected representatives each, but prominent office holders are usually selected.

Up to fifty members can be appointed directly by Franco. In principle he has to appoint prominent ecclesiastical, military and administrative figures who have rendered outstanding public service. In practice this sector is used to ensure that the régime's major support groups are represented. Thus the group is almost entirely comprised of people with immediate access to the Government and many have held important public offices.

An apparently more independent sector is made up of the Presidents or elected representatives of professional and business associations. These are statutory bodies created at the end of the last and the beginning of this century. After the Civil War they were brought under strict government control and the State directly appointed the office holders. But from about 1950 controls were relaxed and members were granted a voice in the selection of leaders. Indeed, one body, the college of lawyers, has become a vehicle for expressing dissent from important aspects of official policy.[4] Nevertheless, ultimate control of these organizations remains with people closely linked to the régime's political élite. Thus 56 per cent of their elected representatives in the Cortes have been or continue to be office-holders in the central administration, the Movement or the *Sindicatos*.

[4]Cf. Chapter 2 for a reference to this.

A much larger group represents local corporations. It is formed by one representative for the municipalities of each province, a representative for every municipality with a population of over 100,000 and one representative for each provincial council. They total 115. Their election is in the hands of representatives of the local corporation themselves and so this sector could provide an element of popular representation. In practice, however, those elected are nearly always the Mayors of large municipalities or the Presidents of provincial councils who owe their jobs to government appointment.

The largest group of all is constituted by representatives of the official *Sindicatos*.[5] They are 150 in number. Of these a large proportion hold their seats by virtue of appointments in the syndical hierarchy. The remainder are indirectly elected but the elections are held in several stages which enable union leaders to influence the outcome. Thus the majority of those chosen also occupy some centrally appointed office in the Syndical structure or in the Movement.

The one major change in the Cortes' composition since 1943 came with the Organic Law of 1966. This provided for two members from each province to be directly elected by those legally defined as the heads of families and by married women. They ostensibly represent the family unit but in reality the creation of this sector signified a gesture toward the notion of popular sovereignty. Initially the Government's opponents hoped this would provide an opening through which their spokesmen could pass into the Cortes. But such hopes have been disappointed. During the first elections, held in 1967, the Movement's control over the selection of candidates deterred or prevented the régime's outright opponents from standing. Moreover, a 41 per cent abstention rate suggests considerable public apathy toward the experiment in its present form.[6]

The background of successful candidates indicates the degree of reliance upon official sponsorship. Twenty-nine had previously been Cortes members and sixty have some kind of public office. Nevertheless, this

[5]This group is sometimes known as the "Syndical third" for in principle it can occupy up to one-third of all seats.

[6]Elections held in Sept. 1971 presented essentially the same picture. Regional differences in abstention rates make interesting reading. Thus in 1971 the lowest turnout was in the Basque Province of Guipúzcoa. Despite the area's traditionally high level of political awareness there was only a 26 per cent vote.

sector contains the largest percentage of wholly new members and the biggest percentage too young to have been implicated in the Civil War. A minority also believe they have a special mandate to question official policies. Therefore the "family" sector has, in a small way, renewed and modified the Cortes' composition.

Some other sectors are characterized by considerable continuity in their membership. It is particularly true of the Movement's representatives, the Syndical sector and those appointed by Franco. For example, 35 per cent of the latter have been present since 1943. But the underlying stability of the membership contrasts with fluctuations in the total number of *Procuradores*, which may even change during one legislative session. In principle the entire assembly is renewed every three years but the *ex officio* and nominated sectors may expand or contract at any time according to political circumstances. To cite just one example, a provincial Governor arraigned for wrongful arrest was added to the list of appointed members in 1968 to enable him to claim "parliamentary immunity". There are also times at which one member may be entitled to two or more seats that will be held separately on other occasions. For example, eight ministers holding office during 1969 are also appointed National Councillors and the loss of one appointment would not necessarily entail the loss of the other.

These features of the Cortes' membership are the consequence of a selection system based largely upon co-option. Co-option also helps to explain some distinctive features of its social composition.

In principle the Cortes represents all sections of society but in practice some social groups are heavily over-represented. For example, 65 per cent of the Cortes belonged to civil service, military, business and other professional groups which form only 5 per cent of the total Spanish population. Moreover, the concentration of these elements tended to be greatest in appointed sectors with close access to the government. By contrast only 8 per cent of all members are of working-class origin and even within the syndical sector they remain in a minority of 10 per cent. Likewise, urban interests were heavily over-represented at the expense of the countryside. Approximately 31 per cent of the whole population are engaged in agriculture but only forty-two members (8 per cent) are engaged in this pursuit and several of these are probably absentee landowners.

Some regions are also over-represented. It is particularly true of Castile.

This is partly due to the heavy concentration of professional élites in Madrid. It is also to be explained by the large number of public officials recruited from the region and the strength of the Falangist party's appeal, during the Civil War, to the Castilian middle classes. At almost the other extreme is Andalusia. Nearly all members originating from this region represent specifically local interests. Strong Basque representation appears surprising but it is chiefly due to the presence in the appointed sectors of industrialists and financiers who opposed the separatist movement. On the other hand, Catalonia, excluding Barcelona,[7] is under-represented.

The strength of particular groups sheds light on their capacity to exert influence and upon lines of conflict within the assembly. The accent is theoretically placed upon harmonizing interests but in reality there are many cross-cutting cleavages. In most cases these do not coincide with the formal section divisions. For example, Franco's appointees constitute a microcosm of the principal political tendencies and interest groups incorporated into his régime. Indeed, this sector's membership normally indicates the current balance of political forces. But most sectors contain a similar diversity of views. Likewise, nearly all members are linked to special interests quite apart from those they officially represent. One-fifth of all members, for example, are directors of important enterprises or banks. They are concentrated in the appointed and professional sectors but even some syndical representatives are in the same category. Special mention must also be made of the 30 per cent of all members belonging to one of the administrative corps. They are most frequently found amongst the high office-holders, and the nominated or professional sectors. But even some elected National Councillors and a handful of the "popularly" elected group have posts in the bureaucracy. This obviously mirrors the régime's reliance upon the bureaucracy, and the way in which the nation's political élite has been replenished from that source.[8] It also means that intra-administrative disputes may be sustained within the Cortes by spokesmen for rival interests. Most sectors therefore lack cohesion and this is paralleled by the absence of formal organization or discipline. The partial exceptions are to be found in the sectors with the fewest high-ranking officials and which are consequently furthest removed

[7]Barcelona is an exception because it supplies a large percentage of the nation's professional and economic leaders.
[8]Cf. Chapter 3.

from official policy-making. Local government representatives sometimes combine to defend common interests. But solidarity is greatest in the Syndical sector. Whilst most members of the Cortes are concerned with a limited range of issues, affecting their immediate interests, nearly every issue impinges upon syndical activities. Moreover, members of this group share similar values. Thus they form the only sector to meet regularly to discuss tactics and to possess its own permanent secretariat. This explains why they have provided the only steady opposition to official economic and social policies.

The directly elected sector is new but its special position has helped to create a certain *esprit de corps* amongst some of its members. Attempts have been made to give the group institutional form. For example, meetings of the group have been organized in various parts of Spain to debate public issues. Subsequently the Minister of the Interior used his powers to ban one of these meetings and the President of the Cortes made it clear that future meetings required his approval. The effort to create an instrument for exerting popular pressure on the Government and for stimulating public debate has therefore suffered a reverse. But reactions to the incident suggest that, in the future, public criticisms of the Government are most likely to come from this quarter.

The same incident also illustrates the extent of formal government control over the Cortes. Such control supplements the strong informal pressures to which members are subjected as a result of their official backgrounds or their modes of appointment.

Responsibility for exercising discipline lies primarily with the Cortes' President. This is a political appointment lying in the Head of State's hands. Since 1943 there have only been three appointees and they have all been figures of major political importance enjoying Franco's special confidence. Their background indicates the special importance attached to the office.[9]

[9]This is underlined by the fact that the President of the Cortes is also President of the Consejo del Reino. This body contains a representative of all other major institutions and groups linked to the régime. It now formally ratifies major decisions like declaring a national state of emergency. It is also expected to handle any future succession crisis. The first two Presidents were both ex-ministers of Carlist background. The present President was appointed in Nov. 1969. He was Vice-Secretary-General of the Movement and so his appointment has been interpreted as compensation to Falangists for the ministerial changes of Oct. 1969.

The President summons and dissolves the Cortes. He constitutes the specialized commissions which examine legislative proposals and resolves doubts about the commission to which a proposal should go. He can also withdraw "bills" at any time. Above all, he, in consultation with members of the Government, determines the agenda. This not only means deciding which measures should have priority in the timetable but also means that initiatives from the Chamber cannot prosper without Presidential assistance. Lastly, the President presides over plenary sessions of the Cortes.

Since 1958 the President has been assisted in the use of his powers by a small commission representing the assembly's various sectors but it is dominated by government appointees. Official control over procedure therefore remains. An examination of procedure will confirm this.

Practically all legislative proposals emanate from government departments. Since 1943 only two laws have been enacted as the result of initiatives within the assembly itself. Moreover, official proposals almost always have a smooth passage. If serious difficulties are anticipated the Government will probably hold back its measure. For example, recent trade union reforms were long held up by dissatisfaction within "the Syndical sector".

Once bills are formally received by the President they are sent to specialized commissions. Eighteen of these, each corresponding to major policy-making areas, have a permanent existence. Their membership is largely determined at the start of legislative periods. The choice of members, including the Chairman, lies with the President, but as all *Procuradores* belong to at least one commission it is obviously expedient for appointments to take account of specialized interests. Most commissions therefore include a cross-section of the Cortes, but official pressure also plays a part in shaping their composition. For example, ministers secure the appointment of allies likely to facilitate the passage of their measures. Likewise, officials seek entry to commissions in whose proceedings their department or administrative corps has a stake.

Sometimes proposals are referred to "special commissions" created on a purely *ad hoc* basis. They are ostensibly established because of an issue's overriding importance or because it does not clearly fall within the competence of a permanent commission. In reality it is often a device for retaining some official control over the discussion of controversial measures. For example, a special commission handled anti-monopolistic legislation that antagonized business interests represented in the Cortes.

The composition of commissions is important, for their deliberations provide members with their one officially recognized chance to influence legislation. They are the only bodies able to pass amendments.

Commissions infrequently challenge the basic principles of official proposals. If this happens, the measure is usually technical in nature and it is withdrawn for further study. Indeed, procedure is designed to inhibit fundamental criticisms. Chairmen appoint small sub-committees whose reports serve as a basis for discussion in the full commissions.[10] Nevertheless, this stage has always produced some activity for members manoeuvre to get amendments accepted. They usually concern points of detail. Sometimes they close loopholes or improve drafting. But they may also secure concessions or protection for special interests.

It is these opportunities which make a study of the Cortes' composition relevant. Without anything corresponding to party discipline alliances can fluctuate according to the issues involved and competing groups can participate in a "log-rolling" process.

The absence of party organization also means that most members are not mobilized for or against proposals unless their immediate interests are involved. This combined with a relative lack of publicity permits determined minorities to agree privately on the slipping in of favourable changes. Business interests can obtain tax concessions in this way. Above all rival administrative interests manoeuvre to modify agreements reached at an earlier stage. Their cohesion, expertise and privileged access to information make it particularly easy for them to dominate discussions. Consequently much of the conflict within the Cortes mirrors intra-administrative disputes. There is one commission, concerned with finance, which is permanently controlled by officials of the relevant ministry.[11]

[10]In the early days of the Cortes at least, these sub-committees were frequently composed of the same reduced group of members. Most of these were close to Franco himself and included, for example, Admiral Carrero Blanco. This and other observations about the behaviour of the Cortes is based on a study of *El Boletín Oficial de las Cortes Españolas*.

[11]The task of determined minorities is also probably facilitated by the frequent absenteeism of many members. Such absenteeism, probably stemming from apathy and a general sense of impotence, makes it marginally easier for the Government to manage the Cortes.

Plenary sessions of the Cortes are relatively infrequent and they simply vote upon the recommendations of the commissions. Sponsoring ministers may defend their measures and the commissions appoint *rapporteurs* to explain their actions. There is, however, no general debate. Votes are taken but bills have never been rejected at this juncture. An opposition vote of over fifty is rare.

It is permissible, however, to question ministers or to initiate inter-pellations in plenary sessions, provided the chair's permission has been obtained. Questions have always been theoretically possible whilst inter-pellations were formally introduced in 1958. Initially these devices were little used but they have been employed more often in the past five or six years. In 1965, for example, a Syndical representative initiated an inter-pellation censuring the Agricultural Minister for deficiencies in his department's policies. But ministers are not responsible to the Cortes and they can also usually count upon protection from the chair when seriously attacked. Thus most ministerial answers are very general and detailed replies are not given.

It is clear from this account that the Cortes can, at best, exert very limited control over the Government. Most changes in policy which do occur result from the private and informal pressure of small groups of members. Some fields of policy are completely beyond its influence. Foreign policy, for example, has been conducted with practically no reference to the Cortes. But the Chamber has not been uniformly quiescent throughout its history. Paradoxically there were more manifest-ations of dissent from 1943 to 1945 than in most subsequent years. This arose from the presence of a vocal Falangist group whose independence was curtailed after 1945. In the past decade, however, the intensity of conflict within the commissions has grown. The relaxation of press censorship has also focused attention upon their discussions and has encouraged freer debate within the régime's élite. Developments in the "family" sector in particular indicate a striving after greater independence. Sections of the present government will, however, resist these trends and for the foreseeable future the Cortes is bound to occupy a secondary position. As long as this is the case it is unlikely to command much popular respect or contribute much to political debate.

LEGAL CONTROLS

Spain's administration works within a framework of public law which is enforced by special courts. Public officials, when acting in their official capacities, are subject to the control of the specialized courts and not of the ordinary civil courts.

In common with other Spanish administrative institutions the system of administrative courts and public law was first borrowed from France. Thus in 1845 a traditional Royal Council (Consejo de Estado)[12] was reorganized in imitation of the Conseil d'Etat and at the provincial level, equivalents of the Conseils de Prefecture were created. These bodies were intended to advise governmental authorities upon the drafting of laws and regulations and to hear appeals against administrative decisions and acts. The ordinary courts were denied control over administrative activities. It was maintained that such control would represent a usurpation of the administrative function and a departure from the idea of a separation of powers.

An influential body of political and legal opinion, looking to Britain rather than France for guidance, felt that the Napoleonic system gave the administration exorbitant privileges and they argued for control by the civil courts. The upheaval of 1868 gave them the chance to dismantle the system of administrative courts. Later, as part of the Restoration political settlement, a hybrid system was created that attempted to reconcile the two rival conceptions. The Consejo de Estado retained responsibility for judicial control of the administration but the responsibility was assumed by a special section of the Consejo recruited from both civil servants and civil lawyers. At the provincial level special divisions of the ordinary provincial courts were established on the same basis. In 1904 the system of administrative courts took more or less its present shape when the section of the Consejo de Estado handling litigation became a specialized division of the Spanish Supreme Court—or Tribunal Supremo. Such a step was a reminder of the political influence and prestige of Spain's legal profession.[13]

This hybrid system has contributed toward difficulties experienced in

[12]In 1845 this body was called el Consejo Real but in 1860 it was renamed el Consejo de Estado.
[13]Cf. L. Jordana de Pozas, *El Consejo de Estado español y las influencias francesas a lo largo de su evolución*, Madrid, 1953.

developing a coherent body of administrative law and in compelling the administration to behave predictably. These problems have several facets. Firstly, the divorce between the Consejo de Estado and the administrative courts has had adverse consequences for both. The Consejo lost prestige. Though it retains advisory functions it carries less weight than its French counterpart. Judges of the administrative courts, for their part, lack the stimulus and insight that come from close contact with every-day administrative problems. The courts are therefore at a disadvantage in their dealings with the officials whom they are expected to control. Equally, it is probable that the administration resists "outside" control more than it would self-imposed controls. Secondly, the judges of the administrative courts have often been ill qualified to erect effective barriers against arbitrary administrative action. The civil servants amongst them have not necessarily been well-equipped specialists in administrative law and have tended to be deferential toward the State. The civil lawyers who staffed the courts in their formative years were the product of a formalistic legal tradition which stressed the observance of outward legal forms. Their training also inclined them to use legal categories inappropriate for handling relationships between the citizen and the State. They thought in terms of disputes between two relatively equal parties and paid little heed to the distinctive problems posed by extensions of administrative activity. Thus the courts failed to produce the bold and creative jurisprudence necessary for the establishing of effective judicial controls. They ignored many of the questions of administrative ethics and efficiency which preoccupied the Conseil d'Etat and they were slow to develop a coherent body of doctrine capable of creating a new balance in the relationship between the citizen and the State.

Because of this, advances in the system of judicial control have come from legislation rather than the courts themselves. New legal concepts have come into use via laws which the courts have subsequently been expected to apply. The biggest advance of this kind came in 1956.[14] After about 1950 a new generation of administrative lawyers reawakened interest in French (and Italian) practices as a result of which a law was passed that opened up fresh possibilities for the control of official institutions.

[14]Cf. "Ley Reguladora de la Jurisdicción Contencioso-Administrativa" (*B.O.E.*, 28 Dec. 1956).

Finally, it must be noted that the severing of formal links between the administration and the administrative courts led the former to retain its own special system of appeals which has to be used before legal redress can be sought. Before appeals can be lodged with the courts against administrative acts or decisions, the administration must first be asked to reconsider its position. Complaints go to the official responsible for the act or decision and if he has a "hierarchic superior" a further appeal may be necessary. In principle this system enables the State to revise its own actions and so avoid the need for litigation. In practice it provides opportunities for obstruction that make it hard to gain access to the courts.

It is clear from this that the problem of developing adequate judicial controls over the administration is perennial and cannot solely be attributed to present political arrangements. Indeed, the reform of 1956 has opened up the possibility of controlling aspects of administrative behaviour once regarded as beyond the reach of the courts. On the other hand, political circumstances do obstruct the process of extending controls. Some sensitive issues are kept outside the jurisdiction of the courts and judges are unlikely at present (by virtue of the mode of their appointments and of their backgrounds) to press the administration on fundamental questions of policy.[15] Above all there is currently no provision for a formal separation of powers. All the powers of the State are vested in the Head of State's hands. This means in practice that if the administration contests the competence of the courts to hear a case, the dispute is not resolved by a judicial body but by the *Presidencia*. The implications of this are obvious. Nevertheless, an unspectacular struggle for legality is going on within the framework of existing institutions.[16]

The "Consejo de Estado"

Before examining judicial controls more closely the present position of the Consejo de Estado must be briefly discussed. The Consejo de Estado no longer exercises judicial controls but it is still of some importance as an advisory body.

After ceasing to function, during the Civil War, the Council was

[15]Cf. below for a reference to the appointment of judges.
[16]For a brief account of the evolution of the system of administrative courts cf. F. Garrido Falla, La Evolución del Recurso Contencioso-Administrativo en España", *Revista de Administración Pública*, No. 55, Madrid, 1968, pp. 9–26.

revived in 1940 in a reorganized form. Its membership is now composed of eight *ex officio* members, representing such major national institutions as the Church and the Movement, and an unspecified number of "permanent" members chosen by the Head of State from amongst Spain's political, military and ecclesiastical leaders. The Council's President is normally a figure of some political consequence.

The President, the permanent councillors and the Council's senior permanent official (or Secretary-General) form a "Permanent Commission" which conducts most of the Council's business. Plenary sessions are normally only held to ratify particularly important items of business. The Permanent Commission works through eight specialized "Sections" each of which handles the affairs of one or more ministries. Every Section contains one permanent Councillor and several legal advisers belonging to a Corps of "Letrados". Letrados prepare reports on matters currently before the Section which normally serve as the basis of the latter's recommendations to the Permanent Commission. The reports explore the legal issues raised by enquiries from the administration. The Permanent Commission's final recommendations may also contain advice on substantive issues.

The Council's advice is principally sought on the drafting of laws by the administration following grants of legislative power from the Cortes; the drafting of administrative regulations designed to enforce already existing laws; the interpretation, modification or rescinding of administrative contracts and concessions; the voting of supplementary grants; and in exceptional circumstances, on the interpretation of treaties.

In many of these cases the administration is bound to seek advice but only in few cases is it bound to follow it. In practice the State appears to follow its advice on legal technicalities but rarely on major matters of policy.[17] The Letrados are highly competent legal specialists whose views are respected, but they are only auxiliaries of the members of the Consejo. The latter tend to receive their appointments as rewards for past service and they are often largely honorific in kind. This inevitably affects the Council's practical influence and importance. It helps to regularize some

[17]In cases where a ministry has had to seek advice but then wishes to reject it, the Council of Ministers must be informed. As all ministers may wish to reserve the right to override the Consejo de Estado's decisions it is unlikely, at present, that this makes much practical difference.

aspects of administrative behaviour but it lacks the independence and prestige needed profoundly to affect the *modus operandi* of public authorities. Some commentators foresee an important role for the Council in checking misuse of delegated legislative powers but circumstances are not yet propitious for this.[18]

Judicial controls

For the moment the Consejo de Estado provides a limited form of administrative control to supplement the more significant judicial controls of the administrative courts. The law of 1956 maintains that the courts may handle all litigation arising from "those activities of the administration which are regulated by public law and from the administration's use of its own rule-making authority". This assertion seems straightforward but it leaves several unresolved problems. Firstly, it does not refer to an important category of decisions or acts which are excluded from the courts' jurisdiction. These are *actos políticos del gobierno*. At present they include measures which "affect the defence of the national territory" and "the internal security of the State". In practice there are doubts about which authorities can use the concept of *actos políticos del gobierno* to claim exemption from judicial controls and about the precise scope of the activities covered by the term. The extent of the courts' jurisdiction remains unsettled at this point. Secondly, the line of demarcation between the administrative and civil courts is sometimes unclear. Lack of clarity in the law can create doubts about the authority competent to handle cases involving the award of damages or the implementation of contracts. Thus two courts may declare themselves incompetent to deal with a particular case, or two courts may arrive at contradictory judgements. Such disputes are resolved by a special *Sala* (division) of the Tribunal Supremo. It is formed by judges representing the conflicting parties and presided over by the Supreme Court's President. This is Spain's nearest equivalent to the French Tribunal des Conflits. It decides which is the competent authority or which of two contradictory findings should stand.[19]

[18]On the subject of the Consejo de Estado cf. Cordero Torres, *El Consejo de Estado*, Madrid, 1944, and A. Pérez Hernandez, *El Consejo de Estado*, Madrid, 1965.

[19]For these and other points concerning the organization and procedure of the courts cf. H. Courbe Courtemanche, *Les Recours contre les Actes Administratives en Droit Espagnol*, Paris, 1960.

The respective jurisdictions of the Tribunal Supremo and of the lower administrative courts are more clearly delimited. The former hears cases involving administrative agencies with nation-wide authority, namely ministries and their dependencies. The lower courts hear cases involving local authorities (when these are acting as autonomous rule-making bodies).

The Tribunal Supremo contains three *Salas* handling administrative disputes. Each one has a presiding *Magistrado* (Judge) and ten other *Magistrados*. All are appointed by the Council of Ministers on the Minister of Justice's recommendation. They are recruited, in fixed proportions, from amongst career Judges specialized in civil law, *magistrados* promoted from subordinate administrative courts and from civil servants holding specified posts.

Before 1956 each Province also had an administrative court. Some, however, had relatively little business. There was also a tendency for the nature of decisions to vary with the Province. Thus the reform of 1956 replaced the provincial courts with specialized *Salas* in each of Spain's fifteen *Audiencias Territoriales* (divisional courts). These *Salas* are staffed by Judges who are recruited through competitive examinations in which preference is given to specialists in administrative law. In this way it was hoped to introduce better-qualified personnel into the system who would eventually be promoted to the Tribunal Supremo and who would, over a period, produce more rigorous case law.

In all courts procedure is essentially the same. First, the possibilities of appealing to the administration itself have to be exhausted. As already noted, this can turn the process of getting to the courts into something of an obstacle race. Once access to the courts has been gained, cases are largely decided on the basis of written evidence. A Judge prepares a legal report on the basis of the evidence submitted and this is made available to the parties to the dispute in question. Prior to 1956 the parties to a case could do little more than make general observations about the Judge's report. The litigants can now play a more active part; in examining witnesses for example. Partly as a result of this the courts have begun to take into account issues wider than the observance of outward legal forms. There is no guarantee, however, that the administration will not keep pursuing an otherwise hopeless case with the hope of wearing down opponents. Procedural changes will be needed to eliminate this form of obstruction.

The Court's final decision, or *Sentencia*, is based on the original Judge's report as modified by subsequent procedures. Appeals are in all cases open if it is maintained that a *Sentencia* contradicts decisions handed down in similar cases; if new evidence comes to light; if evidence has been withheld; or if false testimony has been alleged. Finally, the State's representatives can initiate special appeals designed to sort out anomalous legal situations.[20] Such appeals give citizens significant guarantees but, by the same token, they enable the State to impose lengthy and costly actions upon plaintiffs.

The courts can exercise two main forms of control over the administration. They can hear appeals against administrative decisions or they can exercise controls over the administration's actions.[21]

Appeals against decisions can be made on two grounds. A citizen may allege that a decision infringes one of his civil rights and that he is therefore entitled to compensation, or he may maintain that it is illegal and should be annulled. In reality it is now always the second of these actions which is brought against decisions, though a second subsidiary action can be brought to recover damages.

The one category of decisions which cannot be annulled are those labelled *actos políticos del gobierno*. As already noted there are practical difficulties in defining this concept. On the face of it only decisions taken by the Council of Ministers would seem to be covered by the term, but in practice it has had a wider usage. The Ministry of the Interior, for example, has claimed the title of an *acto político del gobierno* for decisions taken by local authorities when acting as guardians of "public order".[22] The courts have generally proved unwilling to pursue the point when politically sensitive issues have been at stake. Thus citizens have little redress if the State feels its security is being threatened. On a few occasions

[20]Generally the State is represented by Abogados del Estado.

[21]Mention should also be briefly made of special actions concerning the interpretation of contracts, the use of public property and disputed elections which the administrative courts may handle. There are also specialized tribunals, most notably those dealing with taxation, which are directly dependent upon ministerial departments.

[22]Maintenance of public order can of course cover the prevention or repression of opposition political activities. For a discussion of this and related problems cf. E. García de Enterría, "La Lucha Contra las Inmunidades del Poder", *Revista de Administración Pública*, No. 38, Madrid, 1962, especially pp. 181–95.

recently the courts have required the State to demonstrate that a particular decision was necessary for the maintenance of order. A change of political system is necessary, however, before the courts can exert really effective controls in this area.

Before 1956, at least, there were serious obstacles to the effective judicial control of those decisions which could, technically, be impugned. Checks on legality tended to be of a formalistic kind. The law provided for appeals based on "manifest" breaches of legality; for appeals against decisions taken by legally incompetent authorities or enacted without observing the prescribed legal norms. The checks were adequate in the relatively few cases of powers so minutely regulated that there was little room for the exercise of discretion. The courts, however, did little to control the use of discretionary powers. These could be used by the competent authority, observing the correct procedures and yet discriminate against particular individuals or groups. Likewise, discretionary powers could be used for personal or other purposes not foreseen by the legislator, who had granted them. To correct such arbitrary behaviour required the development of legal concepts which would enable the courts to go beyond the scrutinizing of outward forms to the assessment of facts and motives. Periodically the courts took up instances which indicated the possibility of this sort of development, but these cases were infrequent.

Since 1956 some steps have been taken to tackle these problems. The law of that year explicitly widened the basis upon which appeals against administrative decisions could be made. It states that ". . . any breach in the legal system . . ." justifies the annulment of a decision. In particular it singles out decisions vitiated by a *desviación de poder* (a literal translation of the French concept of *détournement du pouvoir* or misuse of power).[23] The law did not spell out what was entailed but in bold hands it could clearly remedy many of the traditional deficiencies of Spanish administrative justice. Some of the possibilities inherent in the new legislation have already been drawn out. The old caution has not been entirely abandoned and the courts have sometimes vacillated, but they have shown some tendency to subject the administration to new and more vigorous forms of scrutiny. Thus the concept of *desviación de poder* has been used to bring the assessment of facts and of underlying motives within the purview of the

[23]Cf. S. Martín Retortillo, "La Desviación de Poder en el Derecho Español", *Revista de Administración Pública*, No. 23, Madrid, 1959, pp. 129–74.

courts. It has been established, for example, that decisions should be annulled if they have been taken on the basis of wrong facts or a mistaken evaluation of the facts, even if those responsible acted in good faith. Equally, the courts have acknowledged that illegal decisions cannot be justified simply because they have been taken in pursuit of legitimate ends. This could have considerable significance in the Spanish context for authorities frequently justify their actions on the grounds of administrative need or urgency and in the past the courts have tended to accept such pleas in a rather literal minded way without further probing. The affirmation that illegal powers cannot even be used for the best of ends could, in the long term, prove salutory and help to curb many existing administrative irregularities.

Judicial controls over the legality of administrative decisions are supplemented by controls over the actions of administrative authorities. The subject of these latter controls will be reviewed under two main headings. Firstly, the cases in which the administration or its officials accept responsibility (in the form of damages) for harm done to citizens as a result of administrative activities. Secondly, some attention will be paid to the courts' efforts to limit the use of the administration's "Police Powers".

Until a law of 1954 on compulsory purchase and, still more, legislation enacted in 1957, the State was rarely forced to accept responsibility for its actions. Spanish practice in this realm lagged far behind most other European countries.[24] The legislation of 1957, however, accepted that "private citizens will have the right to be compensated for any harm done to their property and rights, except in cases of *force majeure*, provided the damage done is a consequence of the normal or abnormal functioning of public services, . . ."[25] This marks a potentiallys ignificant step forward. But in practice the courts have frequently reacted to claims for compensation with much of their traditional caution. Sometimes they have defined the extent of the State's responsibility very narrowly. On other occasions

[24]Local authorities constituted a partial exception to this. The legislation governing local authorities made them, in principle at least, more liable to accept responsibility for the consequences of their actions.

[25]Ley de Régimen Juridico de la Administración del Estado. The law of 1954 was the Ley de Expropriación Forzosa "(*B.O.E.*, 17 Dec. 1956). For comments cf. E. García de Enterría, *Los Principios de la nueva ley de Expropriación Forzosa*, Madrid, 1954, and L. Martín Retortillo, "Responsibilidad Patrimonial de la Administración y Jurisdicción", *Revista de Administración Pública*, No. 42, 1963, pp. 169–224.

they have disclaimed all responsibility for hearing cases on the grounds that the administration, in the cases in question, has been acting as a private entity subject to civil law and not as a provider of public services subject to administrative law.[26]

Such doubts about the competence of the courts may ultimately be resolved but only at the cost of lengthy and costly litigation which tends to bring them into disrepute. On the other hand, there have been instances in which the courts have taken a more generous view and these suggest that, in the future, citizens may have stronger guarantees than have hitherto existed.

The administration's use of its Police Powers has been another of the courts' more recent concerns. Traditionally they have held that the Police Power was a discretionary one to be used when and how the administration judged fit.[27] Their formalistic legal traditions led them to maintain that discretionary powers were, by definition, a matter solely for the administration and that attempts to control their use would be an infringement of the administration's own prerogatives. The furthest that they went was to verify that action had been taken by competent authorities who could claim a legal warrant for their activities. The dangers in this situation have been inevitably increased by the creation of an authoritarian political system in which popular pressure cannot usually be brought to bear upon the arbitrary users of public power. Any efforts to erect standards against which uses of the Police Power can be judged have an added significance in such circumstances.

One advance has been the affirmation that there is no such thing as an entirely discretionary act. It is now argued that administrative acts are complex phenomena compounded of several elements some of which the courts may scrutinize and some of which the administration must necessarily be left free to determine. Thus it is now asserted that acts must only be performed for the end intended by the legislator when first conceding discretionary powers. It is recognized that the administration must have

[26]One example of this was a case in which a municipal bus knocked down a pedestrian whilst taking municipal employees to work. It was held that, in this case, the bus was not involved in an act of public service and the administrative courts were therefore not competent to handle the matter.

[27]Cf. E. García de Enterría, *La Lucha contra las Inmunidades de Poder, op. cit.*, pp. 159–209 for the traditional attitudes of the courts to the use of discretionary powers.

some freedom to select its own means for achieving prescribed ends and must also be free to decide on the timing of its actions. Nevertheless, it has been maintained that the courts are at liberty to determine if the choice of means and of time are consistent with the stated objective. In judging actions according to these criteria the courts have begun to develop relatively sophisticated judicial techniques not previously used in Spain. They have begun to move away from the mechanistic interpretation of isolated legal precepts to an invocation of the general principles underlying the entire legal system. They have turned their attention to the doctrine of the "general principles of the law" which maintains that any corpus of law and legal institutions presupposes and embodies a minimum of rationality and equity. Such values may only be implicit in the existing legal system, but it is the job of the courts to articulate them and draw out their implications for specific cases.[28]

Amongst the general principles applied to appeals against uses of the Police Power is that of the proportionality of ends and means. Thus it has been asserted that when several means are available for securing a specified end, then the administration should select the one least restrictive of individual liberty. Likewise, the principle of equality before the law has been invoked. It has been used, for example, to prevent the withholding of an official licence in a given case when in another but identical set of circumstances it had been conceded. Such principles are relatively elementary but in the hands of capable jurists they could have significant implications for the future.

At present, however, there are political obstacles to major advances in the realm of judicial control. This is made plain by one feature of the present legal position to which reference must finally be made. It is a feature that strikes at the root of the whole notion of judicial control of the administration and is particularly serious because the problem arises in cases involving criminal proceedings against public servants. Thus officials (making use of the strained interpretation of an isolated legal provision) have been known to claim that criminal courts cannot act because the case in question raises matters which have to be decided by the administrative courts before further steps are possible. They have turned to the Presidencia

[28]For a discussion of the general principles of the law cf. E. García Enterría, "Reflexiones sobre la Ley y Principios Generales del Derecho", *Revista de Administración Pública*, No. 40, 1963, pp. 191–221.

del Gobierno as the appropriate organ for resolving such demarcation disputes. The Presidencia has several times upheld such protests and that, in practice, may put an end to the matter. The accused official becomes, *de facto*, immune from further proceedings. In this way functionaries have been rescued from prosecutions for a variety of offences, including wrongful arrests and misappropriation of funds. The arbitrary nature of the procedure requires little comment. It is no less arbitrary for giving the administration the power to decide which of its servants shall be specially protected. Such cases are infrequent but the possibility of their existence highlights the shortcomings of the present system of legal controls.[29]

Financial controls

Finally, brief mention must be made of the organ charged with *post hoc* control of the State's financial activities. This is the Tribunal de Cuentas which, in its modern form, emerged in 1851.[30] Since then it has been reorganized several times but its functions have remained essentially unaltered.[31]

Control of current expenditure is the responsibility of the office of the Interventor General which is part of the Finance Ministry. The Tribunal de Cuentas subsequently audits the State's accounts to check that funds have been used for purposes approved by the Cortes. A report of its findings is sent to the Head of State and to the Cortes. It can draw attention to cases in which public funds may have been misused and recommend the State to bring prosecutions where this seems relevant. It may also indicate to the Finance Ministry malfunctionings in the system of financial administration and indicate possible reforms.

In practice controls exercised by the Tribunal have been very imperfect. This was true before the Civil War and was certainly the case afterwards.

[29]Cf. J. R. Parada Vázquez, "La Responsibilidad Criminal de los Funcionarios Públicos", *Revista de Administración Pública*, No. 31, 1961, pp. 121–46.

[30]It is now regulated by the "Ley Organica del Tribunal de Cuentas" (*B.O.E.*, 4 Dec. 1953).

[31]Since 1951 the *post hoc* financial control of local authorities has been the responsibility of the Servicio Nacional de Asesoramiento y Inspección de Corporaciones Locales which is a dependency of the Ministry of the Interior. Prior to that there had been an almost complete breakdown of control over the financial activities of local authorities—the Tribunal de Cuentas was too overworked adequately to discharge this responsibility.

A large backlog of business combined with uncertain political conditions to accentuate traditional difficulties. Several special factors underlie these long-established problems. Firstly, the Tribunal has lacked a staff large and well trained enough to cope with rapid expansions of state activity. Its members have been grounded in traditional accounting procedures but have lacked the specialized technical knowledge needed for checking the activities of an increasingly complex state. Equally, understaffing has led to such long delays in the handling of business that the practical value of the Tribunal's findings have frequently been much reduced. Secondly, the Tribunal has suffered from a lack of co-operation with the Interventor General. Insights and information available to the latter have not necessarily been available to the former. Finally, the Tribunal has lacked the prestige needed to command the administration's respect and active co-operation. This situation is partly the result of the technical deficiencies which have already been mentioned but it also results from a lack of genuine independence. The Head of the Tribunal is appointed by the Head of State and can only be removed with his agreement, but the senior technical staff are appointees of the Minister of Finance. Thus the Tribunal effectively depends upon the Ministry whose activities it is most concerned to control. A body answerable only to an authoritative legislature could perhaps command greater respect, but this cannot be expected in present political circumstances.

The Tribunal's weaknesses were most spectacularly reflected in the corruption which characterized portions of the administration immediately after the Civil War. The "Matesa" scandal demonstrates that such corruption has probably not been wholly eliminated. The publicity given to the Matesa affair and the charges brought against some of those allegedly implicated would have been almost unthinkable at an earlier stage in the Nationalist Régime's history, but the exposure of this scandal probably owed as much to the feuds of rival factions within the régime as to the administration's own self-controlling mechanisms. An effective system of institutionalized controls probably demands a Tribunal de Cuentas with much greater independence than is currently possible.[32]

[32]For comment on the Tribunal cf. A. J. De Juan Alad, "El Control de la Gestión Financiera del Estado", *Documentación Administrativa*, No. 40; cf. also R. De Mendizábal Allende, "Función y Esencia del Tribunal de Cuentas", *Revista de Administración Pública*, No. 46, 1965.

CONCLUSION

During and just after the Civil War there was an almost complete collapse of the barriers erected to guard against arbitrary behaviour on the part of the State and its servants. This period (lasting until about 1943 or 1944) saw corruption at its height and coincided, in large part, with the period of the Nationalist Régime's most active repression. Subsequently, and particularly during the past decade, institutions charged with controlling the administration's activities have shown certain very limited signs of independence. Thus the State has been compelled in some relatively small but significant ways to behave more predictably and equitably. But the very nature of the present political system precludes any spectacular increases in the guarantees available to the citizen. The conditional nature of civil rights, the possibility of arbitrary arrest, and even torture, and the impunity with which public officials can sometimes flout legal norms, all highlight the nature of the relationship currently existing between the citizen and the State.[33] Without more searching public criticism of the administration and more effective institutionalized controls, such abuses of power are unlikely to be eliminated. In the long run their elimination could contribute to the creation of a more stable polity. At present significant sections of Spanish society continue to feel alienated from official institutions because these often seem to be remote, unpredictable, arbitrary and even repressive. Their legitimacy will only be widely accepted when these suspicions have been removed and when there is a more general belief in the possibility of effectively controlling the Government's activities.

[33]Particularly in the Basque Country, there have only recently been frequent allegations of very arbitrary police behaviour against which there has been no effective redress. It is also important to note that the effectiveness of legal guarantees tends to ebb and flow according to changing political circumstances. If the Government invokes its emergency powers then most "constitutional rights" can be suspended and its political opponents dealt with accordingly. The behaviour of the courts, including criminal courts, also tends to vary from region to region, in a rather arbitrary fashion.

Epilogue

THE Nationalist Régime has provided Spain with a lengthy period of political stability unprecedented in modern Spanish history. The past decade, in particular, has also witnessed a period of rapid economic growth surpassed by only a few other nations. Partly as a result of the latter, significant social changes have been set in train. Large-scale migrations have perhaps done something to lower traditional regional barriers. Equally, Spain now has social structures and consumption patterns closer to those of its northern neighbours than was the case before the Civil War. Partly as a result of such social changes and partly because of the impact of changes within the Roman Catholic Church, it seems probable that significant sections of Spanish society are more obviously secularized and take more pragmatic attitudes to basic political issues than they did prior to 1936. There are therefore reasons for thinking that, in some respects, Spain has become a more effectively integrated society whose cleavages may prove less destructive in the future than they have in the past. By the same token, any future essay in representative government, though fraught with difficulties, may have greater chances of success than previous experiments of that sort. The Second Republic was launched in a society whose politically active members did not possess that minimum of shared values necessary for the survival of a political system ultimately resting on popular consent. The bitter experience of a Civil War together with recent socio-economic changes may, eventually, make it easier to limit the extent and intensity of traditionally disruptive political conflicts.

Nevertheless, several questions have to be posed concerning the likely legacy of Franco's régime and several reservations expressed concerning the state of Spain's political development. Firstly, despite some efforts to provide for the future, there is in practice widespread uncertainty. The present régime survives, in part, because of inertia, habit and the prestige of its creator. His departure will leave a vacuum very difficult to fill and will deprive the Nationalist Régime of a significant proportion of that legitimacy which, with some reason, it can now claim to possess. The installation of a monarchy is the official answer to this problem but there must be doubts about the long-term effectiveness of such a solution. It seems likely that most Spaniards are at best indifferent and at worst hostile to the idea of a monarchy and within the régime itself it has its opponents. Moreover, it has to be recalled that most Spaniards now have no memory of the country's erstwhile monarchy (including most of those technocrats currently in power) and so have little reason to be sentimentally attached to the institution. In these circumstances it is difficult to see how the present power-holders can continue without making some major adjustments. Their general aim has been to conduct an élite-directed programme of economic and administrative modernization, accompanied where necessary by a modicum of political liberalization, whilst leaving the nation's social or political structures essentially unchanged.[1] Evidence accumulated during this study indicates the inherent difficulties and limitations of this approach. On the one hand, economic change and (mild) political reforms can arouse expectations which, being frustrated, can lead to a heightening of tensions. The mere fact of experimenting with economic planning, for example, means the adoption of official objectives that can subsequently be used to measure the success of government policies. On the other hand, there are reasons for believing that a thorough-going modernization of economic and administrative structures presupposes changes in values and popular political participation on a scale which is currently impossible. A régime which emerged from a reaction against threats to traditional interests and values must necessarily have an ambivalent attitude to the challenge of modernization. Policy-makers may wish to modify existing institutions and structures, but they have no coherent ideology, in terms of which goals can be defined and priorities ordered. Equally, there is no inclination actively to involve the society at large in the reform process. On the economic front attempts at "indicative planning" run into difficulties because of industrial unrest caused by a labour force that, to a large extent, feels alienated from official

---

[1]As has been noted, political "liberalization" has not been a linear process but a question of tentative advances sometimes followed, in practice, by partial retreats. Much has depended on the current balance of forces within the Government. Also, when the results of liberalization have become apparent, groups within the Government have reacted against them.

institutions and because of feet-dragging or inertia on the part of powerful pressure groups to whom the régime must look for much of its most substantial support. Similarly, the efficacy of administrative reforms is bound to be limited when they have to be implemented with the aid of affected interests. The mobilization of public opinion through active political parties (or a party) would appear to be the only way of drastically curbing the influence of the now semi-autonomous administrative corps and of reducing the frustration that builds up as the result of the operations of an apparently remote and high-handed bureacracy. This possibility, however, has been ruled out by those currently holding power. The most conservative amongst them tend to look askance at any form of dissent whilst the more moderate appreciate that a thorough-going policy of liberalization might, in present circumstances, release forces over which they could quickly lose control. A minority within the Movement would be prepared to recognize some form of official opposition but most would hesitate to take the risk entailed in such an experiment. At present, policy-makers can perhaps avoid having to face squarely up to the dilemmas inherent in this situation. With the departure of Franco, how-ever, the dilemmas seem likely to become more acute. Opposition pressures may then compel a clearer definition of the régime's inten-tions. There are essentially two responses that can be made.

The Government may rely heavily on repression and so perhaps further radicalize portions of those groups actively committed to the régime's transformation or destruction. Alternatively, it can seek some form of dialogue, or even co-operation, with opposition groups and so run the risk of a right-wing reaction that could conceivably take the form of a military coup.[2] Moderate opposition elements (including Christian Demo-crats, Social Democrats, the heirs of the pre-Civil-war Socialists and perhaps even sections of the Spanish Communist Party) see the monarchy as a short-term solution under cover of which they will have the chance to press for more drastic long-term political changes. They believe that the monarch will inevitably have to seek some sort of popular base and that this will give them their opening. Their degree of success could partly depend on the nature and extent of opposition demands. Opposition intransigence or a breakdown in order is likely to provoke military intervention.

[2] As noted in Chapter 2 direct military rule is unlikely to be a lasting solution.

At the time of writing there are some indications that, initially at least, some strengthening of repressive measures might be expected.[3] Some commentators even maintain that Spain is already, in effect, in the post-Franco era and that some recent aspects of official behaviour represent foretastes of the future. They point to the day to day management of affairs by Admiral Carrero Blanco, rather than by Franco himself, and believe the former has inspired some relatively new but significant measures such as a reversion to stricter press censorship and increases in the penalties attached to opposition activities.[4]

In gauging the likely efficacy of a repressive policy, a number of factors have to be weighed in the balance. On the one hand, there are indications that the Government can continue to count on the acquiescence of considerable sections of the society, even amongst the working classes, who remain largely indifferent to political issues. Equally, it can count on the positive support of relatively small but influential and vocal groups within the army and amongst ultra-conservative civilian elements. Finally, it can depend on an extensive, if not always highly efficient, repressive apparatus which has until now enabled it to contain militant opposition elements. More moderate opponents, for their part, have been unable to mobilize mass support, in any sustained fashion, and in some cases find themselves embarrassed by contacts sustained with the régime and by the semi-legal existence which, *de facto*, they possess. On the other hand, the crisis of Christmas 1970 (precipitated by the trial of Basque Nationalists at Burgos) pointed to some potentially new developments. Though the crisis provoked some manifestations of support for the régime it also provoked unprecedented manifestations of dissent. They were striking because of their frequent spontaneity and because they revealed an unusual degree of solidarity amongst groups of differing ideological persuasions and regional backgrounds. A destructive factionalism has traditionally characterized Spain's political culture and has continued to plague the opposition to Franco's régime, but there are now grounds for believing that some shift in attitudes has occurred or, at the least, that sustained repression would have the effect of driving previously divided groups into a temporary alliance. Interest in the crisis amongst the general public (as registered

[3]These words are being written in Jan. 1972.

[4]These are included in a law regulating "Public Order" passed by the Cortes in July 1971.

by sharp increases in newspaper circulation) also may indicate that the indifference to politics, which has helped to sustain the régime, might in some cases result from the stifling of public debate rather than any fundamental disinclination to confront political issues.[5] Finally, the crisis provided some intimations of the part foreign pressures could play in the shaping of Spain's political future. Moderate elements within the Government then showed themselves very susceptible to foreign pressure which, by contrast with similar past occasions, proved a very important factor in the resolution of the crisis.[6] Spain's anxiety to win friends within the E.E.C. and possible revisions of United States policy could therefore have repercussions inside Spain to the embarrassment of those favouring repression.[7]

Some commentators have pointed to Portugal to support the view that Franco's departure need not produce any significant changes. In the short run this might be true. Spanish society, however, is more developed and relatively more politicized than its neighbour. Thus its immediate political future involves more imponderables. Nevertheless, it is clear that Franco's successors will inherit (albeit in modified form) political dilemmas that, at the outset, his régime purported to eliminate. Equally, they will inherit much of the administrative machinery and some of the commitments that the Nationalists inherited or subsequently developed.

[5] Due to the many foreign pressmen covering the trial the authorities were compelled to lift reporting restrictions. This applied to Spanish as well as overseas reporters. Thus those who staged the trial in a sense fell into a trap of their own making. Spaniards obtained an unusually full press coverage of the trial and it was this that perhaps brought to the surface a latent interest in fundamental political issues.

[6] In the celebrated Griman affair of 1964 foreign pressure to save the life of a Communist leader, sentenced to death for activities during the Civil War, proved counterproductive.

[7] United States military and economic aid has been of great assistance to Franco's régime. In recent years, however, the United States has shown an increasing reluctance to provide military aid and has shut down some of its bases. Thus, in future, the Nationalist Régime may not be able to count on the reserves of moral and material help that have previously been forthcoming. It should be added that, as far as is known, the United States Government exercised no direct pressure on the Spanish Government during the Burgos crisis. The pressure came mainly from European governments. But the crisis did indicate how an uncertain government could be vulnerable given a shift in attitude on the part of its most powerful ally.

Short of a full-scale revolution it is safe to predict that the Spanish state, irrespective of political systems, will, in many respects, continue to be structured and to operate along the lines first laid down by its nineteenth-century architects. The Nationalist Régime has added to the State's traditional commitments, but it has not completely altered its *modus operandi*. The victors in the Civil War ostensibly liquidated the legacy of the "liberal" state. In reality there has been an underlying continuity in patterns of administrative behaviour. Any future changes in the structure of the State are likely to be contained within limits set by the experience of the past.

Bibliography

THIS is merely a list of suggestions for further reading and in no way purports to be exhaustive. Many of the books cited contain detailed bibliographies on particular topics.

Section 1

Primary Sources and Official Publications

Anuario Estadistico de España—an annual official compilation of statistics (Instituto Nacional de Estadistica, Madrid).

Anuario Estadistico de las Corporaciones Locales—intermittent statistical compilations concerning local administration (Instituto de Estudios de Administración Local, Madrid).

Boletín de las Cortes Españoles (Madrid).

Boletín del Movimiento (Madrid).

Boletín Oficial del Estado (Madrid).

Franco, Francisco. *Palabras del Caudillo, 19 Abril 1937–31 Diciembre 1938* (Ediciones Fe, Madrid, 1939).

Franco, Francisco. *Discursos y Mensajes del Jefe del Estado*
1951–1954 (Madrid, 1955).
1955–1959 (Madrid, 1960).
1960–1963 (Madrid, 1964).
1964–1967 (Madrid, 1968).

Franco, Francisco. *El Movimiento Nacional: Textos de Franco* (Ediciones del Movimiento, Madrid, no date, but after 1966).

Fundamental Laws of the State. The Spanish Constitution (Servicio Informativo Español, Madrid, 1967).

Los Impuestos en España (Ministerio de la Hacienda, Madrid, 1967).

Libro Blanco de Educación (Ministerio de Educación y Ciencias, Madrid, 1968).

Ministerio de Información y Tourismo—Annual Reports (Madrid).

O.E.C.D. (Organization for Economic Co-operation and Development)
The Mediterranean Regional Project (Paris, 1965).
Science and Development—Spain (Paris, 1968).
Technical Assistance and the Economic Development of Spain (Paris, 1968).

Plan de Desarrollo Económico y Social para el Periodo 1964–1967 (Boletín Oficial del Estado, Madrid, 1963).

Plan de Desarrollo Económico y Social (Boletín Oficial del Estado, Madrid, 1969).

Resumen Legislativo del Nuevo Estado, Vol. I (Editora Nacional, Barcelona, 1939).
Vol. II (Editora Nacional, Madrid, 1942).

An excellent compilation of major legislative provisions affecting the organization and operation of Spain's governmental and administrative institutions is contained in

GARCÍA DE ENTERRÍA, EDUARDO. *Código de las Leyes Administrativas* (Madrid, 1968).

Section 2

General Historical and Background Works

AGESTA, L. SÁNCHEZ. *Historia del Constitucionalismo Español* (Instituto de Estudios Políticos, Madrid, 1955).

BOLLOTEN, BURNETT. *The Grand Camouflage, The Spanish Civil War and Revolution* (Pall Mall Press, London, 1968).

BORKENAU, FRANZ. *The Spanish Cockpit. An Eye Witness Account of the Political and Social Conflicts of the Spanish Civil War* (Faber & Faber, London, 1938).

BRENAN, GERALD. *The Spanish Labyrinth. An Account of the Social and Political Background of the Civil War* (Cambridge University Press, Cambridge, 1950).

CARR, RAYMOND. *Spain 1808–1939* (Clarendon Press, Oxford, 1966).

CARR, RAYMOND (editor). *The Republic and the Civil War in Spain* (Problems in Focus Series, Macmillan, London, 1971).

CATTELL, DAVID, T. *Communism and the Civil War* (University of California Press, Berkeley, 1956).

CHAMBERLAIN, JOHN. *El Atraso de España* (Valencia, 1912).

COSTA, JOAQUÍN. *Oliquarquía y Caciquismo* (Madrid, 1902).

CROZIER, BRIAN. *Franco. A Biographical History* (Eyre & Spottiswoode, London, 1967).

FERNÁNDEZ-CARAVAJAL, RODRIGO. *La Constitución Española* (Editora Nacional, Madrid, 1969).

FINER, SAMUEL E. *The Man on Horseback. The Role of the Military in Politics* (Pall Mall Press, London, 1962).

GARCÍA, NIETO, JUAN N. *El Sindicalismo Cristiano en España: notas sobre su origen y evolución hasta 1936* (Universidad de Duesto, Instituto de Estudios Económicos-Sociales, Bilbao, 1960)

GARCÍA VENERO, MAXIMIANO. *Historia del Nacionalismo Vasco, 1793–1936* (Editora Nacional, Madrid, 1945).

GARCÍA VENERO, MAXIMIANO. *Historia del Nacionalismo Catalán, 1793–1936* (Editora Nacional, Madrid, 1944).

GIL ROBLES JOSÉ MARÍA. *No Fue Posible la Paz* (Ediciones Ariel, Barcelona, 1968).

HENNESSY, C. ALISTAIR. *The Federal Republic in Spain. Pi y Margall and the Federal Republican Movement. 1868–1874* (Clarendon Press, Oxford, 1962).

HILLS, GEORGE. *Franco. The Man and his Nation* (Robert Hale, London, 1967).

HILLS, GEORGE. *Spain* (Benn, London, 1970).

HOBSBAWM, ERIC. J. *Primitive Rebels. Studies in Archaic Forms of Social Movements in the Nineteenth and Twentieth Centuries* (Manchester University Press, Manchester, 1959).

JACKSON, GABRIEL. *The Spanish Republic and the Civil War, 1931–1939* (Princeton University Press, Princeton, 1965).

JOLL, JAMES. *The Anarchists* (Eyre & Spottiswoode, London, 1964).

MADARIAGA, SALVADOR DE. *Spain. A Modern History*, 3rd ed. (Jonathan Cape, London, 1961).

ORWELL, GEORGE. *Homage to Catalonia*. (Penguin Books, London, 1962).

ORTEGA Y. GASSET, JOSÉ. *España Invertebrada* (Revista de Occidente, Madrid, 1921).

PAYNE, STANLEY G. *Politics and the Military in Modern Spain* (Oxford University Press, London, 1967).

PAYNE, STANLEY G. *The Spanish Revolution* (Weidenfeld & Nicolson, London, 1970).

PEERS, E. ALLISON. *The Spanish Tragedy 1930–1936. Dictatorship, Republic, Chaos*, 3rd ed. (Methuen, London, 1936).

PEERS, E. ALLISON. *Spain, the Church and the Orders* (Eyre & Spottiswoode, London, 1939).

PUZZO, DANTE A. *Spain and the Great Powers 1936–1941* (Columbia University Press, New York, 1962).

RAMA, CARLOS M. *La Crisis Española del Siglo XX* (Fondo de Cultura Económica, Mexico, 1960).

RAMA, CARLOS M. *Ideología, Regiones y Clases Sociales en la España Contemporanea* (Ediciones Nuestro Tiempo, Montevideo, 1968).

RAMOS OLIVEIRA, ANTONIO. *Politics, Economics and Men of Modern Spain, 1808–1946* (Victor Gollancz, London, 1946).

ROBINSON, RICHARD A. H. *The Origins of Franco's Spain. The Right, the Republic and Revolution, 1931–1936* (David & Charles, Newton Abbot, 1970).

ROGGER, HANS and WEBER, EUGEN (editors). *The European Right* (Weidenfeld & Nicolson, London, 1965).

ROMERO MAURA, J. "The Spanish Case". Article in APTER, DAVID E. and JOLL, JAMES (editors). *Anarchism Today* (Papermac, London, 1971).

SÁNCHEZ, JOSÉ MARIANO. *Reform and Reaction. The Politico-religious Background of the Spanish Civil War* (University of North Carolina Press, Chapel Hill, 1964).

SCHAPIRO, J. SELWYN. *Anti-clericalism* (Van Nostrand, Princeton, 1967).

SMITH, RHEA MARSH. *Spain. A Modern History* (University of Michigan Press, Ann Arbor, 1965).

SOLÉ-TURA, JORDI. *Catalanismo y Revolución Burguesa* (Cuadernos para el Diálogo, Madrid, 1970).

SOUTHWORTH, HERBERT, R. *El Mito de la Cruzada de Franco* (Ruedo Ibérico, Paris, 1963).

THOMAS, HUGH. *The Spanish Civil War*, 2nd ed. (Penguin Books, London, 1965).

TRYTHALL, J. W. D. *Franco* (Rupert Hart-Davis, London, 1970).

TUÑÓ DE LARA, MANUEL. *La España del Siglo XX* (Librería Espanola, Paris, 1966).

VICENS VIVES, JAIME. *An Economic History of Spain* (Princeton University Press, Princeton, 1969).

VICENS VIVES, JAIME. *Cataluña en el Siglo XIX* (Editorial Rialp, Madrid, 1961).

VIGÓN, JORGE. *El Espiritu Militar Español* (Ediciones Rialp, Madrid, 1956).

WOOLF, STUART J. (editor). *European Fascism* (Weidenfeld & Nicolson, London, 1968).

Section 3
Political Forces and Dilemmas under Franco

ANSALDO, JUAN ANTONIO. *¿Para qúe . . .? (De Alfonso XIII a Juan III)* (Buenos Aires, 1954).

ARRESE, JOSÉ LUIS DE. *Capitalismo, Communismo, Cristianismo* (Ediciones Radar, Madrid, 1947).

ARRESE, JOSÉ LUIS DE. *Hacia una meta Institutional* (Ediciones del Movimiento, Madrid, no date).

ARTIGUES, DANIEL. *El Opus Dei en España*, 2nd ed. (Ruedo Ibérico, Paris, 1970).

BENEYTO PÉREZ, JUAN. *El Nuevo Estado Español. El Régimen Nacional-Sindicalista ante. Tradición y los demás sistemas totalitarios* (Biblioteca Nueva, Madrid, 1939).

BUSQUETS BRAGULAT, JULIO. *El Militar de Carrera en España. Estudio de Sociología Militar* (Ediciones Ariel, Barcelona, 1967).

CARRO MARTÍNEZ, ANTONIO. "Relaciones entre los altos organos del Estado." Published in *Revista de Estudios Políticos*, No. 152 (Madrid, March–April, 1967).

CLARK, CLYDE L. *The Evolution of the Franco Régime*, 3 vols. No publisher, no date.

CONDE, FRANCISCO JAVIER, *Contribución a la Doctrina del Caudillaje y Representación Política y Régimen Español Ensayo Politico* (Ediciones de la Subsecretaría de Educación Popular, Madrid, 1945).

EBENSTEIN, WILLIAM G. *Church and State in Franco's Spain* (Centre of International Studies, Princeton, 1960).

FARGA, MANUEL J. *Universidad y Democracia en España* (Colección Ancho Mundo, Mexico, 1969).

FEIS, HERBERT. *The Spanish Story: Franco and the Nations at War* (Knopf, New York, 1948).

GARCÍA VENERO, MAXIMIANO. *Falange en la Guerra de Espana: la Unificación y Hedilla* (Ruedo Ibérico, Paris, 1967).

GARRIGA, RAMÓN. *Las Relaciones Secretas entre Franco y Hitler* (Buenos Aires, 1965).

HALIMI, GISÈLE. *Le Procés de Burgos* (Collections Temoins Gallimard, Paris, 1971).

HERMET, GUY, "La Presse Espagnole depuis la suppression de la censure." *Revue Française de Science Politique*, XVIII, No. 1 (Paris, February 1968).

HERMET, GUY. *Les Communistes en Espagne* (Armand Colin, Paris, 1971).

HUGHES, EMMET J. *Report from Spain* (Holt, New York, 1947).

IGLESIAS SELGAS, CARLOS. *Los Sindicatos en España* (Ediciones del Movimiento, Madrid, 1965).

IGLESIAS SELGAS, CARLOS. *La Via Española a la Democracia* (Ediciones del Movimiento Madrid, 1968).

INTERNATIONAL COMMISSION OF JURISTS. *Spain and the Rule of the Law* (Geneva, 1962).

INTERNATIONAL LABOUR OFFICE. *The Labour and Trade Union Situation in Spain* (Geneva, 1969).

JATO, DAVID. *La Rebelión de los Estudiantes (Apuntes para una historia del alegre S.E.U.)* (Cies, Madrid, 1953).

JOBIT, PIERRE. *L'Eglise d'Espagne a l'Heure du Concile* (Editions Spes, Paris, 1965).

KINDELÁN, Lt.-Gen ALFREDO. *Mis Cuadernos de Guerra, 1936–1939* (Madrid, 1945).

LINZ, JUAN J. "An Authoritarian Régime Spain", published in ALLARDT, ERIK and LITTUNEN, YRJE (editors). *Cleavages, Ideologies and Party Systems, Contributions to Comparative Political Sociology (Transactions of the Westermark Society*, Vol. X, Helsinki, 1964).

LINZ, JUAN J. "The Party System of Spain, Past and Future", in LIPSET, SEYMOUR M. and ROKKAN, STEIN (editors). *Party Systems and Voter Alignments* (Free Press, New York, 1967).

LINZ, JUAN J. "From Falange to Movimiento Organization", in HUNTINGDON, SAMUEL P. and MOORE, CLEMENT H. (editors). *Authoritarian Politics in Modern Society. The Dynamics of Established One-party Systems* (Basic Books, New York, 1970).

LINZ, JUAN J. "Opposition in an Authoritarian Régime", to be published in a forthcoming volume "Emerging Oppositions" edited by DAHL, ROBERT (Yale University Press, New Haven).

LINZ, JUAN J. "The Inauguration of Democratic Government and its Prospects in Spain", to be published in a forthcoming volume edited by DE GRAZIA, ALFREDO.

MARÍN PÉREZ, PASCUAL. *El Caudillaje español* (Ediciones Europa, Madrid, 1960).

MARTÍNEZ CUADRADO, MIGUEL (editor). *Anuario Político Español* (Cuadernos para el Diálogo, Madrid, 1970).

MARTÍNEZ CUADRADO, MIGUEL (editor). *Anuario Político Español 1970* (Cuadernos para el Diálogo, Madrid, 1971).

MEDHURST, KENNETH N. *The Basques* (Minority Rights Group, London, 1972).

PAYNE, STANLEY G. *Falange, a History of Spanish Fascism* (Oxford University Press, London, 1962).

PAYNE, STANLEY G. *Franco's Spain* (Routledge & Kegan Paul, London, 1968).

PEÑA BOEUF, A. *Memorias de un Ingeniero Político* (Madrid, 1954).

RIDRUEJO, DIONOSIO. *Escrito en España*, 2nd ed. (Losada S.A., Buenos Aires, 1964).

ROMERO, EMILIO. *Cartas a un Principe* (Afrodisio Aguado, Madrid, 1964).

ROMERO, EMILIO. *Cartas al Pueblo Soberano* (Afrodisio Aguado, Madrid, 1965).

SALABERRI, KEPA. *El Proceso de Euskadi en Burgos* (Ruedo Ibérico, Paris, 1971).

SERRANO SUÑER, RAMÓN. *Entre Hendaya y Gibralter. Frente a una leyenda* (Ediciones y Publicaciones Españolas, Madrid, 1947).

SOUTHWORTH, HERBERT, R. *Antifalange: Estudio critico de Falange en la Guerra de España* (Ruedo Ibérico, Madrid, 1967).

VILAR, SERGIO. *Les Oppositions a Franco* (Editions Denoel, Paris, 1970).

WELLES, BENJAMIN. *Spain, The Gentle Anarchy* (The Pall Mall Press, London, 1965).

WHITAKER, ARTHUR P. *Spain and the Defence of the West. Ally and Liability* (Praeger, New York, 1962).

WITNEY, FRED. *Labor Policy and Practices in Spain. A Study of Employer–Employee Relations under the Franco Régime* (Praeger, New York, 1966).

YNFANTE, JÉSUS. *La Prodigiosa Aventura del Opus Dei* (Ruedo Ibérico, Paris, 1970).

242   *Government in Spain*

Section 4

Governmental and Administrative Institutions—History, Structure,
Problems and Checks upon them

ALBI CHOBI, FERNANDO. *La Crisis del Municipalismo* (Instituto de Estudios de Administración Local, Madrid, 1966).

ALVAREZ GENDIN, SABINO. *Problemas sobre decentralización y autonomía administrativa* (Real Academia de Jurisprudencia y Legislación, Madrid, March–April, 1969).

ALVAREZ GENDIN, SABINO. *Tratado General de Derecho Administrativo*, 2 vols. (Bosch, Barcelona, 1958).

ANALES DE MORAL SOCIAL Y ECONÓMICA. *Sociología de la Administración Pública Española* (Centro de Estudios Sociales de la Santa Cruz del Valle de los Cáidos, Madrid, 1968).

BENZO MESTRE, FERNANDO. *La Organización de la Hacienda Española* (Ediciones Duesto, Bilbao, 1967).

CALVO DE ALCOCER, RAMÓN. *Las Comisiones Provinciales de Servicios Técnicos* (Ministerio de la Gobernación, Madrid, 1966).

CHAPMAN, BRIAN. *The Profession of Government* (Allen & Unwin, London, 1959).

CORDERO TORRES, JOSÉ MARÍA. *El Consejo de Estado* (Instituto de Estudios Políticos, Madrid, 1944).

COURBE COURTEMANCHE, N. *Les Recours contre les Actes Administratives en Droit Espagnol* (Paris, 1960).

DIETTA, JAVIER. *Las Secretarías Generales Técnicas* (Centro de Formación y Perfeccionamiento de Funcionarios, B.O.E., Madrid, 1965).

FABREGAS DEL PILAR Y DIÁZ DE CEVALLOS, JOSÉ MARÍA. *El Control de la Actividad Fiscal del Estado según el Derecho Español* (Real Academia de Jurisprudencia y Legislación, Madrid, 1956).

FERNÁNDEZ RUIZ DE VILLEGAS, ANTONIO. *Secretarías Generales de Prefecturas y de Gobiernos Civiles* (Ministerio de la Gobernación, Madrid, 1963).

FRAGA IRIBARNE, MANUEL. *El Reglamento de las Cortes Españolas* (S.I.P.S., Madrid, 1959).

GALLEGO BURIN, A. *Manual de la Policía Municipal* (Instituto de Estudios de Administración Local, Madrid, 1950).

GALLEGO BURIN, A. *Manual de Alcaldes y Concejales* (Instituto de Estudios de Administración Local, Madrid, 1953).

GARCÍA DE ENTERRÍA, EDUARDO. *Los Nuevos Principios del Nueva Ley de Expropiación Forzosa* (Instituto de Estudios Políticos, Madrid, 1954).

GARCÍA DE ENTERRÍA, EDUARDO. *Problemas Actuales de Régimen Local* (Instituto García Oviedo, Seville, 1958).

GARCÍA DE ENTERRÍA, EDUARDO. *La Administración Española*, 2nd ed. (Instituto de Estudios Políticos, Madrid, 1964).

GARCÍA DE ENTERRÍA, EDUARDO. *Agentes de Derecho Administrativo*, 3 vols. (Facultad de Derecho, Madrid, 1966–7).

GARCÍA PASCUAL, PEDRO. *Los Cuerpos de Funcionarios de la Administración Pública Española* (Centro de Formación y Perfeccionamiento de Funcionarios, B.O.E., Madrid, 1960).

GASCÓN Y MARÍN, JOSÉ. *Administración Provincial Española* (Instituto de Estudios de Administración Local, Madrid, 1942).

GARRIDO FALLA, FERNANDO. *Tratado de Derecho Administrativo*, 3 vols. (Instituto de Estudios Políticos, Madrid, 1958, 1960, and 1963).

GARRIDO FALLA, FERNANDO. *Las Transformaciones del Régimen Administrativo*, 2nd ed. (Instituto de Estudios Políticos, Madrid, 1962).

GARRIDO FALLA, FERNANDO. *La Nueva Legislación Sobre Funcionarios Públicos en España* (Centro de Formación y Perfeccionamiento, B.O.E., Madrid, 1964).

GILBERT, RAFAEL. *El Consejo del Reino* (Centro de Formación y Perfeccionamiento de Funcionarios, B.O.E., Madrid, 1961).

GÓMEZ ANTON, FRANCISCO. *La Ley de Régimen Jurídico de la Administración del Estado* (Centro de Formación y Perfeccionamiento de Funcionarios, B.O.E., Madrid, 1959).

GÓMEZ ANTON, FRANCISCO. *El Consejo Foral Administrativo de Navarra* (Ediciones Rialp, Madrid, 1962).

GONZÁLEZ BERENGUER, J. L. *La Actividad de Policía en la Esfera Municipal* (Instituto de Estudios de Administración Local, Madrid, 1959).

GONZÁLEZ PÉREZ, JESÚS. *La Sentencia Administrativa. Su Impugnación y Efectos* (Instituto de Estudios Políticos, Madrid, 1954).

GUAITA, AURELIO. *El Consejo de Ministros* (Centro de Formación y Perfeccionamiento de Funcionarios, B.O.E., Madrid, 1959).

GUAITA, AURELIO. *Derecho Administrativo Especial*, 4 vols. (Librería General Zaragoza, 1960–6).

HERRERO TEJEDOR, FERNANDO. *Memoria elevada al Gobierno nacional en la solemne apertura de los Tribunales* (Institut. Editorial Reus, Madrid, 1970).

INSTITUTO DE ESTUDIOS DE LA ADMINISTRACIÓN LOCAL. *Guía General de la Administracion Local Española* (Madrid, 1968).

INSTITUTO DE ESTUDIOS DE ADMINISTRACIÓN LOCAL. *Problemas Políticos de la Vida Local*, Annual volumes (Madrid, 1961–).

INSTITUTO DE ESTUDIOS DE ADMINISTRACIÓN LOCAL. *Centenario de los Iniciardores de la Ciencia Jurídico—Administrativa Española* (Madrid, 1944).

INSTITUTO DE ESTUDIOS DE ADMINISTRACIÓN LOCAL. *Ideario de D. Antonio Maura sobre la Vida Local* (Madrid, 1954).

INSTITUTO DE ESTUDIOS DE ADMINISTRACIÓN LOCAL. *Problemas de los Aereas Metropolitanas* (Madrid, 1969).

INSTITUTO DE ESTUDIOS POLÍTICOS. *La Administración Publica y El Estado Contemporaneo* (Madrid, 1961).

JORDANA DE POZAS, LUIS. *Homenaje a Jordana de Pozas* (Instituto de Estudios de Administración Local, Madrid, 1961).

JORDANA DE POZAS, LUIS. *El Consejo de Estado Español y las Influencias Francesas a lo Largo de su Evolución* (Publicaciones del Consejo de Estado, Madrid, 1953).

LOPEZ MEDEL, JESÚS LÓPEZ. *El Problema de las Oposiciones en España* (Euramerica, Madrid, 1957).

LÓPEZ RODÓ, LAUREANO. *La Administración Pública y las Transformaciones Socio-economicas* (Real Academia de Ciencias Morales, y Políticas, Madrid, 1963).

MARQUES CARBO, LUIS. *El Derecho Local español*, 3 vols. (Barcelona, 1957–8).

MARTÍN MATEO, RAMÓN. *Manuel de Derecho Administrativo* (Madrid, 1970).

MARTÍN MATEO, RAMÓN. *La Comarcalización de los Pequenos, Municipios* (Ministerio de la Gobernación, Madrid, 1964).

MARTÍNEZ CALCERRADA, LUIS. "Independencia del poder judicial" (*Revista de Derecho Judicial*, Madrid, 1970).

MEDHURST, KENNETH N. "The Political Presence of the Spanish Bureacracy", article published in the journal *Government and Opposition*, London, Spring 1969.

MEDHURST, KENNETH N. The Legal and Political Institutions of Spanish Local Government (unpublished thesis, Manchester University, 1969).

MERCADER RIBA, JUAN. *La organización administrativa francesa en España* (Zaragoza, 1959).

MESA, SEGURA ANTONIO. *Labor Administrativo de Javier Burgos* (Instituto de Estudios de Administración Local, Madrid, 1946).

MEYLAN GIL, JOSÉ LUIS. *La Función Pública Española en la Doctrina Científica* (Centro de Formación y Perfeccionamiento de Funcionarios, B.O.E., Madrid, 1962).

MINISTERIO DE LA GOBERNACIÓN. *La Coordinación de la Administración Periférica en España* (Madrid, 1969).

MINISTERIO DE LA GOBERNACIÓN. *Las Provincias y sus Comarcas. Estudio sobre delimitación comarcal en las Provincias españolas* (Madrid, 1965).

MINISTERIO DE LA HACIENDA. *Los Impuestos en España* (Madrid, 1965).

MONTERO PUERTO, MIGUEL. *Régimen Disciplinario en la ley de Funcionarios Civiles del Estado* (Centro de Formación y Perfeccionamiento de Funcionarios, B.O.E., Madrid, 1965).

MORALES MARÍN, JOSÉ. *Los Sistemas de Formación de los Funcionarios Publicos* (Centro de Formación y Perfeccionamiento de Funcionarios, B.O.E., Madrid, 1962).

NIETO, ALEJANDRO. *La Retribución de los Funcionarios en España* (Revista de Occidente, Madrid, 1967).

OLIVÁN, ALEJANDRO. *De la Administración Pública con relación a España* (first published in 1843, republished by Instituto de Estudios Políticos, Madrid, 1954).

PARADA VAZQUEZ, JOSÉ RAMÓN. *Sindicatos y Asociaciones de Funcionarios Publicos* (Colección Acueducto, Madrid, 1963).

PÉREZ DE LA CANAL, MIGUEL ANGEL. *Notas sobre la evolución de Régimen Legal de los Gobernadores Civiles 1812–1958* (Ministerio de la Gobernación, Madrid, 1964).

PÉREZ GALDÓS, BENITO. *Miau* (a novel) (Penguin Classics, London, 1966).

PÉREZ HERNANDEZ, ANTONIO. *El Consejo de Estado* (Centro de Formación y Perfeccionamiento de Funcionarios, B.O.E., Madrid, 1965).

PÉREZ SERRANO et al. *Discursos Léidos en el Primer Centenario de D. Juan Bravo Murillo* (Real Academia de Ciencias y Políticas, Madrid, 1952).

PLAZA NAVARRO, MANUEL DE LA. *Las Garantias de la Independencia Judicial* (Real Academia de Ciencias Morales y Políticas, Madrid, 1954).

POSADA, A. *Evolución Legislativa del Régimen Local* (Madrid, 1910).

PRESIDENCIA DEL GOBIERNO. *Guía de la Administracion del Estado* (Madrid, 1965).

PRESIDENCIA DEL GOBIERNO. *Entidades Estatales Autónomas* (Madrid, 1966).

PRESIDENCIA DEL GOBIERNO. *I, II, y III Semana de Estudios sobre la Reforma Administrativa* (Madrid, 1958, 1959 and 1963).

PRESIDENCIA DEL GOBIERNO. *Classificatión de Puestos de Trabajo* (Madrid, 1965).

PUGET, H. *Le Governement Local en Espagne* (Paris, 1920).

RETORTILLO BAQUER, SEBASTIAN M. *De las Administraciones Autónomas de las Aguas Públicas* (Instituto García Oviedo, Seville, 1960).

RUIZ-JARABO BAQUERO, FRANCISCO. *Jurisdicción social y especialización Judicial* (Real Academia de Jurisprudencia y Legislación, Madrid, 1964).

RUIZ RODRIGO, F. *El Submunicipio Español* (Santander, 1960).

SECRETARÍA GENERAL DEL MOVIMIENTO. *Nuevo Horizonte de las Haciendas Locales* (Ediciones del Movimiento, Madrid, 1966).

VALLINA VELARDE, VICENTE DE LA. *La Provincia, Entidad Local en España* (Oviedo, 1964).

VARIOS. *Conmemoración del Centario de la Ley Provisional sobre Organización del Poder Judicial y del Código Penal de 1870* (Real Academia de Jurisprudencia y Legislación, Madrid, 1970).

Section 5

The Spanish Economy and Spanish Society

ANALES DE MORAL SOCIAL Y ECONÓMICA. *Promoción Social en España* (Centro de Estudios Sociales de la Santa Cruz del Valle de los Caídos, Madrid, 1966).

ANALES DE MORAL SOCIAL Y ECONÓMICA. *La Educación en España* (Centro de Estudios Sociales de la Santa Cruz del Valle de los Caídos, Madrid, 1970).

ANDERSON, CHARLES W. *The Political Economy of Modern Spain. Policy Making in an Authoritarian System* (University of Wisconsin Press, Madison, 1970).

ANLLÓ, JUAN. *Estructura y Problemas del Campo español* (Cuadernos para el Diálogo, Madrid, 1967).

ANZAR, SEVERINO, *Estudios religioso-sociales* (Instituto de Estudios Políticos, Madrid, 1949).

CANDEL, FRANCESC. *Els Altres Catalans*, 10th ed. (Edicions 62, Barcelona, 1967).

CAPELLA, MIGUEL. *La autarquía económica en España* (Editorial Vimar, Madrid, 1945).

CARO BARAJA, JULIO. *Los Vascos* (Ediciones Istmo, Madrid, 1971).

COMÍN, ALFONSO C. *España del Sur* (Editorial Tecnos, Madrid, 1965.)

DUOCASTELLA, ROGELIO. *Problemas Sacerdotales en España* (Caritas Española, Madrid, 1959).

FERNÁNDEZ CAMPOS, JOSÉ LUIS. *El Apremio de la Enseñanza en España* (Bilbao, 1968).

HERMET, GUY. "La Sociologie Empirique en Espagne." Published in *Recherche Mediterraneenne*, No. 4 (Centro de Documentation Mediterraneenne, Paris, June 1967).

246 *Government in Spain*

INFORME SOCIOLÓGICO SOBRE LA SITUACIÓN ACTUAL DE ESPAÑA (Fundación Foessa, Madrid, 1970).

INTERNATIONAL BANK, for Reconstruction and Development. *The Economic Development of Spain* (Johns Hopkins Press, Baltimore, 1963).

KENNY, MICHAEL. *The Spanish Tapestry* (Cohen & West, London, 1961).

KENNY, MICHAEL. "Patterns of Patronage in Spain" in *Anthropological Quarterly*, January 1960).

LAÍN ENTRALGO, PEDRO. *El Problema de la Universidad* (Madrid, 1968).

LATORRE, ANGEL. *Universidad y Sociedad* (Ediciones Ariel, Barcelona, 1964).

LINZ, JUAN J. Estructura y dinamica de los grupos sociales en España (unpublished volume prepared for the Comisaría del Plan de Desarrollo. Madrid, 1967).

LINZ, JUAN J. Local Elites and Social Change in Andalusia (a recent unpublished study, Madrid, no date).

LINZ, JUAN J. and MIGUEL, AMANDO DE. "Within-nation Differences and Comparisons: the eight Spains." Published in MERRITT, RICHARD L. and ROKKAN, STEIN. *Comparing Nations. The Use of Quantitive Data in Cross-National Research* (Yale University Press, New Haven, 1966).

LINZ, JUAN J. and MIGUEL, AMANDO DE. *Los Empressarios ante el Poder Público* (Instituto de Estudios Políticos, Madrid, 1966).

LISÓN-TOLOSANA, CARMELO. *Belmonte de Caballeros. A Sociological Study of a Spanish Town* (Clarendon Press, Oxford, 1966).

LÓPEZ MUÑOZ, A. and GARCÍA DELGADO, S. L. *Crecimiento y crisis del capitalismo español* (Madrid, 1968).

LORA SORIA, CECILIO DE. *Juventud Española Actual* (Ediciones y Publicaciones Españolas, 1965).

MARAVALL, J. M. *El desarrollo económico y la clase obrera* (Ariel, Madrid, 1970).

MARTÍN LOBO, MANUEL. *Realidad y Perspectiva de la Planificación Regional en España* (Nuevo Horizonte, Madrid, 1962).

MARTÍNEZ ALIER, JUAN. *La Estabilidad del Latifundismo* (Ruedo Ibérico, Paris, 1968).

MIGUEL, AMANDO DE. *Diferencias Regionales en España e Italia* (unpublished paper, Madrid, 1968).

MURILLO FERROL, FRANCISCO. *Estudios de Sociología Política* (Tecnos, Madrid, 1953).

PINILLA DE LAS HERAS, ESTEBAN. *Los empresarios y el desarrollo capitalista* (Madrid, 1968).

PITT-RIVERS, JULIAN A. *The People of the Sierra* (University of Chicago Press, Chicago, 1963).

RUBIO, JAVIER. *La Ensenañza Superior en España* (Editorial Gredos, Madrid, 1969).

TAMAMES, RAMÓN. *Estructura económica de España*, 2nd ed. (Sociedad de Estudios y Publicaciones, Madrid, 1964).

TAMAMES, RAMÓN. *España ante un segundo plan de desarrollo* (Editorial nova terra, Barcelona, 1968).

TAMAMES, RAMÓN. *La Lucha contre los Monopolios*, 2nd ed. (Editorial Tecnos, Madrid, 1960).

TORRES, MANUEL DE. *Juicio de la actual política económica española* (Aguilar, 1956).

Vazquez, Jesús Maria. *Realidades Socio-religiosas de España* (Editora Nacional, Madrid, 1967).

Periodicals

Anales de Sociología (Madrid).
Anales de Económia (Madrid).
Boletín de Información de la Vida Local (Madrid).
Cuadernos para el Diálogo (Madrid).
Documentación Administrativa (Madrid).
Ficheros de Altos Cargos (Madrid).
Hispanic American Review (Stanford).
Información Comercial Española (Madrid).
Revista de Administración Pública (Madrid).
Revista de Estudios de la Administración Local (Madrid).
Revista de Estudios Políticos (Madrid).
Revista Española de la Opinion Pública (Madrid).
Revista Internacional de Sociología (Madrid).
Revista de Política Social (Madrid).
Revue Francaise de Science Politique (Paris).
Revue International des Sciences Administratives (Brussels).

Newspapers

A.B.C. (Madrid).
Arriba (Madrid).
Madrid (publication suspended 1971) (Madrid).
Nuevo Diario (Madrid).
Pueblo (Madrid).
La Vanguardia (Barcelona).
Ya (Madrid).

Index

Abogados del Estado 106n, 110, 113, 223n
Acción Católica 16, 43, 46, 47, 63, 71
Acción Nacional Católica de Propogandistas 16, 43, 74
Active Administration 122–32, 136–7
Actos Políticos del Gobierno 221–3
Administración Periférica see Perepheric Administration
Administrative corps ch. 5 *passim*, 121–2, 123, 126, 128, 131, 133, 134, 136, 137, 138, 160, 189, 197, 198, 212, 214
Administrative courts 217–19, 221–8
see also Administrative law
Administrative law 160, 184, 217–28
Administrative reform 77, 85, 87, 93, 95–101, 115–17, 118, 124–5, 127–8, 130–33, 135–7, 206
Advisory councils 134–7
see also Consejo de Estado
African territories 63
Agrarian structure (of Spain) 8–9
Agricultural Minister 95, 216
Agricultural Ministry 120–1, 129, 130, 131n, 134–5, 136, 149, 163, 173, 175
Agricultural policy
pre-Civil War 18–20, 141, 143
under Franco 145–9, 174–7
Alava 15, 21, 41, 182
Alfonso XIII 5–6n, 26
Alonso Vega, Lt. Gen. 66
Anarchism 9, 35, 37n
Anarcho-syndicalism 11
Andalusia 8–9, 11, 173, 212
Anti-clericalism 14–15, 16, 18, 48
Arab powers (relations with Spain) 25n, 81

Aragon 11
Armed forces 77, 78, 120–1
Army Minister 64, 66, 82
Army Ministry 88n
Arrese, José Luis de 72, 77, 157
Asaltos 18, 88n
Association (Right of) 28, 58
Asturias 11, 37
Asturias (1934 rising) 19
Audiencia Territorial 222
Autarchy 25, 75, 145–9, 151, 155, 162, 166
Autonomous administrative entities 122, ch. 7 *passim*
see also Instituto Nacional de Colonización; Instituto Nacional de Industria; Instituto Nacional de Previsión; Instituto Nacional de la Viviendae R.E.N.F.E.; Servcio de Concentración Parcelaria y de Ordenación Rural; Servicio Nacional de Cereales
Axis powers 24, 31, 59, 64, 69
Ayuntamientos 183, 189, 191, 192, 193, 202

Bachillerato 168, 170
Badajoz (Plan) 175–7
Banco Popular 44
Banks (Private) 10–11, 66, 79, 141, 144, 155, 162, 164, 166, 172, 212
Bank of Spain 66, 154, 155, 164
see also Official Banks
Barcelona 13, 58, 182, 212
Barroso, Lt. Gen. 66, 72, 80
Basques 8, 12–14, 15, 21, 41–42, 179

Basque Country   8, 10–12, 16–17, 21–
    22, 41–42, 122, 150, 173, 194, 210n,
    212, 230n
Basque Nationalism   12–14, 21, 41–42,
    234
Basque Nationalist Party   12, 41
Benelux Countries (attitudes to Spain)
    63
Black market   151
Blue Division   24
Bourbons   1
Bravo Murillo, Juan   103
Brigada Social   88n
Broadcasting   28n, 109, 150
    see also Censorship; Communications;
    Radio; Television
Budget (autonomous administrative en-
    tities)   163
Budget (local authorities)   200, 203
Budget (State)   50n, 56, 86–87
Burgos (*polo de promoción*)   177
Burgos (trial)   41–42, 234
Business (as interest group)   10–11, 19,
    25, 31, 34, 44–45, 61, 65–67, 73, 78,
    79–80, 100, 126, 140, 144, 155, 159,
    161, 165–7, 172–3, 178, 186, 191,
    209, 212, 215
By-Laws   88n, 197

Caciques   4, 8
Caciquismo   185, 186
Calvo Serer, Rafael   45n
Calvo Sotelo, José   19n
Captains General   48–49
Carlists   3, 14–15, 19, 21, 24, 29–30, 46,
    61, 63, 64, 70, 125–6, 213n
Carlist Wars   3, 15
Carrero Blanco, Admiral   68, 74, 84,
    94n, 234
Castiella, Fernando María   69, 88, 94
Castile   8, 13–14, 108, 122n, 211–12
Catalans   4, 8, 12–14, 21–22, 41–42

Catalan Nationalism   4, 12–14, 41–42,
    179
Catalonia   4, 7–8, 10–12, 13–14, 16–19,
    22, 41–45, 122, 150, 173, 177, 179,
    182, 184, 187, 192, 194, 212
Catholic Church   8, 14–17, 18–19, 25,
    36, 42–48, 62, 65–71, 73, 78, 80, 81,
    231
Catholic Church and education   15–16,
    43, 80–81, 168–9, 171
Catholic Church's Workers Organiza-
    tions   15, 36
Catholic Kings   1
Caudillo (Franco)   30
Cavestany, Rafael   94
Censorship (ecclesiastical)   43
Censorship (State)   28, 32, 94, 120,
    136, 150, 216, 234
Ceuta   63
Chambers of Commerce   79
Charles III   1
Charter of Spanish People   58–60
Christian Democrats   16, 39, 40, 43, 48,
    70, 233
Civil aviation   142
Civil Guard   3, 9, 18, 88n, 191
Civil Responsibility of Administration
    225–6
Civil servants   Ch. 5 *passim*
Civil servants (number of)   121
Civil service   9, 61, 66, 72, 73, 75, 76,
    Chs. 5, 6 *passim*
    see also Administrative corps; Elite
    corps; General corps; Special corps
Civil service, deployment   113–14
Civil service, pay   105, 107, 110, 112,
    114, 116, 117
    see also Extra budgetary Income, *Tasas*
Civil service, pensions   110
Civil service, promotions   103, 109–10,
    116
Civil service, recruitment   103, 107–9,
    116
Civil service training   106
    see also Higher Technical Schools

Civil War 6, 20–23, 29–31, 43, 48, 55, 60, 64–65, 75, 77, 107, 119–20, 144, 146, 156–7, 186, 195, 209, 211, 212, 219, 230, 231

Codification of Law (19th century) 3

Clases medias 9–10, 13, 20–21, 23, 29–30, 32, 42, 101, 117

Collective bargaining 36, 159, 180

College of Lawyers 40, 209

Comisaría Nacional del Paro 156

Comisión Para la Distribución del Carbon 151

Comisión Superior de Personal 116, 118

Comisiones Provinciales de Servicios Técnicos 196–7, 205–6

Commerce Ministry 77, 120, 125, 133, 153

Commissariat of Economic Plan 98–100, 162

Communications (government control) 150–51

Communión Traditionalista 22–23

Communist Party 19, 22–23, 35–36, 39, 53, 233

Compañía Arrendatoria del Monopolio de Petróleos. S.A. (C.A.M.P.-S.A.) 142–3, 160, 166

Compañía Telefónica Nacional de España 150

Concessionaires (official) 140, 144–5, 159–60, 166, 195

Concordat (1851) 15

Concordat (1953) 25, 43, 47

Confederación Española de Derechas Autonomas (C.E.D.A.) 18–19, 61n, 63

Confederación Nacional de Trabajo (C.N.T.) 11, 19, 22, 29

Confederaciones Hidrograficas 141, 174

Conseil d'Etat 217, 218

Consejo de Economía Nacional 135

Consejo de Estado 135, 137, 217, 218–21

Consejo del Reino 27, 213n

Consejo Superior de Investigaciones Cientificas 44

Conservative Party 4, 6

Consultative administration 122–3, 132–7

Control of administration Ch. 9

Corruption 31, 151, 229, 230

Cortes 27, 43, 56–59, 94, 98, 202n, 207–16, 228

Cortes, President of 213–14

Cortes of Cadiz 2–3

Council of Ministers 54, 56, 59, 68, 86–87, 89–95, 96–97, 135, 208, 220n, 222, 223

Council of Ministers (Committees of) 91, 96–99

Criminal responsibility of civil servants 227–8

Cuadernos para el Diàlogo 39n

Decrees 56, 57, 91, 126

Decree laws 57–8, 92

Defence expenditure 50n, 87

Delegación del Gobierno en la Industria del Cemento 151

Delegado Provincial 128, 130

Desviación de Poder 224–5

Devaluation (of Peseta) 25, 26, 125n

Diputación Provincial 183–4, 190–3, 195–6, 202n

Diputación Provincial, President of 183, 190, 193, 201, 210

Dirección General 123–4, 126–7, 129, 135

Directors General 123–4, 126

Economic planning 26, 97–101, 111, 147–8, 149, 155, 157, 164–79, 232

Economic Planning (Minister of) 77, 86

  See also Commissariat of Economic Planning

Economic policy 25–6, 89, 97, Ch. 8 *passim*

Economists (Corps of) 113–4

Education and Science, Minister 38–9, 44, 45, 70, 81, 112, 138

Education and Science, Ministry 77–8, 109, 112, 114, 120–1, 129, 135, 138, 150, 173

Education system 3, 10, 79–81, 122, 139, 168–71, 176–9

Elections (Cortes) 209–10

Elections (local) 191–3

Elections (trade union) 33–34, 36

Electricity supply 152–3

Elite corps 105, 107–108, 110–13, 116–17, 118, 128, 129, 136, 138

Emigration 167n

Empresa Nacional 161, 162

Engineers 9, 104–5, 111, 164

Equatorial Guinea 63n

E.T.A. (*Euzkadi Ta Azkatasuna*) 41–42, 49n

European Economic Community (E.E.C.) 26, 62, 69n, 72, 235

Extra-budgetary income of civil servants 112, 116, 117, 121

Extremadura 8, 173, 182

Falange Espanola y de las J.O.N.S. (The party and its members) 19, 29–33, 35–36, 38–39, 42, 61–65, 67, 70–74, 76–79, 83, 144–5, 155, 157–8, 166, 168, 169, 171, 208, 213n, 216

See also The Movement, *Sindicatos*

Federal Republic (1873–1874) 3

Fernando Poo 63n

Finance Minister 66, 86, 87, 112, 132, 202

Finance Ministry 77, 86–87, 93, 97–98, 106, 112, 114, 117, 119, 127, 128, 134, 138, 142n, 162–3, 174, 188, 200, 202–5, 215, 228–9

Financial Inspectorate 114

Fiscal monopolies 140, 141, 143

Foreign Affairs Ministry 43n, 69–70, 78, 88, 108, 119, 121–2

Foreign investment (in Spain) 10, 25, 142, 160, 167

Foreign Legion (Spanish) 5n

Foreign Minister 61, 69, 70–71, 73, 82

Foreign relations 24–25, 31–32, 69–70, 73, 75, 78, 88, 91, 216, 235

France (influence on Spanish institutions) 1, 98–100, 122–3, 181–2, 217–18

France (relations with Spain) 21–22, 63n, 81–82

Franco Bahamonde, Francisco 5n, 19, 23–27, 30–32, 48–50, 52–53, Chs. 3, 4 *passim*, 144, 207–9, 212–3, Epilogue, *passim*

Franco's régime *See* Nationalist régime

Fuero de los Españoles See Charter of the Spanish People

Fuero de Trabajo See Labour Charter

Fueros (local) 12

Fundamental Laws 59

Fundamental Principles of the Movement 32, 56

Gabinetes (ministerial) 132–3

G.A.T.T. (General Agreement on Trade and Tarrifs) 25

General corps 105–6, 115–16, 181, 126

"Generation of '98" 4n

Germany (relations with Spain) 22, 24, 27, 29–30, 61, 88, 96, 153

Gibraltar 24, 25, 63, 69–70n, 70, 96, 179

Gobierno Civil 185, 187, 196

Grands Corps (of France) 114

Grimau (affair) 235n

Guerillas of Christ the King 48n

Guipúzcoa 41, 210n

Hapsburgs 1

Head of State (office of) 24, 55–60, 68, 85, 90n, 207, 213, 219–20, 228–9

Higher technical schools (of elite corps) 108, 169

Hitler 24

Hospital services 95

Housing Ministry 70, 72, 77, 94, 120, 137–8, 157, 178

Housing policy 99, 156–7, 160

Iberia (air line) 142, 161
Ifni 63, 82
Industrial policy (of Franco régime)
   144, 151–5
   See also Economic Planning
Industries of national interest 144, 152,
   166
Industry Minister 131n
Industry Ministry 77, 120, 125, 131,
   135, 165, 173
Industry (structure of) 10–11, Ch. 7
   passim
Industry and Commerce, Ministry of
   77
Inflation 25, 110, 144, 151, 159
Information and Tourism, Minister of
   28n, 73–74, 94, 132
Information and Tourism, Ministry of
   77, 109, 120, 125, 135, 150, 174
Inspectorates, of Ministries 124, 133–4
Institución Libre de Enseñanza 16
Instituto Nacional de Colonización 146–7
Instituto Nacional de Industria 151–5,
   158, 161–6
Instituto Nacional de Previsión 142–3,
   157, 160
Instituto Nacional de la Vivienda 156–7
Instituto de Reforma Agraria 143, 146
Integristas 15, 17, 43, 46
Interior Minister 61, 64, 66, 187, 190,
   197, 213
Interior Ministry 69, 77, 88, 94, 95,
   105, 110, 119, 120–2, 124, 127–8,
   133, 135, 160, 174, 182, 188, 198,
   200, 204, 223
Irrigation 9, 95, 113, 141, 146–7, 174–5
Isabella II 3
Italy (relations with Spain) 22, 27, 29–
   30, 61

Jaén (Plan of) 175
Jefe Provincial 128
Jesuits 16, 46n
Journalists 10

Juan Carlos, Prince 26
Juntas (local administrative) 189, 194,
   196
Junta Política (of Falange) 30
Justice Minister 125, 126, 222
Justice Ministry 70, 78, 95n, 119, 127,
   138

Labour Charter 30, 59, 157
Labour courts 34
Labour Minister 70
Labour Ministry 34–35, 70, 78–79, 92,
   95n, 120, 128, 133, 136, 156, 158,
   159, 160, 167n, 173
Labour relations 11, 18, 33–38
Landowners (as interest groups) 8–9,
   66, 78, 94, 130, 140–1, 143, 146,
   148–9, 186, 211
Latifundia 8, 149
Latin America (relations with Spain) 25n
Laws 57–59
Law on Political Responsibilities 31
Law of Succession (1947) 58–60
Lawyers 8–10, 40, 104–5, 119, 217–18
Letrados, Corps of 220
Liberal Party 4, 6
Liberalism 1, 2, 15, 17, 27–28, 140, 236
Liberalization (economic) 25, 44, 75,
   154, 163–4, 231
Liberalization (political) 26, 33, 50, 52,
   231
Libro Blanco de Educación 170
Local administration 119, 120, 178, Ch.
   8 *passim*, 213
Local finances 203–5
Local officials 198–201
Local services 194–7
López Bravo, Gregorio 69, 131n
López Rodó, Laureano 45n, 85–86,
   98–101
Lotteries 189

Madrid 11, 13, 17, 42, 48, 122n, 129,
   178, 182, 185, 187, 212

Madrid (the newspaper) 28, 45n
Madrid University 65
Marshall Plan 24
Martín Artajo, Alberto 31, 69
Matesa (scandal) 45, 46n
Mayor 182–3, 189, 190–3, 201, 210
Medical profession 10, 77
Melilla 63
Migrations (internal) 42, 149, 156, 231
Military (pre-Civil War) 5, 17–18, 18–20, 105
Military (in Civil War) 20–21, 29–30, 43, 55
Military (since Civil War) 31, 42, 48–51, 61–62, 64–65, 66–67, 70–71, 78, 80–82, 92, 96, 153, 162, 164, 186, 209, 211, 233–4
Military courts 31, 40–41, 48–49n, 90
Minifundia 8, 147
Mining (interests of State) 140
Ministerial orders 57, 160
Ministers 43, 56–57, 67, 69–70, 72, 74–81, Ch. 4 *passim*, 110
Ministries *See* references to separate departments, Chs. 5 & 6 *passim*
Monarchists 21, 24, 33, 60, 63, 64, 65, 66, 71–73
Monarchy 5, 24, 26, 59, 62, 65, 119, 232
Monopolies 152–3, 215
Morocco (French) 81
Morocco (Spanish) 5, 18, 55, 62, 81–82
Movement, The 32–33, 186, 190–2, 208–9, 210–11, 233
Municipalities Ch. 8 *passim*, 210
Mussolini 22
Mutualidades Laborales 158

Navy Ministry 125n
Napoleon 1–2
Napoleonic State 57, 102, 181, 184, 217
National Council of the Movement 30, 32n, 208–9
National Press Council 137

National Referendum Law 59
National Syndicalism 29, 33–38, 78
National War of Independence 1, 7, 14, 17, 103
Nationalist Régime 9, 23–54, Chs. 3 & 4 *passim*, 102, 107
Economic Policy 144–80, 186, 231–6
N.A.T.O. (North Atlantic Treaty Organization) 25n, 51
Navarra 15, 29, 41, 46, 182
Negociado 127

O.E.E.C. 25, 169
Office of Economic Coordination and Programming 97
Official Banks 141–2, 143–4, 155, 162, 165
Oposiciones 38, 108–9
Opposition to Franco's régime 22–24, 27–28, 31, 52–53, 58, 64, 67, 69, 71–72, 88, 150, 197, 210, 233, Epilogue *passim*
by Catholic Church 46–48
of regions 41–42
by universities and intellectuals 38–40
working class 33–38
Opus Dei 16, 38, 43–46, 48, 63, 66, 70–72, 74–75, 76n, 77–78, 80, 83–86, 93, 97, 100–1, 115, 118, 125, 126, 133n, 155, 162, 165, 169, 170, 173, 178
Organic Democracy 191, 208
Organic Law (1966) 26, 33, 56, 59, 60, 68, 210
Overseas territories (administration) 85

Patimonio Forestal del Estado 147–8
Perepheric Administration 122, 128–32, 182, 187–8, 189, 194, 196
Pius XII 44
Police 35, 48n, 67, 88n, 119, 120
Police powers 57, 184, 226–7

Political Crisis (1956)   39, 65, 71–73, 169
Political Crisis (1969)   40, 83–84
Political Crisis (1970)   41–42, 50, 54, 58, 83–84, 90, 234–6
Political culture   6–7
Polos de Desarrollo   177–8
Polos de Promoción   177–8
Popular Front   19–20, 144
Population (size and structure)   37, 157n
Portugal   25n, 235
Postal services   120, 159–60
Postal workers   114
Prefect (French)   182, 186
Presidency (*Presidencia del Gobierno*)   77 84–86, 89–90, 93, 95–96, 97, 105n, 114, 115, 116, 120, 132, 161, 175, 219, 227–8
Press   28, 69, 94
Prices and incomes   36, 92, 114–15, 158–9, 171–3
Prime Minister   59, 68, 75, 85
Primo de Rivera, José Antonio   29
Primo de Rivera, Lt. Gen.   5, 9–10, 38, 63, 107, 135, 139, 141–3, 150, 156, 160, 161, 174, 183, 186, 198, 208
Prisons   119
Professional organizations   40, 209
Pronunciamientos   17, 20, 23, 55
Protestants   43
Province   129, 181–206, 210
Provincial Governor   182–93, 196–7, 199, 201–3
Public health   120, 168, 189
Public order   17, 19–20, 57, 62, 69, 88, 91, 120, 127, 139, 182, 190, 197, 203, 223, 234
Public sector (organization)   159–64
Public Works, Minister of   138
Public Works, Ministry of   92, 95, 106, 112, 120, 121, 129, 138, 173–4, 195

Radio   28n, 150
Railway system   3, 140, 142, 150–1

Rationing   145
Real Patronato   15, 43, 47
Referendum (1947 and 1966)   58–59
Regional administrative units (of Ministries)   129, 131
Regional conflict   4, 11–14, 17, 41–42
Regional planning   173–9
Religious liberty   47, 94
R.E.N.F.E. (*Red Española Nacional de Ferrocarilles*)   151, 161, 163, 165–6
Renovación Española   19, 63, 66, 208
Republic *see* Second Republic
Republican parties   6, 10, 11, 20
Research (Government)   153–4, 160
Restoration (1874)   3, 4, 104
Road engineers   138
Road system   3, 92, 95n, 99, 129, 138, 141, 150n
Ruiz Jiménez, Joaquin   39, 71, 80

School teachers   10, 114
Sección   127, 128
Second Republic   4n, 6, 16, 18–20, 21–23, 62, 107, 120–1, 135, 143–4, 147, 160, 169, 186, 231
Second World War   24, 31, 62, 96, 145
Secretarías de Despacho   119
Secretary General of the Movement   30, 33, 70, 74, 187
Secretaría General Técnica   132–3
Serrano Suñer, R.   61n, 64, 69
S.E.U.   38–39
Servicio Nacional de Cereales   148, 161
Servicio de Concentración Parcelaria y de Ordenación Rural   147
Shop Stewards   36
Sindicatos   29, 31, 33–38, 66, 69, 78–79, 98, 136–7, 144, 147, 149, 159, 172–3, 175n, 176, 186, 191, 192, 209–10, 211, 213–14, 216
Social Democrats   39, 233
Social policy   142–4, 155–9
Social security   62, 68, 95n, 145, 157–8
Socialist Party   6, 10–11, 19, 22–23, 35–36, 233

Socio-economic change (post-Civil War) 37, 42, 156–9, 167–80, 231–2
Soria 190
Soviet Union 22
Spanish America 2, 10
Spanish Sahara 62n
Spanish Guinea 62n
Special Corps 104–6, 109, 115, 121, 124, 129
Stabilization Plan (1958) 52, 97, 154, 157, 159, 172
Statistics (official) 85, 99, 189
Strikes (under Franco régime) 34–38, 46–47, 78, 197
Subalternos, Corps of 106
Sub-Dirección General 127–8
Sub-Director General 128
Subsecretaría 123–5
Subsecretario 94, 123–5

Tariff protection 11, 79, 140, 144, 154
Tasas 112–13, 134, 161, 163
Taxation 3, 7, 56, 87, 112, 140, 144, 159
Taxation (local) 203–5
Telecommunications 120
Television 28n, 150
Tourism 92, 120, 142n, 167
Town planning 120, 137, 189
Trade associations 34, 79, 173
Transport (local) 195
Transport policy 150–1
Tribunal des Conflicts 221
Tribunal de Cuentas 163, 204, 228–9
Tribunal of Public Order 49n
Tribunal Supremo 217, 221–2

Tutelage 184–5, 200–4

Under-secretary *see Subsecretario*
Unemployment 158n
U.T.G. (*Unión General de Trabajadores*) 11, 19
United Kingdom (relations with Spain) 22, 179
United Nations 24, 25, 63
United States (relations with Spain) 24, 35, 62, 69–70n, 73, 82–83, 96, 153, 235
Universal suffrage 4
Universities 38–40, 44, 67, 71, 106, 122, 168–70, 209
University Professors, Corps of 112
University districts 129
Urban development 149, 173, 178, 195

Valencia 11
Vallodolid 177
Varela, Lt. Gen. 64–65
Vatican 25, 43n, 47, 48
Vatican II (Council) 47, 94
Veterinary services 134
Vizcaya 41
Voluntary associations 7, 88

War Ministry 5, 119, 121
World Bank 26, 112n, 163n

Zaragoza 177